Praise for

American Pie

"Pascale Le Draoulec's engaging account of driving through our country's hinterlands in search of pie . . . will move pie enthusiasts to dust off their rolling pins and get busy."   —*Chicago Tribune*

"As satisfying as a slice of homemade pie, Le Draoulec's cross-country journeys in search of 'the real stuff' are an armchair traveler's heaven. Le Draoulec is an enthusiastic tour guide with a quirky sense of humor and a personal life as unpredictable as pie crust. *American Pie* takes the reader into the heart and soul of a fading icon and inspires us to get out the rolling pin and take to the road."   —*Library Journal* (starred review)

"*American Pie* is to be savored, slice by slice, chapter by chapter."
—*San Diego Union-Tribune*

"A rich, satisfying account of one woman's cross-country search for the age-old dessert."   —*Entertainment Weekly*

"Le Draoulec is a natural-born reporter. . . . She's curious, she likes people, and she has an instinct for where the most interesting story might lie. Pie, as this book charmingly demonstrates, is complicated, a mystery and metaphor, 'the Madonna-whore of the dessert world.'"   —*Washington Post Book World*

"Le Draoulec explores America's relationship with pie with a journalist's instinct and curiosity. This book, which is more memoir than cookbook, takes readers across the country and into some forgotten corners of the country that are all connected through this one dessert."   —Associated Press

About the Author

PASCALE LE DRAOULEC, the restaurant critic for New York's *Daily News*, has been writing for newspapers for fourteen years, concentrating for the last six years on food features. An award-winning journalist, she has worked for the *San Diego Union-Tribune, Marin Independent Journal,* and Gannett Newspapers in New York. Her work has also appeared in *USA Today* and in national magazines. In 2001, she joined the *Daily News,* where she also writes a quirky weekly food column. In 2002, she received the James Beard Award for Newspaper Restaurant Criticism. This is her first book.

About the Author

PREPARED BY BEN OFTEDON the reference editor for the New York's Daily News, has been writing for newspapers for four seven years, concentrating for the last six years on food features. As a veteran beauty journalist, she has worked for the San Francisco, Boston, Miami, Indianapolis Journal, and Gannett Newspapers in New York. Her work has also appeared in USA Today and in national magazines. In 2001, she joined the Daily News, where she also writes a quirky weekly food column. In 2002, she received the James Beard Award for Newspaper Restaurant Criticism. [The Editor] american pie

american pie

slices of life (and pie)

from America's back roads

PASCALE LE DRAOULEC

Perennial

An Imprint of HarperCollinsPublishers

To my parents
who fed me stories with every meal
and who see beauty and truth in small things . . .

ACKNOWLEDGMENTS

I wish to thank all the people I met on America's pieways who took the time to share a slice of life and/or pie with me. Thanks, also, to all those who pointed me toward pie and to the bakers who contributed recipes. Together, we've assembled quite a collection.

I can't thank Kris enough for sticking with me through twenty-four states, for her beautiful photographs, her sense of humor, and for scraping the bugs off the windshield at every fill-up.

Thanks also to my other co-"pie"-lots: Nicole, for her lean and keen observations and for turning me on to BBQd corn chips in South Carolina; Teri, for running away to eat pie with me a month before her wedding; Liz, though Maine didn't make the cut—I will never forget your waking up at 4 A.M. to go lobstering for pie.

Thank you, also, to friends old and new, in Livingston, Montana, Houston, Texas, Thornton, Iowa, Hammond, Louisiana, Ripon, Wisconsin, Traverse City, Michigan, and Orleans, Massachusetts, who took road-weary pie travelers in for the night and fed them something other than pie.

Thanks also to my mechanics, Tim, in Yonkers, New York, and Clay, in Marin County, California, who made sure Betty and Betty Blue were ready to rumble. Thanks to Rodney, the shy cowboy in the pepper-red jumpsuit who stopped to fix my thermostat near Roswell, New Mexico.

I am grateful to my editors at the *Daily News* for their patience while I baked this book. Hanna O'Clair: thank you for testing all those recipes and making the pies look so pretty.

Elena, thank you for coming into my life at the tail end of yours. Thanks for my bowl and for Judy's number. Nancy Bronstein and Olivia Barker, thank you for being such caring friends and back readers.

Thanks to Mike and Andrea for introducing me to Gordon Kato, my agent, who "got it" right away and who gave me great tunes for the trip; and to Larry Ashmead and Krista Stroever, my editors at HarperCollins, for their insights and for understanding that writing a first book is a lot like making pie: you just can't rush it . . .

Un grand merci to my family for their constant cheerleading and, finally, to Ty, for patiently working on "dough" with me until we got it just right.

CONTENTS

part one

part two

part three

part one

*"Everything in life is somewhere else,
and you can get there in a car."*

—E. B. WHITE

"Fro-Joy," ONE MAN'S MEAT

my huckleberry friend

. . . Two drifters,
Off to see the world,
There's such a lot of world to see.
We're after the same
Rainbow's end
Waitin' round the bend,
My huckleberry friend,
Moon River
and me.

—JOHNNY MERCER, "MOON RIVER"

On November 16, 1982, a state bear trapper named Dave sat in his living room in Whitefish, Montana, with a loaded .357 Magnum in his lap and his dog, Pip, curled at his feet.

Most marauding bears can be snared and relocated, never to be seen again. But some pesky bears keep coming back.

On that icy November night, under the cold, stern eye of the Northern Rockies, Dave knew his personal grizzly had returned one too many times. He reckoned he had only two choices: live dry or die drunk.

The state fish-and-game warden, a hardened bachelor of 43, stared at the gun in his lap. His thoughts drifted to those endless nights frittered away on bar stools. The way Pip cocked his head at the sight of him teetering home through knee-deep snow. So many boyhood dreams, dissolved, like ice in whiskey.

Then Dave passed out.

When day broke, he cracked open his slate eyes. The gun had not moved. Neither had Pip, a Saint Bernard mix, named for J. R. R. Tolkien's most statuesque hobbit.

Dave pushed himself up from his easy chair knowing that nothing about the days and months ahead would be easy. He'd have to keep busy. No idle hands.

With Pip at his heels, he marched into the kitchen to look for a rolling pin.

And he made a huckleberry pie.

And then he made another.

Growing up in the foothills, in Choteau, Dave used to watch his mother make pie. He'd lay his head on the kitchen table and stare as she'd roll out her dough, pushing the large rolling pin away from her belly with the sure, even strokes of a rower. From this cheek-to-flour angle, the rolling pin came straight at him.

He must have picked up a lot this way, because those first pies came pretty naturally to him. He tried all sorts of recipes. Bourbon pecan made him want to lick the slope of his wooden spoon. But huckleberry quickly became his favorite.

"Another trait I share with the grizzlies," he says with an impish grin.

A huckleberry, the grizzly's late-summer snack, is a wild bluish-black berry that is often confused with the tamer, sweeter blueberry. Only found in the wild and at high elevations, the huck has a thicker skin and packs ten small hard seeds. Grizzlies gorge on the berries to fatten up for winter's long hibernation.

Since it was the dead of winter, Dave used frozen huckleberries for those first pies and, after all these years, he insists that frozen hucks make just as good a pie filling as fresh. Dave baked pies as gifts for the town bartenders and waitresses who'd kept him company all those years. The companionship, it turns out, was a lot harder to give up than the beer and bourbon.

When Pip died a year later, Dave didn't think he'd bounce back. Pip had saved him from scrapes with mountain lions and armed poachers, but Dave was most grateful the dog had stuck it out through the toughest part of his recovery.

A year later, a waitress in town surprised Dave on his birthday with a six-week-old golden retriever pup wearing a red bow. Pretty soon, Dave graduated to seven goldens, most of them rescued. He called them "The Magnificent Seven."

The dogs liked nothing better than to watch Dave make pie, he says. They'd lie down in the kitchen, muzzles resting on crossed forepaws, and wait for a stray scrap of dough. By then, Dave was baking nearly every night. Friends who owned a popular café in Whitefish had asked him to bake for the restaurant. Eventually, Dave was making fifteen covered pies a day and putting an extra $12,000 a year in his pocket.

Tourists who had discovered Dave's crimped huckleberry pies while skiing in Whitefish had them FedExed to their homes as far away as London, Australia, and Japan. But Dave says the compliment that meant the most came straight from his mother—a woman of few words and, I gather, even fewer displays of affection. She had come from Choteau to visit him in Whitefish, and he had invited a few friends over for dinner. He made a huckleberry pie. "This is as good as Mom used to make," a guest said after tasting the tart pie with a sturdy crust, to which Dave's mother replied:

"I never made a pie *this* good."

Dave eventually retired from his state job and moved with his pack of dogs back to Choteau, a town of 1,800, where he now builds and sells aluminum bear traps. Something about growing older made Dave, now 62, want to be close to his flatland roots. "As a kid, I couldn't wait

to get out of here . . . but something drew me back. I guess I needed to complete the circle," he muttered under his breath, the night I met with him, and his dogs, to talk about Zen and the art of making pie.

He was working on his truck when we pulled up at dusk after driving across the same wide Montana prairie where dinosaurs once came to breed, using Ear Mountain as our beacon.

"I hear you make a mean huckleberry pie," I said.

"Well, that depends on what you mean by mean," Dave growled.

"I mean damn good."

"Damn right."

Dave was gruff at first. But when he saw how I took to his dogs, letting them lick my face and my toes, and when he saw the rolling pin attached to the front grille of my car, he opened the screen door and invited us inside.

"This is their home. I live here but by their grace," he said, as each of the dogs took its respective spot.

All pie bakers will tell you that the real trick to crust is knowing exactly when to stop working the dough. Overworking the dough makes for a tough, plaster crust. Once you've reached that point, there is no turning back.

"It's a make-or-break point," said Dave, "and I had reached that point in my drinking."

He recounted the details of that November night and, with his chin, pointed to my chair. "That's the chair I was sitting in," he said. Silence.

I asked Dave if baking pie was a form of therapy. He winced.

"Baking pie was just a way to keep me busy—and away from the bottle"—on those long, lonely nights after trapping, he said.

Dave had trapped about five hundred bears in his lifetime, a third of them grizzlies. Dave hated to see bears cozying up to civilization, and was always happy to return a bear to its natural element—even if it meant fewer huckleberries for pie.

For all of his bluster, Dave clearly had a gentle heart, and I asked him why he'd never married. He drew back in silence. And, as if they knew something I didn't, the dogs stopped their panting. There had been one woman, Dave said. She was married to someone else.

And he left it at that.

It was as good a time as any to turn to the rules of pie. Dave prefers shortening to butter or lard. He always adds a touch of vinegar to his dough and he never makes a pie unless all of his ingredients are very cold. He slips his rolling pin in a cheesecloth glove to prevent the dough from sticking. He's a crimper, though not a fussy one.

Had he not been leaving town so early to deliver a bear trap in Arizona, he would have baked me a huckleberry pie for sure.

"Will you settle for the recipe?" he asked.

Dave pulled the recipe from a dented *Ladies' Home Journal*

index-card box decorated with daisies, which, I presume, had once belonged to his mother.

It was past midnight when we finally found a room for the night at the shabby Wagons West Hotel just off the highway in Augusta, near the Scapegoat Wilderness Area and the Continental Divide.

It had been a long day but I wasn't ready to sleep, so I threw on a sweater and sat on the wooden bench directly outside my room. A low maple moon popped out of the black sky like a gold button.

The motel manager, a tall, tumbleweed blonde, stepped out for a smoke. She propped herself against one of the decorative wagon wheels, facing the desolate highway, one leg in a flamingo tuck.

"So you're driving across America looking for pie," she said matter-of-factly. She paused to blow smoke at the moon.

"Bet you're finding *a lot* more than pie . . ."

DAVE'S HUCKLEBERRY PIE

CRUST

1¼ cups of butter-flavored Crisco

3 cups of flour

1 raw cold egg

1 tablespoon of ice-cold vinegar

1 teaspoon of salt

6 tablespoons of ice-cold water

FILLING

3 cups of fresh (or frozen) huckleberries rinsed and picked clean

1 cup sugar

¼ cup flour

⅛ cup of heavy whipping cream

Cut your shortening into your flour in a large mixing bowl. Using your fingers or a pastry cutter, incorporate the fat into the flour until the consistency is that of cornmeal or tiny peas. In a separate bowl, combine the beaten egg with the vinegar, salt, and water. Add this wet mixture to the flour very slowly, until the dough holds together. Work the dough with the heel of your hand until it forms a smooth ball. Divide the ball into 3 pillowy discs. Dave says 2 discs should be plenty for one double-crust pie, so wrap the extra disc in clear plastic and freeze or refrigerate it for your next pie.

Before rolling out your dough, line your work surface with cheesecloth. Slip some extra cheesecloth over your rolling pin and, working from the center, roll out each disc into a circle about ⅛ inch thick. Line the bottom of a 9-inch pie pan, leaving enough dough around the edges for crimping. Trim off any excess dough.

For the filling, combine all the ingredients in a large mixing bowl and mix gently. If the berry mixture is too runny, add some flour. (If you plan on making your filling ahead of time, Dave suggests you set it aside, high on a shelf, away from dogs.) Spoon the filling into the lined pie pan. Drape the top crust over the pie. Crimp edges. Cut slits into the top crust to release steam. Bake at 425 degrees for 15 minutes, then reduce heat to 350 degrees and bake for 35–45 minutes longer.

why pie?

*"A lot of people have never really had the chance to taste
a decent apple pie, but after a minute's sensual reflection will know
positively what they would expect if they did. They can taste it on
their mind's tongue . . ."*

—M. F. K. FISHER, "MOM, THE FLAG, AND APPLE PIE"

I never set out to find the *best* pie in America.

I was moving from San Francisco to New York for a newspaper
job and decided to drive, rather than fly, into my new life.

It occurred to me that in switching coasts, I was trading one
extreme for the other and it seemed important that I spend some
time in the middle getting there.

Truth is, I've always wanted to take a back road across America.

As a journalist, I was all too familiar with the America that makes
headlines. I'd often wondered about the America that wakes up to
them. Not the slick USA packaged in sitcoms and strip malls, but
the America that still buys eight-penny nails at hardware stores,
shucks peas on a weather-beaten porch, and boxes Little League
scores on the front page of the local paper.

I bought a map of the United States and for weeks it sat splayed
on my kitchen table. The bold blue interstates, thick as veins,
jumped off the map with the subtlety of a cheesy come-on line. They
could get you from A to Z all right, no exploration necessary. But the

myriad "two-lanes," faint filaments of muted gray and red, they offered miles and miles of mystery.

I considered each squiggly line on the map with the same gravity with which I'd considered some of the men in my life. I didn't have much time for the trip, less than three weeks, so I'd have to choose my route carefully. I knew that whichever route I chose, it would offer a completely unique scenario. I had never given Nebraska much thought, but it suddenly looked sexy there, sandwiched between Kansas and South Dakota.

Too many options can be paralyzing. Rather than choose a route, I wanted it to choose me. I needed some sort of peg, a thread, to pull me from one coast to the other and, at the same time, deliver the raw America I was seeking.

As a news reporter turned food writer, I thought it made sense to turn the journey into a culinary quest. I flirted with barbecue, but that sounded geographically limiting, not to mention leaden.

Then it hit me one night as I sat at the kitchen table, staring at the map. Pretend it's a cake or a pie, I told myself. Just make the first cut; the rest of the journey will follow.

Pie.

Although the Egyptians first imagined it and the British brought it across the Atlantic, pie—the sweet staple of pioneers—is *the* quintessential American dessert. There isn't a state in the union that doesn't boast a signature pie, from Georgia peach to Florida Key lime to Pennsylvania shoofly. Pie transcends all lines of race, color, and class. A rhubarb pie feels as much at home in a blue-collar diner in Flint, Michigan, as it does in a lacy autumn inn in Vermont.

And while no two Americans bake their pie exactly the same way, most would agree that nothing screams USA better than a wedge of apple or sweet-potato pie served warm on a plate.

My grail would be pie.

Just saying it out loud made me surrender a smile. I would drive to small towns looking for pie bakers, pie recipes, and pie lore. I'd seek out pies with character and characters who love pie.

Perhaps examining the state of pie in America would also take me back to the essence, the roots of this country, and just maybe help me get to the bottom of mine.

As a first-generation American born to two faithfully-French immigrants living in Los Angeles, I had straddled two cultures most of my life. The plan was that we'd move back to France someday. So, I attended a French school, spoke only French at home, and ate smelly cheese after dinner. When it rained, we'd dive into the back-yard laurel bushes for snails, which my mother would prepare *à la bordelaise*. We celebrated Bastille Day and played petanque on the Fourth of July.

I still don't know the words to the "Star-Spangled Banner," and my mother never learned to make pie.

"A pie is not a *tarte,*" she would say, shrugging her slight shoulders in that typically French way that suggests a conversation has no place to go. I never questioned it, just as I never questioned the dictum that a baguette placed on its back brings bad luck or that all French women "just know" how to wear a scarf.

My parents never did move back to France, though we visited often. And, on either continent, I always felt like an extra, never part of the main cast. I look like an Easter egg whenever I try to wear a scarf *and* I missed out on all those family debates pitting lard against butter, Pyrex against pie tins.

I didn't even taste my first slice until I was in college. It was pecan. Store-bought. Uneventful.

I had a lot of catching up to do.

Some of my more jaded San Francisco friends didn't understand my quest. They deemed it frivolous—and, God forbid, fattening.

"Who bakes pies from scratch anymore?" asked a colleague. "Who has that kind of *time*?"

Was she right? Had the spirit of pie gone out with the old kitchen guard, the pin-curled grandmothers with their wooden potato mashers and ceramic mixing bowls? Had working mothers everywhere traded their pastry cutters for briefcases and panty hose? Maybe I had missed the boat entirely on pie, and, like Don McLean who mourned the death of rock 'n' roll in the song "American Pie," I, too, was "out of luck."

I knew I was on the right quest when I floated my idea past the couple seated next to me on the plane during a last-minute business trip. The woman nearly choked on her honey-roasted peanuts. "Our entire relationship was based on a shared passion for pie," she said. Her beau grabbed her hand. "I recently proposed to her," he said, "and before she said yes, she asked if we could have pie at the wedding."

As I dismantled my California life, I reread books by other road-trippers. Skimming Alexis de Tocqueville's *Democracy in America*, I was struck by how contemporary some of his observations were. Americans had, in fact, changed little in the two centuries since the Frenchman took to the road with his traveling partner, Beaumont. The following passage, about the purely American notion of "drive," seemed particularly apt:

> An American will build a house in which to pass his old age and sell it before the roof is on. He will plant a garden and rent it just as the trees are coming into bearing; he will clear a field and leave others to reap the harvest; he will take up a profession and leave it, settle in one place and soon go off elsewhere with his changing desires. . . . Death steps in in the end and stops him before he has grown tired of this futile pursuit of that complete felicity which always escapes him.

As a woman in her mid-30s who wanted children but hadn't yet paused long enough to have them, I knew all too well about how time, and drive, can play tricks on you. And maybe my thirst for a two-lane slice of America, for a place where people still took time to bake pies from scratch, spoke to something deeper.

In the days before my departure, I cast my pie line out at dinner parties, at my mechanic's, even in line at the post office, to see what I could reel in.

My doctor told me it wasn't a real pie quest if I didn't stop in Montana, his wife's home state, for some huckleberry pie. Everyone had a pie-baking relative named after a leafy plant (Fern, Iris, Rose) in some small town that I just *had* to add to my route.

At my office going-away party, several coworkers scribbled favorite pie stops on business cards. A group of men argued over whether strawberry had any business shacking up with rhubarb, putting to rest all theories about this being a purely feminine quest.

"Nothing is more honest than pie," said Scott, the photo editor at the small Marin County newspaper that I was leaving. "Pie," he said, "is like a comfortable pair of shoes.

"And no cross-country pie journey would be complete without a stop in Hurricane, Utah, for their famous bumbleberry pie," he added. His wife bakes him a pie every year on his birthday. I had worked alongside Scott for four years and never knew of his passion for pie. What had I tapped into here?

The next day, I drew a red pie dot on the town of Hurricane and other "must-hit" towns. For the rest, I'd rely on intuition.

That made sense, since intuition—knowing exactly when to stop working the dough or when to pull a pie out of the oven—is a large part of baking pie.

I knew this intuitively because I had never baked a pie.

I had baked a handful of tarts but had somehow managed to live 35 years dodging the trauma of the all-American pie crust. Many of my friends confessed to the same subterfuge. They, too, had mastered profiteroles and tiramisu, but pie? Well, pie was too intimidating.

Pie stands for "motherly love," and who wants to fail at that?

My plan was to turn up in small towns, seek out the most typical locals, and ask them where they'd go for a good slice of pie. I promised myself that, to stay true to my mission, I would go wherever they sent me, which is how I landed deep in the Ozarks one night when the locusts were running.

Since the berries in the northern states were two months shy of ripe, I decided to stay on the lower half of the country, in the belly and legs of the beast.

I went to the Automobile Association of America to pick up some state maps. The woman behind the desk tossed her head back in laughter at my quest—a sweet deviation from the "Route 66" itineraries she usually prepares for members.

"Pie route? We don't have a *pie* route," she said, "but if you find a good cherry pie on the road, will you bring me back a slice?"

She leaned back into her chair and, within seconds, was taking a little pie trip herself, stirring up memories of the latticed cherry pies her former mother-in-law used to bake for her on her birthday. The pie, she confessed, was the sweetest memory she had of that marriage.

Pie does that: loosens tongues and inhibitions. Tell someone you're looking for a good slice of pie and their countenance changes: shoulders sigh, brows soften, eyes open wide as a barn door. Memories drift to a spiced sweet-potato pie cooling on the kitchen sill, to backyard picnics and church bazaars and Ma's favorite rolling pin, worn handles faded artichoke-green.

Pie brings even the crustiest people out of their shells.

All lovers of pie can remember exactly where they ate their favorite slice as clearly as they remember their first kiss.

And all pie lovers, I would soon discover, have a story to tell.

De Tocqueville had his Beaumont, and as my departure date neared, I realized I needed mine. What a shame to discover a great slice of blueberry pie and have no one to share it with. Who would warn me about gruesome roadkill up ahead or play the state-capital game on those long stretches between pie stops?

I called my friend Kris to see if she would join me on the American pieways. A producer of commercials, Kris is always game for adventure. She, too, has traveled the world, from Dar es Salaam to the Australian bush, but had yet to explore the American outback. And, like me, who had just broken up with someone serious, Kris was untethered. She had grown disenchanted with advertising and was tiring of San Francisco, where, she insisted, she would never find a man. She could use a good road trip to clear her head.

Kris had one concern.

"I'm hypoglycemic and can't eat too much sugar," she said.

"Is that going to be a *problem*?"

We made a pinkie pact to run every day on the road to keep pie thighs at bay. We tossed our running shoes in the trunk—and that's exactly where they stayed for the next three weeks.

dawn

"Morning is when I am awake and there is a dawn in me."
—HENRY DAVID THOREAU, *WALDEN; OR*
LIFE IN THE WOODS, 1854

Any veteran of the road will tell you it's always best to get an early start. There's nothing like beating the sunrise on a desert highway with that first cup of steaming coffee coaxing your senses back to life.

A dawn departure makes the day's possibilities seem endless. It means you will be able to "motor" instead of just drive. "Driving" means you will be efficient: you will stop to relieve yourself at the same place you stop for gas. "Motoring" means you can dawdle: you can pull over when you see a sign for a tag sale or poke around a cool rock shop. Motoring means leaving yourself enough time to get lost and secretly hoping that you will.

Most veteran pie bakers will also tell you it's best to bake a pie first thing in the morning, before the house, or the day, have come to life. There's a stillness to dawn that keeps your dough from acting up. Maybe it's a stillness of spirit that radiates right down through to your fingertips. Before that first telephone call, that first glance at the morning headlines, your mind hasn't started racing yet, hasn't filled up with lists.

Similarities end where temperature is concerned. While it's best to let your engine warm up before you clock that first mile, the opposite is true for pie ingredients. "Chill" is the pie-baker's mantra. Your fat of choice—butter, lard, or shortening—should be as hard and cold as the slate floor against your bare feet. Whether you use milk or water in your dough, it, too, should be ice-cold so that when your knuckles bear down on the mealy mound in your bowl, you'll be reminded of the earth in your geranium pots when it's time to bring them in for the winter.

Even your mixing bowl should be as cold as your ears when vanity prevents you from wearing a hat in winter, and some bakers even refrigerate their mixing bowls overnight before making a pie. All this requires some forethought, of course, something that went out of style when we learned to point and click. But the number-one rule of the art of pie—and there *are* rules, I learned—is that you can't rush a pie any more than you can hurry on a two-lane road with a tractor hauling hay up ahead . . .

on the road

> *"There is a time for departure even when
> there's no certain place to go."*
>
> —TENNESSEE WILLIAMS, *CAMINO REAL*

Jack Kerouac had no trouble finding pie when he was on the road. His daily dose of apple pie à la mode was a steadfast source of nutrition, he wrote. No doubt that familiar wedge of pie also had a grounding effect on the rambling poet.

It seemed like a good omen to begin my journey by driving past the small unassuming house on Russell Street where Kerouac is believed to have penned a draft of *On the Road*.

I lived in a sunny studio right around the corner, on Russian Hill, so it wasn't much of a detour.

Pescadero, a two-hour drive south of San Francisco, now *that* was a detour. But it was where Richard P., a seasoned cable-car operator, had suggested we go for good pie. In the spirit of the hunt, Kris and I had set out to find a cable-car operator for a pie recommendation in San Francisco. What could be more typical than a grip man?

We'd found Richard at the Bay Street turnaround. He was on a break, in his empty trolley, eating a Fuji apple. Behind him, the Golden Gate Bridge's twin vermilion towers were being swallowed up by a meringue of dense fog.

"Do you know where I could find some good pie around here?" I asked, testing my pie handshake for the first time.

Richard seemed relieved that we weren't asking for the nearest rest rooms. He smiled.

"Pie? San Francisco isn't a pie town," he croaked. "Pie's too pedestrian. For a good pie, I'd get out of the city and go down the coast south a ways, to Duarte's in Pescadero," he said. "Try the olallieberry pie. They grow the berries right there behind the restaurant."

I had heard of Duarte's Tavern (pronounced Do-Arts), a roadside diner in San Mateo's coastal farming community, famous for its buttery artichoke soup, but had never been there. We weren't crazy about backtracking from the get-go—but going where we were told was part of the pact. Besides, neither one of us had ever heard of olallieberries.

A crowd of Japanese tourists gathered around the cable car. Richard looked at his watch and reached for the grip.

"Hey, you two ladies have a safe trip now," he said above the sound of clanging bells. We didn't know it yet, but this farewell, thrown out as casually as a banana peel, would become a leitmotif of the trip. There wasn't a person we met on this journey, from the woman who ran the rock shop in Springdale, Utah, to the 79-year-old antiques dealer in Russellville, Arkansas, who didn't send us off with that singsong road-luck blessing.

So, the next morning, we pointed the piemobile south instead of east. On U.S. 280, we rode alongside latte-sipping commuters bound for Silicon Valley. We left them at the Half Moon Bay turnoff and followed the seven-mile narrow road past sleeping Christmas-tree farms to the water's edge. For the next 15-mile stretch of Highway 1, the Pacific ocean sprayed the tall bearded iris lining the road.

Pescadero, "fisherman" in Spanish, is a small, one-street town with old frame houses whose roots date back to the pioneer Yankees who made their way west. Duarte's Tavern is right on Stage Road, once the main artery along the California coast. Ron Duarte himself was out sweeping the sidewalk when we parked beneath the tavern's retro neon sign.

Barely taller than his broomstick, Ron was tickled that Duarte's was to be the first stop on our pie tour and that a longtime cable-car operator had urged us to try the olallieberry pie his mother, Emma, made famous.

"Have you girls ever seen an olallieberry vine?" he asked.

We shook our heads.

Broom still in hand, Ron escorted us to his home, directly across the street, and opened the latch on the white picket fence brimming with peonies, delphiniums, and daisies. He led us to the rear, where trained olallieberry vines, dotted with white star-shaped flowers, stood tall on the verge of summer ripeness.

An olallieberry is a cross between a loganberry and a youngberry. It grows primarily on the West Coast and has a distinct fruity flavor, much sweeter than its blackberry cousin. Ron, a dead ringer for Mickey Rooney, said his family had planted several vines "as an experiment" years ago and that they took remarkably well to the foggy coastal climate.

Indeed, ruthless El Niño storms had just pummeled the California coast, wiping out his strawberry crop and toppling cliffside homes, but the olallieberry vines were thriving.

Kris and I were eager to taste our very first pie of the trip, particularly since neither one of us had eaten breakfast. But Ron wanted to show us the artichoke patch behind the restaurant. He explained the difference between a tubular artichoke, which has more heart and more flavor, and the more common seed variety. Then he took us to see a batch of baby goats, still wobbly on their Q-tip legs, that his son was raising to make cheese.

I was wondering why Ron was being so friendly when he pulled me aside and extracted a small, tattered, spiral-bound notebook from his chest pocket.

"I really understand what you girls are doing," he said, handing it to me. Every page had a recipe or a description of a meal. Turned out Ron and his wife traveled extensively and Ron liked to collect recipes as souvenirs. He made me look up the rhubarb-and-marionberry pie he'd tasted in Alberta, Canada, and still woke up some nights dreaming about.

"I'll give you the recipe for your collection, if you'd like," Ron said. I told him thank you, but I had to *earn* mine, as he had his.

Maria Huerta, one of thousands of Mexican immigrants drawn to this fertile, agricultural area for work, had just pulled a batch of pies out of the oven when we entered Duarte's kitchen through the back door. She usually bakes between fifteen and thirty pies a day, depending on what's in season and on the time of year. In broken English, Huerta said she'd never eaten pie as a child, but here she was, whipping them out with no apparent stress.

In the kitchen, two younger women with long, flowing ponytails, also from Mexico, were cracking steamed Dungeness crab for the cioppino, and the milky smell of sweet crab competed with the aroma of just-baked olallieberry pies.

By the time we sat down at the counter, it was lunchtime, so we ordered some creamy artichoke soup before our pie. Kathy Duarte, Ron's daughter, told us the Duarte's story, which began in 1894 when Ron's grandfather, Frank, brought a barrel of whiskey up from Santa Cruz, placed it on top of the wood bar, and sold shots for ten cents a pop. In 1934, Ron's parents took over the tavern and added a barbershop and a sandwich parlor. Ron's mother, Emma, baked pies every morning from 7 A.M. till noon. Old-timers still talk about Emma's way with pie.

Kris and I had decided that we'd share each and every slice of pie on this trip to keep her hypoglycemia and our waistlines in check. Kathy understood, but her father would hear nothing of it and sent out two thick slices of olallieberry pie. Maria had not skimped on the deep-purple filling, which spilled out on either side of the wedge like the flowers in Ron's garden. The crust was on the tender side. Flaky, fragile, and slightly sweet.

"The secret," Kathy said, leaning across the counter, "is to put milk in the dough instead of water."

Ron was happy to give me the recipe for his mother's pie, my first.

I still had olallieberry seeds in my teeth when we took the mind-numbing I-80 toward Reno, and Kris could feel a sugar rush coming on. But we both had a very good feeling about our first pie out. That night, we passed several truck-weigh stations on the road and toyed with the idea of getting weighed at the start of the trip.

Naaaaaaaah.

THE LATE EMMA DUARTE'S OLALLIEBERRY PIE, FROM DUARTE'S TAVERN, PESCADERO, CALIFORNIA

DOUBLE CRUST

¾ cup of shortening

2 cups all-purpose flour

1 teaspoon salt

⅓ cup of cold milk

FILLING

1 quart olallieberries (raspberries or boysenberries will do)

1¼ cups of sugar

a handful (approximately ¼ cup) of flour

With a pastry blender, cut the shortening into the flour. Add salt and milk. Stir well; if too dry, add more milk. Roll out half of the dough and use it to line the bottom of a 9-inch pie pan. Roll out the remaining dough for the top crust. Set aside. In a heavy bowl, mix 1 quart berries with 1¼ cups sugar and the flour. Fill the pie shell and rest the remaining dough on top. Seal it well and bake at 375 degrees for an hour or until brown. Put a pan underneath the pie while it's baking, to catch the drippings. Serve warm with fresh clotted cream or vanilla ice cream.

no-luck nevada

*pie-alley: a bowling term which refers to a
lane where strikes are easily made.*

In the early morning sun, the parched earth—orange and pock-marked along Highway 50, better known as the Loneliest Highway in America—looked like baked corn bread. Up ahead, in the faded-denim sky, snow-capped Pinto and Pancake summits kept a watchful eye on the valley's alkaline flats.

Not much to see out here but the occasional shuttered brothel and tufts of wiry sagebrush skedaddling across the highway. When we saw a sign for the Loneliest Phone on the Loneliest Highway, we pulled over to check in with the parents (had to). "Had any pie yet?" my mother asked in French. I tried to describe an olallieberry to the best of my ability.

"*Très intéressant* [Very interesting]," she said. "*Sois prudente!* [Be safe!]"

We had purchased a CB radio for the trip so we could ask truckers for their pie recommendations on the road. This was as good a place as any to install it. The more-mechanical Kris tackled the job while I ducked behind some sagebrush to answer nature's call.

A series of big rigs thundered past and honked. Back in the car, we immediately set the CB on channel 19, the truckers' channel, to see what we'd retained from those late-night reruns of *Smokey and the Bandit.*

We heard a couple of truckers having a good chuckle at my expense.

Loneliest Highway in America, my foot!

We'd been driving for about an hour, listening to a local country station, when Kris, who was sunning her legs out the window, straightened up and asked:

"What are we going to call her?"

"Who?" I asked, turning down the radio. "Your car," she said. "We can't drive a nameless car across America. It's bad car karma."

"All of *my* cars have had names," she said. There was Felix, her first, a brash and speedy Datsun B-210, and Günther, a spiffy, hunter-green Karmann Ghia, and, finally, Rowdy, her new Audi A4, named after Olympic swimmer Rowdy Gaines.

All of her cars were named after men, and I was thinking about the psychological ramifications of this when she said: "What about Betty?"

I liked it immediately.

Betty is a '50s kind of name that, for me, has always conjured up images of curvy women with broad hips and wide girth . . . signature traits of the 240 Volvo sedan. Plus, there was the whole Betty Crocker connection.

We agreed to make it official by running Betty through a baptismal car wash at the first opportunity. We patted her dash and, from that moment on, Betty became a character, not just a car.

At around 2:30 P.M., we pulled into Austin, a scruffy little town that has experienced a steady melancholy decline since 1873, the year a silver ore mining boom ended. Three hundred people live in Austin, which boasts three cafés, three gas stations, and three motels.

"Maybe we'll find three pies," I said. Our first day out had been so successful, I was feeling confident. In Nevada, I'd made the executive decision to bypass Las Vegas. I told Kris I wanted to find a slice of real desert pie. Not some mass-produced Caesar's Palace pie served up by a chain-smoking waitress in a toga.

We got gas and I walked over to a sheriff's deputy sitting in his parked black-and-white sedan, bronzed forearm dangling alongside the door. "Can you recommend a good place for pie around here?"

Deputy Pete Hegge was young and handsome in a "crunchy" sort of way, a striking contrast to the decaying town he was paid to protect. He rubbed his chin.

"I'm kind of new in town but, you know, who can help you is Darla, our dispatcher. Why don't you follow me to headquarters."

Darla came out of her hutch of an office and icily asked us what our business was. She thawed as soon as we explained our mission.

"I wasn't going to give you two the time of day, but now that I know what you're looking for, I have all the time in the world," she said, taking a seat next to Kris. "I *love* pie."

Two German tourists had just walked in with some serious car trouble. But Darla told them they'd have to wait.

"I have some bad news for you girls, though," Darla said. "There is no good pie in Austin. No good pie at all."

"What about that International Café down the street?" Hegge asked. She shot him a pistol with her eyes.

"I can defrost a pie as well as they can," she said, curling her upper lip. "Which way you two girls headed?"

Hurricane, Utah, for bumbleberry pie, we said. Darla couldn't think of any good pie between Austin and Hurricane. But she was most curious about bumbleberry pie, surprised, even somewhat embarrassed, that as a pie connoisseur and a woman of the law, she hadn't heard of it. She scribbled her address on an office memo pad and wrote in big letters: PLEASE SEND ME INFORMATION ON BUMBLE-BERRY PIE.

Officer Hegge walked us back to the car. "Sorry she wasn't much help," he said. "Say, what are you ladies calling yourselves?" He'd spotted the CB antenna.

"We're thinking the piemobile," said Kris.

Hegge winced. "I don't think you want to go with that," he said. "Two redheads driving across America in a piemobile? That could get you into a whole lot of trouble."

We blew through Eureka and Ely and Connor's Pass where, at dusk, we headed south on desolate US Route 93 toward Utah, with no pie in sight.

"Maybe Nevada isn't a pie state," I sighed. "Maybe we *should* have gone through Vegas."

In the dusty, barren Panaca, a wild mustang came barreling down the highway, headed straight for our car. Kris swerved just in time. Sunflower seeds and baby-carrot sticks—our pie-thigh antidote—flew everywhere. The nervy, dark-chocolate horse bolted, running slanted, as only wild horses can, then disappeared into someone's backyard.

Eerie. A few miles down the highway, we noticed a sign touting the state's mustang protection program. The wild horse had bucked us right out of our funk. I found The Rolling Stones' CD with the "Wild Horses" cut on it and popped it in the player. Kris was cruising at eighty-five, or that's what the clenched state trooper told us he clocked her at when he pulled us over and shined a flashlight in our faces.

"Do you know where we can go for some good pie around here?" I asked the badge as he examined Kris's driver's license. I saw his jaw slacken ever so slightly.

Tammy at the de Veyo Mercantile

"Nope," he said. "Nothing around here for miles."

He handed Kris her license. "This is your lucky day, ladies. I'm going to let you go this time, but you slow down a bit, OK?"

We thanked him profusely and continued on south on state Route 18 toward the Utah border. Lucky? It was 9 P.M. and we still hadn't found any pie in Nevada.

We were both parched from the sunflower seeds, so around 10 P.M. we pulled into the Veyo Mercantile, which is connected to an RV camp and seemed to be the nerve center of a hamlet called Veyo. Kris stayed in the car, and, when I spied the gleaming display case behind the register, I was sorry she had. Wedged between bug repellents and cans of chewing tobacco was a veritable oasis of cream pies: banana cream, lemon meringue, and coconut cream, all lined up like Vegas showgirls.

"I'll tell you what, the pies will kill you here," said Tammy, the long-haired woman in a Harley Davidson T-shirt behind the counter. "People come all the way from Vegas to buy them."

Redeemed, I ran outside to get Kris, who was methodically picking sunflower seeds out of the gear box. "Jackpot!" I said.

The baker, Evaline, 79, wasn't in at this late hour, but Tammy gave me her phone number—after selling a fishing license to a guy in tip-to-toe camouflage.

We shared a generous slice of banana cream in the car, right there in the parking lot. The thick-cut banana slices sat plump and cold on my tongue while folds of freshly whipped cream tickled my palate. I didn't know what was sweeter: the pie or the success of finding pie just when we'd lost hope in Nevada.

Either way, it was a wondrous thing to be tasting my first slice of banana cream pie on a warm spring desert night under a rhinestone sky.

"They all call me the pie lady around here," Evaline said when we spoke. She'd moved from Connecticut to the desert to be near her son. She was only five when she made her first pie—apple. Growing up, she'd had pie for dessert every single day. Making pie was second nature to her. Not so for today's generation of women, she said.

"I have young girls who come into the bakery looking for work and they've never even seen a rolling pin, let alone roll out a crust," she sighed. "Everybody wants everything ready-made and out of the freezer these days."

I was too embarrassed to tell her I had never made a pie myself. I did tell her that her banana cream pie was an inspiration.

"The secret is the *touch*," she said. "I've given my recipe, ounce for ounce, to lots of people and they tell me it never comes out as good."

"I'll take my chances," I said, and I took down the recipe.

The sugar buzz from the pie gave us enough energy to drive on to Hurricane, to find a motel. As I sat up in bed tracing our day's route on the map with a yellow highlighter, I realized that Veyo was technically, though just barely, in Utah—not Nevada.

Oy Vey-o.

EVALINE'S BANANA CREAM PIE

CRUST

1 9-inch pie crust

FILLING

½ cup sugar

¼ teaspoon salt

3 tablespoons cornstarch

1½ cups milk

½ cup light cream (half-and-half)

3 egg yolks, lightly beaten

2 tablespoons butter

1 teaspoon vanilla

¼ teaspoon banana extract

1–2 bananas, depending on size

WHIPPED-CREAM TOPPING

¾ cup heavy cream

½ teaspoon vanilla extract

1 tablesoon sugar

pinch of salt

Combine sugar, salt, and cornstarch in a small mixing bowl and set aside.

Scald milk and cream and slowly beat in the sugar mixture. Cook on low flame until filling thickens.

Beat a small amount of this filling into your 3 beaten egg yolks. Mix thoroughly, then incorporate egg mixture into the filling. Cook at low temperature, stirring constantly, until thick, about 3-4 minutes.

Remove from heat. Add butter and flavorings. Pour ⅓ of filling into prebaked pie shell. Slice bananas on top. Add remainder of the filling.

Let cool. Beat topping ingredients together until thick. Slather on pie.

fumbling toward bumbleberry

"Snozzberry? Whoever heard of a snozzberry?"
—LITTLE MIKE TEAVEE, *WILLY WONKA AND THE CHOCOLATE FACTORY*, BOOK AND SCREENPLAY BY ROALD DAHL

The first thing we learned when we woke up in Hurricane, Utah, was that it was pronounced *Hurry-cun*. The second thing we learned was that it was *not* the home of bumbleberry pie.

My friend and colleague Scott couldn't remember the name of

the café where he'd allegedly tasted this pie, but he'd told me we couldn't miss it: "There are signs for bumbleberry pie all over the town."

Here we were, in the eye of the Hurry-cun, surrounded by strip malls, and there was no such sign in sight. In fact, the only sign that caught our eye was one for a GIANT YARD SALE. Naturally, we pulled over.

Donna P. was trying to clear some space in her 1920s Mission-style home, a refreshing architectural gem in this sea of 1960s stucco. Donna was smiling. She had just sold an old wooden carriage for $100 and two old friends, Vi and Lloyd, had dropped by in their RV to visit and rummage through her toss-aways.

The seventy-something Vi wore a tight T-shirt with these words stretched across her bust: "If you don't like my attitude, quit talking."

She was as plucky as that wild mustang we dodged in Panaca. Surely, she'd tried the local bumbleberry pie, I thought.

"My full name is Violet Rosela," said Vi. "My mother named me after a flower; she'd be whirling in her grave if she knew I'd turned into a weed."

Indeed, Vi had tasted the famous bumbleberry pie, and it was in Springdale, Utah, about 20 miles east, near the entrance of Zion National Park.

"I don't know what the big deal about bumbleberry is," she har-rumphed. "Lloyd and I like the coconut cream pie at Grandma Bishops right around the corner much better. Don't we, Lloyd?"

Lloyd, a retired old driller, who wore one of those mesh baseball caps that could double as a pasta drainer, agreed with his wife, which, I imagined, he did often. Neither Kris nor I had ever tasted coconut cream pie, so we decided to stop at Bishops on our way out of town. It looked like it was going to be a two-pie day, and that made me happy. Three Utah pies would surely make up for striking out in Nevada.

Mel, our waitress, had an attitude and eyes layered thick with powder-blue shadow. We'd barely ordered our eggs when she slapped the check on the table facedown. We took the hint and our slice of coconut cream pie to go and were glad we did. There was enough sugar in this pie to choke every weed from Hurricane to Springdale.

We tossed it in the first trash receptacle we could find and coined the term "Dumpster pie."

Springdale is one of the main gateways to the national park, and holiday traffic was already heavy through town. An outdoor table filled with blue-lagoon calcite rocks caught our eye. We ducked inside the rock-and-gem shop to ask the owner, Sherry, where we could find this bumbleberry pie we'd heard so much about. She tried to suppress a laugh.

We explained that our mission was loftier than merely satisfying a sweet tooth. We were after pies with geographic significance.

"Well, this is Mormon country, ladies," Sherry said. "Mormons rarely go *out* for pie. *Home* is where you go for good pie around here."

Was that an invitation, we asked. "Goodness, no," said Sherry. "I don't bake. But Elva Twitchell, who lives right across the street in that little house, makes great peach cobbler and pie. She sometimes brings some over. Let me give Elva a call and see if she's home."

It was mighty nice of Sherry whose husband had left her for a California tourist who had wandered into the shop one afternoon looking for rocks.

"She says to just go on over," said Sherry, hanging up the phone and pointing to a white clapboard house across the street.

Elva Twitchell's daughter, Sharon, opened the door with a bucket of aqua curlers in one hand. Elva, 88, was sitting in a worn velvet

recliner in the living room. We'd interrupted a Cliff Robertson movie.

"Do you mind if Sharon sets my hair while we talk?" Elva said, muting the television. "We're going to my great-grandson's eleventh birthday today and I want to look my best."

She had a calm, peaceful expression on her face and a slow, deliberate way of blinking that reminded me of the Thumbelina doll I had as a child. She didn't seem the least bit surprised that two strangers would land on her doorstep to talk pie.

"I'm not sure why Sherry sent you over here, though," she said. "Everyone in town knows that my sister Beulah's pie is better than mine."

It was the way she said her sister's name that suggested Beulah was the elder sister. And while the pie seeker in me did want to speak to the better baker, the little sister in me wanted to stay exactly where I was.

She told us that her family had homesteaded in Zion canyon before it became a national park in 1931. She described the days she spent chasing polliwogs in the streams ("we always put them back") and climbing over the park's famous jagged red rocks.

The word "Zion" means a peaceful resting place. But Elva's life didn't sound all that restful. As a Latter-Day Saint, she was raised to be completely self-sufficient, which is why she made all of the clothes for her seven children by hand ("I didn't make the boys' overalls, though") and baked two fresh pies every Sunday. The secret to her peach pie, she said, wagging her curved index finger for emphasis, is to "thicken the filling with a little tapioca."

Elva told us that Mormon pioneers first began to settle in southern Utah in the 1850s. They grew crops, planted fruit trees, and raised livestock in Zion canyon where they lived in dugouts and small log cabins.

"I only wish my own children could have known what it was like to grow up there, too."

When her hair was set in white lamb curls, Elva asked if we wouldn't mind moving into her kitchen. She was more comfortable there, surrounded by all her knickknacks, her collection of porcelain salt-and-pepper shakers, her teapots, the wooden sign that said "Elva's Kitchen." She was crushed that she didn't have any ready-made peach pie for us to try. The peaches in the backyard weren't quite ripe, she said.

"Can you come back in a month?" We told her this was a one-way trip. "My, my, you girls must be having fun," she said.

Elva wondered why we were so fascinated with pie.

"It's really not difficult to make a pie," she said. "You just have to practice until you get that first one right." Then, after a moment's reflection, she said:

"I guess I do feel a sense of pride and accomplishment when I've made a pie first thing in the morning."

Careful not to muss up her new 'do, we gave Elva a big hug on her doorstep and thanked her for her peach pie recipe.

"I sure wish you had time to talk to Beulah," I heard her say from the end of the walkway.

Scott may have been wrong about the town, but he was not wrong about the signs. The Bumbleberry Restaurant was attached to the Bumbleberry Inn, which hosts the Bumbleberry Theater. The owners of the bumbleberry compound were sitting down to a late lunch, and invited us to join them for a slice of pie and a lesson on the mysterious berry.

"The bumbleberry is a cross between a binkelberry and a burple-berry," owner Ken Smith said with a perfectly straight face. "It grows on a giggle bush and can only be picked by a happy, kind-hearted person."

Kris and I laughed politely. Pen to pad, I waited for something useful to jot down.

"The size of the berry is determined by the heart of the picker," Smith went on to say. "It grows only where nothing else can grow. At the precise moment it becomes ripe, the bumbleberry giggles. And if you're eating a bumbleberry at the right time, you will spend the rest of your life giggling."

I put my pen down. Clearly, this was *not* a recipe they were will-ing to part with, although many food writers—and investors—have tried to pry it out of them. Smith explained that the secret recipe came with the restaurant, which his family, also Mormons, bought from a frugal woman of pioneer stock who often mixed her leftover fruit-pie fillings.

"One day, she came upon this combination of berries that was particularly magical," Smith said. "When the customers asked the waitress what was in the pie, she came up with the word 'bumbleber-ries' and it stuck."

According to the Smiths, the recipe does not exist on paper. The current pie baker, Tracie, was whispered the recipe in her ear by her mother, who'd baked for the restaurant for years and had recently retired.

When the pie arrived, the Smiths derived obvious (and, may I say, not very spiritual) pleasure in watching us try to divine the berries in the filling. The beet-purple color and the tug-of-war between sour and sweet made us guess it was a combination of blue-berry, blackberry, and maybe rhubarb.

The crust was puff-pastry light and dusted with powdered sugar. Our teeth stained purple, we laughed our way through the ochre sandstone cliffs and shaled slopes of the national park where the cacti were in peacock bloom. The moon lilies were wilting in the heat like a belle at a barbecue. These can be hallucinogenic, I told Kris, and we wondered if the Smith family didn't have its own private patch.

When we emerged on the other side of the park, we bought some buffalo jerky from a roadside vendor to satisfy a serious craving for salt.

HERE'S HOW ELVA TWITCHELL MAKES PEACH PIE:

CRUST

"I usually make enough dough for three pies at a time, and freeze any pie I'm not going to eat. For five cups of flour, I use about two cups of shortening, but that's rough because I usually don't measure anything. I like the butter-flavored Crisco because it seems to come out flakier. My sister Beulah uses lard and, like I said, her pies are *very* good. I add a little bit of ice-cold water to the dough, and a teaspoon of salt. I also put in a spoonful of vinegar and beat up a whole egg into the dough. It just seems to make the dough handle better and makes it less sticky. I bake it until the crust is brown on top, in a 400–425 degree oven. Careful, if the temperature is too high, the fruit will boil over."

FILLING

"For a nine-inch pie, I peel and cook about three LARGE peaches just until they're tender. But you really don't have to cook them, you could just cut the sliced peaches and lay them in the crust. I usually sweeten them with a little bit of sugar (about two tablespoons, I guess) and season them with cinnamon and nutmeg and throw a bit of tapioca in there, too."

a pie is not a tarte—
vive la difference!

Piebald: *having irregular patches or spots of colors, particularly black and white, as in a piebald cow.*

I've done my share of foolish things for love. And on those long stretches between pie stops, Kris heard about most of them.

The craziest, Kris agreed, was spending a year on a dairy farm in northern France, in a village named Warlus, with a population of 200 and a median age of 72.

I was 23 then, and in that carefree space between college and graduate school. My love interest at the time—an older Frenchman—had been asked to teach at an experimental language school there.

Housing was limited. We landed in a two-room cottage attached to a dilapidated barn. I agreed to simply "play house" for a year in the French countryside.

That meant learning to wash clothes in a tiny portable washing machine and getting used to the occasional piebald cow poking her head through our bedroom window.

When I tell people about my year in Warlus they imagine a bucolic, under-the-Tuscan-sun experience. But Warlus didn't have any of the obvious charms of Cortona. The town was so small, there was no bakery for croissants or even a village grocery or a café. To the villagers, Paris, where we, thankfully, spent most weekends, may as well have been the end of the earth.

Although I spoke French fluently, I stood out like a sore thumb for what the villagers called my "American eccentricities." A few days after moving in, for instance, I decided to wash our muddy Fiat in the open barnyard. I was scrubbing the hubcaps to the beat of Madonna's "Papa, Don't Preach" on my boombox when I sensed I was being watched. I stood up and saw a dozen villagers standing in a half moon around the car, staring.

"We let the rain do that here," a beret-clad farmer said, arms folded across his barrel chest. "Are you gonna wash my tractor next?"

To try and ingratiate myself to the farmers and because I was curious, during calving season, I asked if I could watch the next time a cow gave birth. Two days later, a teenage boy rapped on our bedroom window at 5 A.M. I dressed quickly and followed him to the main barn. Two of the older, red-nosed farmers were standing directly behind the cow, facing each other. Each had one gloved arm buried deep inside the cow's privates, and was trying to pull the calf out by its legs.

Next I knew, I was lying faceup in a pile of hay with four old, whiskered Frenchmen hovering over me. "Quick. Someone get some calvados for *l'Americaine*." The farmers walked me home, my legs wobblier than the newborn calf's.

I stayed indoors a lot after that. I passed the time by writing long, detailed letters to my parents. And I learned how to make a *tarte*.

In fact, this *Americaine* learned to make a *tarte* long, long before she ever tackled her first pie. And there is a difference.

"*Une tarte ne cache rien* [a *tarte* hides nothing]," my mother said when I called her long-distance before my first attempt: a *tarte aux pommes* with Normandy apples and a recipe I'd clipped from *Elle* magazine.

A *tarte* is always topless, or open-faced. Pies, more often than not, are covered, if not with a top crust, then with a mound of meringue or a blanket of whipped cream, making pie slightly more forgiving. Generally speaking, a *tarte* crust is sweet, buttery, and has a crumble to it. It could easily stand alone if it had to. Pie crust, on the other hand, is less sweet, and has a crisp, not crumbly, texture. On its own, pie crust is rather uninteresting.

A *tarte* pan is already fluted and has shorter, non-sloping sides, so the filling-to-crust ratio is larger. *Tarte* pans also have a removable bottom, which makes for a more elegant presentation.

I don't remember the details of making my first *tarte*, but I do remember taking my time and not being stressed. I didn't own a rolling pin, and I used a bottle of Sancerre to roll out my dough. I remember that the Frenchman found it delicious and that we dunked leftover slices in our café au lait the next morning.

The ignorance of youth? Perhaps. But I just don't think making crust is grounds for trauma in France, where a cook is more likely to be judged by her coq au vin or the balance in her vinaigrette.

In America, pie crust is the barometer of a cook's mettle. Susan Westmoreland, food editor at *Good Housekeeping* magazine, says all candidates applying for jobs in the test kitchen must roast a chicken *and* make a pie from scratch.

"Making a pie is the ultimate test of a good cook," she says. "It shows technique *and* heritage."

Emboldened by my first effort, the following week I made a pear tart for my neighbor Monsieur Poulet.

Poulet was the only person in Warlus who didn't make me feel like an outsider. I spent many an afternoon in Poulet's barn, both of us on low-slung stools, me watching him dunk then pluck chickens at record speed.

"Bravo, la tarte!" he said with a thumbs-up sign, when he came by two days later to drop off my weekly order of a just-skinned roasting rabbit.

I'd raised rabbits as pets but I had no compunction about cooking rabbit, having been weaned on my mother's country cooking. One thing, however, made me squeamish—Poulet's habit of leaving one back paw on, its fur still intact.

"Ca porte bonheur, [it brings good luck], *Mademoiselle,"* he'd say whenever I peeled back the *torchon* [damp kitchen rag] and cringed.

I finally told him I had enough good luck to last several lifetimes, but by then the Frenchman and I were headed stateside.

The relationship ended a few years later, and I never heard from Poulet again. But there have been many moments in my life, and on the pie trip in particular, when I was grateful for all the luck those rabbit feet kicked my way.

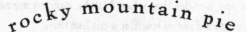

"The rule for overcoming fear is to head right into it."
—ANONYMOUS

Two days into the trip, we had already logged 1,236 miles, eaten four pieces of pie, dissected the men we'd dated, extolled the virtues of navy-blue toe polish, compared biological clocks, and examined our respective relationships with our fathers.

Could we keep up the pace—calorically and conversationally?

In Colorado, the plan was to head toward the canyons above Boulder, but not without stopping to visit our respective families first.

My sister Valerie, and her husband, Jerry, live in Steamboat Springs, in a small house nestled against the mountain, with their daughters, Natalie, 8, and Allison, 5.

I hadn't had a chance to explain the pie quest to my sister before leaving California. With two small children in the house, phone conversations are usually clipped.

She seemed surprised I'd chosen pie as my grail since, like me, she felt pie was a stranger. Although her husband is American, she'd never made a pie either. Still hasn't.

"I don't think it's right to make a pie with a frozen crust," she said defensively. "And since I'm scared of crust, I've never made a pie."

I didn't know my big sister was afraid of anything.

Jerry thinks a frozen-crust pie is better than no pie at all, and so, once a year, for Thanksgiving, he makes pies with the girls using store-bought crusts.

So, is it any wonder that when Natalie handed me an apple pie recipe as we headed out of town, it went like this:

PERFECT APPLE PIE BY NATALIE PEARL

"You get some crust at the store. When you're at the store, you get twelve yummy delicious apples. Peel them and cut them up into triangles. Put a plate under the crust. Put apples on top of the crust and pour ¼ teaspoon of sugar and ¼ teaspoon of cinnamon and then put another crust on top and bake at eighty degrees for twenty minutes."

Kris's parents had prepared a homespun Italian meal for us in Denver. Her father was also perplexed by our journey, though the simple logistics of it were what threw him.

"You mean you just go up to complete strangers and talk to them about pie?" he asked, his spaghetti fork poised like a question mark. "And they talk back?"

Earning the trust of strangers, getting them to talk is key to my job. Maybe to a civil engineer like Kris's dad, I realized, such behavior is as odd and mystifying as Emma Duarte adding milk to her dough.

We rose at dawn, hoping to make up for our lazy Sunday. Kris's dad had been thoughtful enough to pack a few Frank Sinatra CDs for us.

"You can't drive across the country without the Chairman of the Board," he said. Maybe he was telling us he wanted to come along.

On the Peak-to-Peak Highway, bordered by shimmering aspens, a jet-black wild pig lurched in front of the car, sending me into the other lane. We missed the pig—and an oncoming Jeep—by a bristle.

Our nerves jangled, we stopped at the Sundance Café and Lodge for breakfast. One table over, a cool middle-aged couple—cool in that they seemed to genuinely enjoy each other's company—shared a stack of buttermilk pancakes. I leaned over to borrow some syrup and ask where we could get some good mountain pie. Karen, the director of cultural programs at the Boulder Public Library, and her partner, Tom, a contractor, were building a home in nearby Coal Creek Canyon. They liked to carbo-load on pancakes every weekend before pounding nails, they said. They didn't hesitate when we asked them for a local pie recommendation. "You've got to go to the Gold Hill

Inn," they said. Gold Hill, which has no stoplights or pavement, we learned, is the oldest mining town in the Nebraska Territory.

On a sticky napkin, they drew me a map with lots of little fingers for canyons. We followed the rippled index finger for some time until the road switched from pavement to dirt without warning.

I saw a strapping young man in khaki shorts and a T-shirt working in his garden, and pulled over to ask if we were on the right path to Gold Hill and good pie.

He wiped his brow and shook his head.

"Oh, you're headed for Gold Hill all right," said the man, whose name was Bill. "You're also headed straight for pie heaven."

We sat on a boulder and let him explain. It turned out, he too had recently gone on a quest for pie. Banana cream pie. He'd begun the quest as a game, with his ex-girlfriend who shared his lifelong passion for this vintage dessert. They broke up before finding the perfect pie.

Maybe it was his way of keeping the relationship alive, said Bill, an organic herb farmer, but he'd never stopped searching. He had almost given up hope. Then, one day, that previous winter, he was coming down the mountain after a day of cross-country skiing in the Arapaho Recreation Area and he stopped at the general store in Gold Hill for a quick sugar fix.

"There, right in my own backyard, was the most wonderful banana cream pie I'd ever seen," he said. "I sat down and ate it, and I knew I'd found my pie. It's funny, but when I needed it most, that's where it was."

We offered to take him up the dirt hill, known as Lick Skillet, for a slice of this perfect pie, but he declined.

There are 160 people who live in Gold Hill year-round and, at last count, 57 dogs. But on weekends, the town, a maze of low-slung log cabins with flowerpot porches, triples in size as Boulder residents, bikers and hikers, head up the hill for good food and bluegrass.

It was Memorial Day, and the Gold Hill Inn was closed. So we headed straight for the general store to find Bill's banana cream dream.

No one knows for sure when the general store was built, but Hugh Moore, who bought it a few years ago, has a copy of an early bill of sale for $4.25 dating back to the 1880s. The store used to sell hardware, as evidenced by the metal bins lining an entire side wall. Today, it serves as a community center of sorts: video store, fax service, post office, consignment store, grocery store, and café.

Moore said they got many of their pies delivered from a bakery in Boulder—but the banana cream pie is the only one that's made in-house by a young woman on his staff.

On cue, she emerged from the kitchen balancing a hot tray of twice-baked potatoes. Susan, in her early 30s, was wearing a full-length apron with a red-chili-pepper motif over a peasant blouse and a pair of shorts and Birkenstocks. With her mane of floppy curls and her sad, deep-set eyes she reminded me of a cocker spaniel.

She was flattered—albeit surprised—that someone had raved about her pie.

"Did he really say it was the best he'd ever had?"

When we asked her her secret, she blushed.

"I cannot tell a lie," she said. "I got the recipe from the back of a Jell-O pudding box."

Susan never ate pie made with box mix when she was growing up in North Carolina.

"My nana used to make boysenberry pie from scratch when I was a little girl," she said. "All the kids and cousins would go pick the berries on her farm and then we'd bring them to her kitchen and she'd get to work and we'd all watch and wait for the pie to come out of the oven.

"What would my grandma say if she knew I was making pies from a box?" We told her that Nana would just be glad she was still making pie. So few people her age seem to take the time anymore.

There were only two slices of banana cream pie left, so Kris and I shared one on the spot and had the other slice wrapped for Bill. It was much sweeter than the one we'd had in Veyo, and the banana chunks weren't as firm or single-minded. But it had big fluffy mounds of whipped cream worthy of a double-black diamond powder day in the Rockies. Perhaps it was the pure mountain air, Susan's freshness of spirit, or that her nana had somehow passed on "the touch." But the pie didn't taste box-made at all.

Handsome Bill was relaxing on the porch when we pulled into his driveway to deliver his pie. He was grateful, took a bite, then said he'd save the rest for later. We decided it was best not to tell him that it was pudding-mix pie. In the end, did it really matter?

On deadly quiet and arrow-straight Highway 36, going toward Kansas, we passed eerily quiet and flat Colorado towns with names like Last Chance and Cope. We saw our very first silos of the trip that night. In the dusk hour, they glistened like the handlebars on a new bike.

"I think I'm going to move back to Colorado and find myself a man like Organic Bill," said a wistful Kris.

P.S. About a year later, I was in a restaurant bar with a friend in Irvington, just north of Manhattan. We were talking about the pie trip, and a woman three stools down overheard our conversation and wandered over.

"Are you the Pie Lady?" she asked.

(Ever since my articles about my search for American Pie had run in the local Westchester paper along with a picture of me and Kris and the piemobile, readers would often corner me in the supermarket or at the bank and ask me if I was the "Pie Lady" from San Francisco.)

"You interviewed my brother in Colorado," the woman said. "Bill, the herb farmer."

Sometimes the world seems no bigger than an eight-inch pie pan.

Kris still hadn't met anyone and, on her behalf, of course, I asked if Bill was still single.

"I'm not sure, but I think he started dating that gal you mentioned in Gold Hill who made the banana cream pie," she said.

I have both Susan's and Bill's phone numbers in my pie journal. I've considered calling to see if it's true. The romantic in me keeps me from dialing. Best to keep on believing instead.

kansas

"You dare to come to me for a heart, do you? You clinking, clanking, clattering collection of caliginous junk!"

—WIZARD TO TIN MAN, *THE WIZARD OF OZ*

The sky was streaked purple and gray, like a shallot, when we passed the WELCOME TO KANSAS sign around 8:30 P.M. With its beaming sunflower set against a violet backdrop, it was the prettiest state sign yet, so we stopped alongside the highway and took pictures.

Maybe it's because we were leaving the West and entering unfamiliar territory, or maybe we were curious to discover pie in the Land that inspired Oz, but Kris and I, barefoot since Boulder, were feeling giddy.

The dusk air felt warm and wheaty. Neither one of us wanted to get back in the car, which was starting to feel crowded and was strewn with soggy sunflower-seed shells. Suddenly we were doing cartwheels in the middle of the highway, trying to land square on the dotted yellow line.

Kris clicked her heels three times.

Our goal was to make it to Oberlin, in the northwest pocket of the state, where our AAA guidebook promised a clean budget motel and a monument to the nineteen settlers who'd been killed in the last Indian raid.

For a long time, it was just us and the silos on Route 36, then a fleet of June bugs came out of nowhere and slammed their green bulbous bodies against Betty's windshield.

The windshield was so littered with bug goop, we almost missed the sign for the Frontier Motel in Oberlin. The fiftysomething woman behind the counter seemed daisy-fresh at this late hour. "You're lucky we have a room, because there's a fiftieth high school reunion in town," she said, handing us a cartoonish wind-up alarm clock on three legs. (When I picture my biological clock, I picture one just like it.)

We asked her about the June bugs.

"In the Midwest, kids like to tie a string around their legs and fly them like a buzzing kite," she said.

"But I just hate those buzz bombs," she said. "Tell you what: if I get one of those down my blouse, I don't care who's standing in front of me, I'll just rip my clothes off."

The alarm buzzed us awake at 6 A.M. We used a dull plastic knife to scrape dead-bug residue off the windshield before hitting the road.

In 1878, an Indian by the name of Chief Dull Knife led a band of Cheyennes across Kansas, leaving a path of destruction in their wake. Oberlin was the site of their last battle. Neither one of us was keen on seeing the monument, so we headed south on Highway 83. I'd promised Kris that we'd make a stop in Liberal at the very bottom—or stem—of the corn state to visit the Dorothy Museum. Liberal is where Frank Baum is believed to have written *The Wizard of Oz* and where Dorothy Gale allegedly lived. Kris has seen the movie twenty-eight times.

There are 4,606 John Deere retail outlets in North America and my guess is, two-thirds of them are located right along Highway 83, where one mile feels like three. The map had promised "scenic," but only a Kansas farmer could consider the flat, dull promise of corn picturesque.

No wonder Frank Baum had such an active imagination.

For a much-needed diversion, we stopped at Prairie Dog Town petting zoo and freak show. The zoo is home to the world's largest prairie dog (8,000 pounds) and such bizarre attractions as caged city pigeons and a cow with an extra leg coming out of its rear.

We talked to truckers on the CB radio more often in Kansas than in any other state—out of boredom, really. A trucker named Norman waxed "pie-etic" about his mother's peanut butter pie. Norman couldn't recommend any local spots for pie, but he suggested we stop in Oakley to get a feel for a typical small Kansas town.

"OAKLEY?" Kris nearly slammed into Norm's rig filled with corn feed.

Several years back, a woman Kris knew from college had surprised all of her friends by moving to Oakley to marry a farmer. Oakley had always seemed like a mythical place to Kris, even after she'd heard that the friend had dumped the farmer and moved back to Denver. We were so close it was a shame not to stop and visit, she said.

Norm honked and left us at the Oakley exit. It was odd, having spoken to him for so many miles without seeing his face.

The main drag was so quiet, I wondered if the whole town had picked up and gone fishing.

"I can't believe Sabrina lived here," said Kris, scanning the lifeless town. The Carrell Variety Store had a pulse, so we stepped inside where it was nice and cool.

Louise, the cashier, turned from her register to greet us. She had long gray hair and wore glasses that were twice too big for her face, but her skin was translucent and her smile broad.

She was eager to help a new face in town, she said, but couldn't think of any place between Oakley and Liberal that had any good pie.

"You wouldn't consider backtracking, would you?"

Backtracking in Kansas? I went as limp as the Scarecrow.

"Because you just passed the best pie in Kansas about 50 miles northwest of here, in Colby. My husband and I drive to Colby at least once a week just for their pie at the Deep Rock Café."

And then there was no stopping her.

"My husband is a pie connoisseur," she said. "Every time we go on vacation we stop at little cafés to try their pie. He grew up with pie every day, on a farm in Seldon. His mother used to bake them for the church. He doesn't like to go anywhere except to look at and taste pies. He likes coconut cream, I like mincemeat."

By now, a long line of customers had formed at the register—a woman buying beads for a wedding quilt, a girl who looked like a wax bean in cutoffs clutching some Chupa Chups, a man in overalls buying mothballs.

Louise kept talking to us as she rang them up. From Michigan originally, she had moved to Oakley because "I like small towns where everybody knows everybody's business." Louise's husband, Dean, was a retired wheat farmer. On their first date they stopped to check on his crop on their way to dinner.

"I think what he liked about me was that I was willing to go traipsing through the fields in my high heels and panty hose."

I didn't know which vision was more entertaining: the one of Louise running through wheat fields in her panty hose or of the Frontier Motel lady stripping in public to free a buzz bomb from her bra.

"Well, it certainly wasn't my baking skills that won his heart," Louise said, rescuing me from my own thoughts. "I've always been intimidated about baking pie . . . I guess it's because pie has such emotional baggage.

"My mother is a superior pie baker and I wouldn't dare attempt a pie with her around," said Louise. "Whenever she comes to visit she makes her famous apple pies and the smell of warm cinnamon apples just fills up the house."

The people standing in line nodded knowingly.

Interesting, I thought, that after everything we've accomplished as women, it's often their domestic aplomb we admire most about our mothers.

If Louise and Dean braved the drive to Colby every week for pie, then surely we could make the drive just once, I told Kris.

To amuse ourselves on the drive there, Kris made several phone calls to track down her girlfriend Sabrina in Denver.

Sabrina couldn't believe that we'd found Oakley. What drove her out, she said, was exactly what had attracted Louise: "Everybody knew everyone else's business," she said. And we laughed, because she remembered Louise.

It was lunchtime, and the regulars were keeping the waitresses dressed in pink shorts, pink blouses, and matching pink hairbows, hopping at the Deep Rock Café. Between ads for a local muffler shop and auto parts store, the menu boasted no fewer than thirty-five pies.

Pauletta, the pie baker, had just left. "She has a side job pulling wells with her husband," a friendly waitress named Grace explained. Grace was more than happy to sing Pauletta's praises, though.

"When Pauletta makes the meringue, if there's so much as a dot of yolk in the bowl, she'll toss the whole thing out," she said. She turned to greet a customer. "Hey there, I didn't recognize you without your suspenders."

Then she leaned in to our table and whispered:

"You can set your clock by Frank," she said. "He's a corn-and-wheat farmer who comes every day for his fix of Dutch apple pie." Although Pauletta has trained other members of the staff to make pie, Grace said, "we think there are secrets she holds back."

In honor of Louise's husband, Dean, we gave coconut cream another shot. The crust was unusually flaky. But the filling did nothing for me. This had little to do with execution. I just realized right there in Colby, Kansas, that I was not a coconut cream kind of gal. Neither was Kris.

The Colby stop had delayed us, and by the time we arrived in Liberal, the Dorothy Museum was closed. Kris was crushed. There's nothing else to see in Liberal. So, having found pie in Kansas, we wandered into an antiques shop where we had fun looking at old cookbooks before hitting the road.

"Knowing how to make a pie is a certain means to a man's heart," I said, reading aloud from a farm journal cookbook.

"That's it," said Kris, "I'm getting myself a rolling pin."

She bought the book. I bought Ruth Wakefield's 1930 *Toll House Cookbook*.

We ran Betty through an automatic car wash and washed those June bugs right out of her grille.

TREASURE IN THE
BARGAIN PILE

Ruth Wakefield's book turned out to be the best $1 I ever spent. In this excerpt, Ruth examines common "pie failures" and their causes. No mention of "the touch" anywhere.

If your pie burns around the edges:
   a. oven too hot
   b. pastry too thin on rim of plate
   c. pans placed too close to oven side or to other pans on
      same rack

If your top crust is too light in color:
   a. oven not hot enough
   b. insufficient baking time

c. oven too full, cutting off proper circulation

d. pie set too low in oven

If your pastry is tough:

a. not enough fat

b. handled too much when it was rolled out

c. too much flour in dough

d. too much flour used on rolling board

If your pie is soggy on the bottom:

a. set too high in oven

b. shiny tin or aluminum pans intensify condition

c. oven not hot enough, especially during first part of baking

d. pie stood too long before being placed in oven

e. too much liquid in filling

If your double-crusted fruit pies boil over:

a. too much fruit for depth of pan

b. edges not firmly sealed

c. crust punctured near edge of pan

d. oven too hot

e. baked too long

o-k-l-a-h-o-m-a!

*"Away from the superslab, you can still order a piece of pie from the
person who baked it, still get change from the shop owner, still take a
moment to care and to be cared about, a long way from home."*

—MICHAEL WALLIS, *ROUTE 66, THE MOTHER ROAD*

My favorite picture of my parents is the one of them standing cheek-
to-cheek on the top of the Empire State Building. It was taken forty
years ago, when they were both 26, shortly after they moved to
America.

My mother is wearing a strapless cream dress with navy polka
dots big as balloons. My father is clutching her thimble waist tightly,
lest she fly away.

My parents really tried to make a go of it in New York. My father
worked as a waiter in a fancy French restaurant and they rented a
dirt-cheap basement apartment in the heart of Hell's Kitchen. But
after their first snowy New York winter, they decided that perhaps
California was the America they'd dreamed about back home. So
they scraped together enough money to buy a 1957 Chevrolet Bel
Air and drove there.

Funny, the things they remember about the twenty-one-day road
trip along Route 66. The motel swimming pools shaped like kidney
beans. The "Soft Shoulder" road signs, which, they thought, were
there as a gentle reminder to relax their shoulders while driving.

They picked Santa Monica as their final destination, because "it had a pretty ring to it," my mother says. Santa Monica was also where Route 66 came to a full stop, on a palmed bluff overlooking the Pacific Ocean.

It was important to me that we hook up with the historic highway at some point on the trip. Though Route 66 was finally put to pasture, "decommissioned," in 1984, sections of it still remain, often paralleling the superslab that replaced it. Such is the case in West Oklahoma, where we met up with the historic highway in Clinton.

It was late, we needed a room. The sign at the Best Western Trade Winds Inn beckoned shamelessly: SLEEP WHERE ELVIS SLEPT.

Neither one of us were big fans of the black-velvet crooner, but we asked for the Elvis room anyway.

The woman at the front desk, Kay, wore a sherbet-green pantsuit and eye shadow to match. She was sorry but room 215, where Elvis slept four times, was already taken. Would a ground-floor room by the pool do?

Sure, but we wanted to know more about the Elvis connection. Walter Mason Jr., also known as "Doc," owns the franchise and took care of Elvis personally.

Doc told us that Elvis was afraid to fly. So, during the '60s, when he was making movies in Hollywood, Elvis and his entourage would take long road trips between Los Angeles and Memphis, stopping at the Trade Winds for some shut-eye. At The King's request, Doc never told a soul.

Sadly, Doc said, on what turned out to be Elvis's last visit, a maid delivering food to room 215 glimpsed The King through the cracked door.

"She made a Paul Revere ride through the downtown area," said Doc, "and pretty soon all of Clinton was in the hotel parking lot chanting his name."

Elvis stepped out onto the balcony and waved to the crowd. He even tossed a ball with some of the kids but, Doc sighed, "he never came back after that."

After all these years, Doc had kept the Elvis room just the way it was. He said "corporate" had been pressuring him of late to bring the outdated room furnishings in step with the rest of the hotel chain. He wasn't budging.

We asked Kay and Doc if they had any local pie recommendations for us.

"I'll tell you, I fell in love with that pecan delight pie at the Flamingo Restaurant in Elk City," said Kay. "I used to go there all the time with my grandmother. I think it's the best-kept secret in Oklahoma.

"It's been years since I've been there, but I still think about that pie every now and then," she said. "The baker was a sweet old woman with white hair." Elk City was 20 miles behind us, but backtracking seemed to be becoming a habit. Besides, I liked the image of a young Kay sharing pie with her grandma, so we decided to go there after breakfast.

Our 7 A.M. wake-up call the next morning came courtesy of twenty-five Harley hogs being revved up one at a time. A posse of leather-clad German tourists, all Route 66 junkies, had shipped their Harleys stateside for a late-spring ride from Chicago to California. We were grateful for the early start because we had a lot of ground to cover, and finding pie, even bad pie, was proving challenging.

Kerouac didn't know how good he had it.

We walked over to the Route 66 Café connected to the hotel and, going past the Dumpster, we noticed an old, yolk-yellow Best Western sign resting on its side. It bore the hotel chain's former corporate logo—the sparkling royal crown. So much more whimsical and certainly more inviting than its bland replacement, better suited for a bank.

Jimmie, Ferd, and Darrell

We ordered coffee and eggs and dived into our journals to catch up on the events of the last few days.

A brawny man with a polka-dotted scarf wrapped around his black straw hat sauntered in holding a bouquet of fresh-cut roses, yellow and peach, straight out in front of him.

"These are for you," he said, handing them to the waitress behind the counter where he took a seat. "They're from my garden. They're for putting up with me every day."

"Oh, Jimmie, you shouldn't have," the waitress said, flipping his cup over to pour his coffee.

"Now, where are my grits?" he barked.

A few minutes later, an elderly, thin-lipped toothpick of a man climbed right up on the stool next to Jimmie's and also ordered grits.

"Hello, Ferd," Jimmie said, his head buried in his crockpot o' grits. "Hello, Jimmie," Ferd replied. Five minutes later, Darrell arrived and took his seat to the right of Ferd. "Hello, Ferd. Hello, Jimmie," he said.

"Now the trio's complete," said the waitress of the three friends who looked ready to trade Clinton news of the day.

I slid on the stool next to Jimmie and asked him about the flowers.

"Aw, that's nothing. These ladies put up with a lot from regulars like me," he said. "Sometimes I bring horny toads in for their kids."

Surely such a generous soul would point me toward some fine pie.

"Pie?" said Jimmie, pulling on his long beard. "My mama used to make the best rhubarb pie. I can't tell you how good that pie was."

"Rhubarb?" the waitress groaned from behind the counter. "Yuuuuk."

Jimmie sat up straight and wagged an angry finger. "Anybody who don't like rhubarb pie just get out of here right now," he said. He was 12 again; a classmate had just dissed his mama in the schoolyard.

Ferd told his friend to settle down.

"Well, OK, then, not everyone likes rhubarb," Jimmie said. "I'll admit even *I've* grown more fond of coconut cream in my old age."

Indeed. Jimmie told us he often drove the 80 miles or so up Highway 40 (the new Route 66) to the Cherokee in Calumet, a truck-stop chain, "for a slice—or two." He rubbed his taut, protruding belly as evidence.

Ferd, who made us guess his age (86!), pooh-poohed Jimmie's recommendation. "My wife Leoda makes the best coconut cream pie in the world," he said. "That's why I married her.

"Yes, sirreee, it was her coconut cream pie that done me in."

Neither one of them had eaten the pecan delight pie in Elk City, which worried me a little, but at least Darrell, the quiet one, had heard of the place.

Ferd, who works at the car wash across the street, reached into his blue work shirt pocket to give us a token for one free wash.

"You've got to get to West Oklahoma to find Southern hospitality," Jimmie said. "The best people in the world live in this little town of Clinton, which, incidentally, ladies, was named long before that guy ever made it to the White House."

As we loaded the car, one of the maids called out to us from the upstairs balcony. She was outside the Elvis suite, balancing a stack of sheets in the crook of her arm.

"You girls want a peek at Elvis's room?"

The tacky room was exactly as I'd imagined. King-sized bed with a white scalloped headboard, a white vanity, a divan, smoked-glass mirrors, and Viva Las Vegas bathroom fixtures. We took turns, posing on the bed, for a Polaroid picture. The maid giggled, declined our offer to take one of her.

Betty had just gotten a scrub in Liberal, but since we had no plans to return to Clinton in the near future, we used Ferd's token and gave Betty a rinse anyway.

"Pecan delight pie, here we come," I said as we pulled out onto Route 66. Kris had high hopes for this pie, but the word "delight" attached to anything edible always makes me nervous.

I took one look at the refrigerated pie display and, once again, saw only tufts of meringue and cream. This display case had angled mirrors on each shelf, so you could see the top of each pie. Kind of kinky. We asked if we could meet the elderly baker we'd heard so much about.

A woman in her late 50s stepped gingerly out of the kitchen. She seemed too young to be the veteran baker Kay had described, but, then, there was the pecan delight pie in the case, in all its burnt-orange bouffant splendor.

Carla was extremely shy. Like Elva, she failed to grasp the meaning of our mission. Pie was pie. She was too close to it to appreciate its worth or imagine life in America without it. She'd learned to bake when she was only four, using a miniature rolling pin her aunt Cissy had given her.

Tactfully, we asked her if she was the baker Kay had described.

Carla at the Flamingo Restaurant, Elk City, OK

"Oh, no," she said. "That's Gloria. She retired a few years back. She's in a nursing home just north of town. But we still use a lot of her recipes." Still full from breakfast, we bought our slice of pecan delight to go, and slid it in the glove compartment for later.

"Something tells me we should try and find Gloria," I told Kris who knew better than to argue with my instinct.

Elk City is the kind of town where the local newspaper lets parents know on the front page when report cards are ready, so it was easy to find the nursing home on the outskirts of town. Gloria was slumped in a wheelchair, waiting for a nurse to come change her soiled clothes. She was not completely lucid, and it took a while for her to realize that two strangers were in her room.

She caught me admiring a decorative, three-tiered pie stand on her nightstand.

"My son gave me that," Gloria said, her speech slow and slurred. "It's a jewelry box."

I heard myself saying that we were researching the best pies in America and we'd heard from several pie experts that her pies had been voted the best in the state. It was a stretch, especially since we hadn't even tasted the pie yet. Kris looked at me and smiled. "Congratulations, Gloria," she said, shaking her hand.

"That makes me very proud," Gloria said. "Thank you for telling me." A nurse arrived at that moment and wheeled Gloria into the bathroom to change her. We slipped out.

And for the first time since leaving California, Kris and I had nothing to say.

Lucille Hamons was just the gal we needed to see to lift our spirits. If John Steinbeck called Route 66 the Mother Road, then the plucky Lucille, who ran a Route 66 gas station just south of Hydro for sixty years, had to be the mother of the Mother Road.

Lucille and her husband, Carl, bought the gas station in 1941. When World War II erupted, Carl started hauling hay to the northern states to pay the bills. Lucille learned how to pump gas and fix flats. When Route 66 gave way to I-40 in 1985, many businesses tumbled, but the by-then widowed Lucille hung on, selling cold drinks and highway memorabilia.

A stop at Lucille's eventually became a rite of passage for all those cruising the historic highway. A slip of a woman, Lucille was sitting at her kitchen table, showing her beloved scrapbook to three hard-core bikers when we strolled in. One of the bikers wore a Daniel Boone–style hat. The head of a fox was still attached, and its muzzle lay flat on his forehead.

He asked us if we were "66ers," too. We had to tell them the truth, that our quest for pie had only intersected with Route 66. Lucille had zero interest in pie and she made that very clear, immediately bringing the conversation back to the famous highway and her place on it. So we sat down and listened quietly as she made it through to the very last page of the scrapbook.

When she was finished, "Daniel Boone" recommended an unforgettable pie in Hamden, Connecticut, where he grew up. "I've traveled the country," he said, "and it's still the best pie I ever had."

"Any pie in particular?" I asked. "No, they're all good," he said. That should have been a tip-off.

We took pictures of Lucille with the bikers next to the gas pumps and then we rode off in search of Jimmie's Cherokee restaurant off the interstate in Calumet.

Amy, the 18-year-old hostess, sat on a stool, directly under the chin of a wall-mounted bison head, ringing up customers who mechanically handed her the check, then grabbed a toothpick.

Amy has a soft spot for the lemon meringue.

We looked at the pie case and saw only cream pies. My heart sank. Was I ever going to see a fruit pie again?

I couldn't bear to eat another slice of coconut cream. Amy said she had a soft spot for the lemon meringue.

"When I was little, I'd always buy my grandmother lemons at the store and then bug her to make me a pie," said Amy.

Lemon meringue was another first for me. Sadly, the only words I scribbled in my pie journal were: "foamy, yellow, practical."

A trucker we talked to in the parking lot said he stopped for pie at the Cherokee whenever he started to nod off at the wheel. "The sugar picks me right up," he said. So did, I suspected, the fresh-faced Amy.

Exhausted from our pie-packed day, we barreled down a quiet

two-lane back road toward the Arkansas border. As night fell, the first fireflies of the trip flickered around Betty as if to say: "What are you doing way out here?"

"It's like a scene from *Fantasia*," said Kris.

And then we remembered the pecan delight in the glove compartment, which, since it was mostly whipped cream, was no longer delightful or safe to eat.

We tossed it somewhere between Eufala and Spiro on US 9. It was on that lonely stretch of road that we noticed a ramshackle "liquor shack" and pulled over to buy a small bottle of Maker's Mark bourbon, so that we could pour a civilized drink if and when we found ourselves a room that night. We were due.

The store was connected to the owner's living room and we glimpsed him, a bear of a man, watching television in his Barca-lounger with a poodle on his lap. He shuffled into the store in his muscle T-shirt and overalls, the yapping poodle running circles at his feet.

The poodle wore a spiffy pink bow, and when it jumped into its owner's arms, we noticed that its tiny claws were painted fire-engine red. We suppressed a giggle.

"They paint her nails at the beauty parlor," the man said defensively. We paid for our bourbon and backed out of the store.

Lucille Hamons died a few months after our visit. The funeral procession crawled from Weatherford, Oklahoma, down Route 66 to her old store, where she was once photographed kicking up her heels for a "Get Your Kicks on Route 66" postcard.

Here's the recipe for Ferd's wife's pie—the one that made him weak in the knees.

LEODA MUELLER'S
COCONUT CREAM PIE

FILLING

½ cup sugar

½ cup sifted flour

¼ teaspoon salt

3 cups of milk

3 egg yolks, lightly beaten

¾ cup shredded coconut

1 tablespoon butter

1½ teaspoons vanilla

CRUST

1 prebaked pie shell

MERINGUE

3 egg whites

¼ teaspoon cream of tartar

6 tablespoons sugar

¼ cup of shredded coconut

Mix sugar, flour, and salt in a saucepan over low heat. Add milk gradually and keep stirring until smooth and mixture comes to a boil.

Remove from heat and incorporate the hot mixture, in small

batches, into a bowl with the lightly beaten egg yolks. Return this mixture to a saucepan, let boil for two minutes, stirring constantly. Remove from heat, add coconut, butter, and vanilla. Let mixture cool, then pour into a prebaked pie shell.

For the meringue, beat egg whites and cream of tartar until frothy; gradually add sugar as you continue beating until egg whites form stiff peaks. Spread over pie filling, sealing the edges of the pie to prevent shrinkage. Sprinkle coconut over meringue. Bake at 425 degrees for about 5 minutes or until meringue is delicately browned and the coconut is toasted.

# of bowls, buford, and pine bluff

"Flyspecks! Flyspecks! I've been living my life among flyspecks, while miracles have been leaning against lampposts on the corner of 18th and Fairfax."

—DR. WILLIAM CHUMLEY TO ELWOOD P. DOWD
IN THE PLAY *HARVEY* BY MARY CHASE

I have a collection of old ceramic mixing bowls, which I did not have before I drove across America.

Most are displayed in my kitchen, but I keep a butter-yellow bowl I bought in Virginia on my desk as a round reminder of my journey— and as a handy receptacle for divorced pen caps and stray paper clips.

Its sides are scalloped like an Esther Williams swim cap. The interior is crackled, and I like to believe this bowl was a workhorse in its day.

Maybe it was a woman's wedding ring, hitting the side of the bowl as she whipped egg whites, that cracked the glaze. Something tells me this bowl has played a starring role in many lemon meringue productions.

The wide-openness of a worn bowl invites such wanderings.

Although my mother was never a baker, she had—and still has—such a bowl. Hers is sage-green, wide, deep, and remarkably heavy.

For as long as I can remember, my mother served our tossed green salad in that bowl every night. And on special occasions it was the vessel of choice for my mother's famous *îles flottantes*, or floating-islands dessert.

My mother would make this dessert whenever we were invited to a dinner party. I remember her sitting in the passenger seat with the green bowl lodged between her bird legs, cautioning my father to slow down so that the frothy egg-white islands floating on crème anglaise didn't jump ship.

The urge to buy bowls that had once been cradled by our nation's grandmothers surfaced somewhere in Colorado, where, incidentally, more dinosaur fossils have been found than anywhere else on earth. The urge intensified as the journey progressed. Just as in pies, I wasn't looking for pottery with a pedigree. Yellow ware, for example, once deemed utilitarian, is now the ultimate in kitchen chic.

No, I looked for bowls that spoke to me, like poppy-orange and pool-bottom blue bowls that had seen a ball of dough or two in their prime.

Burrowing through dusty, cluttered "antiques" shops was, I realized, a good way to get a fast feel for the history and personality of a region. In Kentucky, for example, much of the antiques were horse paraphernalia: old bridles and bits. In Russellville, Arkansas, antiques shops were cluttered with locally manufactured pottery, and also became a great—albeit convoluted—source for a most memorable lemon pecan pie.

"Pie? You're asking me where to go for pie? Why would anyone go out for pie? Pie is something you should bake at home," Mary B. sputtered as she carefully wrapped in yellowed newspaper a green, thickly ribbed mixing bowl I had just purchased. Mary is a tall woman with Farrah hair and more glitz than, I'm sure, is legal in Russellville, which boasts sixty churches for a town of about 25,000. Mary was running things at the This n' That and Something Else antiques shop, to help out the vacationing owner. It was a good distraction, she said, as she had recently gone from wife to widow and was still adjusting to the emptiness in her life.

"I would never eat pie out because I make the best strawberry pie," she declared. "What do *you* think, Buford, you've had my strawberry pie. Isn't it goooooooooooood?" Buford Smith, a dapper vision in a cream linen suit with a cherrywood cane, had just snuck in the back door. Although a "retired" antiques dealer, Buford still made the rounds at the local shops in town to keep an eye on the lucrative pottery market, she whispered.

Mary explained our situation to Buford and, after some brainstorming, they came up with an artisan bakery in Leslie, in the Ozarks, which mutual friends had recommended to them. They weren't sure if the bakery made pie, but the friends said their bread was "out of this world," said Mary. It wasn't our modus operandi to follow a pie lead once removed, especially one as tenuous as this one. But Kris and I had both expressed a desire to see the Ozarks, and my journalistic nose was all in favor.

Buford wandered about the shop, slow and cautious as a heron, turning his head once in a while in our direction to examine us up and down. So many years in the cutthroat antiques business had made him wary.

When he was convinced that all we wanted was pie, he pulled up a stool next to Mary, planted his cane firmly between his bent knees, and wrapped both hands over the burled handle. For the next half hour words poured from his mouth slow and sure as sap. His father, as it turned out, owned the Little Model Café, one of the first bakeries in Russellville, which opened at the turn of the century. "So I know a thing or two about pie," he said.

"My father's egg custard was so good that all the bakers in Little Rock would come down to Russellville to watch him bake," he said. His father had started out as a sweet-potato farmer, but a series of devastating crop failures led him to open the bakery. "I've seen him bake a hundred pies at a time. He would sell four hundred slices of pie between 11 A.M. Saturday and noon on Sunday. Pie was 10 cents a slice back then."

I don't know if Buford and his father were close, but I could tell by the way he talked he would have liked them to be. I told Buford that listening to him talk was like reading a period novel.

"You should see his house, honey," Mary said. "Buford, why don't you let them take a peek?"

We followed Buford in his white Bentley into a quiet, peaceful neighborhood where majestic magnolia trees in full fragrant bloom offered a real Southern welcome. A large boulder at the start of the walkway was once used by Buford's grandfather to hoist himself upon his horse. "I had to fight tooth and nail to retrieve it from the family estate when my grandfather died," he told us, tapping the rock with the tip of his cane.

Hard to imagine blood relatives fighting over a rock.

Buford gave us a tour of the house, and his suspicions suddenly became clear. Rarely had I seen such opulence, outside of eighteenth-century chateaux in the Loire Valley. Room after room was cramped with gilded mirrors, French and British portraits from Napoleonic times, tapestries, golden mantel clocks, and ballroom chandeliers.

A man much younger than Buford was stretched across a couch in one of the more casual rooms, watching television. Buford introduced him as a fellow antiques buff and "my traveling companion."

Buford finally relaxed, took off his jacket, and pulled out a long nutty cigar, which he smoked on the porch. The two men regaled us with tales of their cross-country escapades visiting antiques fairs, historic cemeteries, and estate sales and eating pie and turtle soup whenever, wherever possible.

We talked until Buford got to the sweet part of his Cohiba, and then we had to push off to the Ozarks.

Arkansas back roads treated us to the most interesting church "message" signs of the trip. WAL-MART: IT'S NOT THE ONLY SAVING PLACE was my favorite. It was also in Arkansas that people started waving to us from their porches. People who seemed to have all the time in the world, sunken in overstuffed recliners with a dog at their terry-cloth slippers. Grand marshals at a parade, we waved back in slow motion.

When we got to the Ozark mountain range in the late afternoon, we could hear a loud crackling sound, like bacon frying in a skillet.

"It's the locusts," a construction worker on the main drag in Leslie said. "They come every seven years."

Locusts are short-horned grasshoppers that migrate in swarms so dense they can sometimes block out the sun. This year's infestation, although raucous, was relatively mild, and we were the only ones who seemed to pay any mind.

The bakery our Russellville friends had recommended in Leslie did indeed make pillowy bread in a wood-fired oven, but, to our chagrin, no pie. We needed to get to Mississippi later that night to stay on schedule, but we couldn't leave Arkansas without finding pie.

"What should we do now?" Kris said, hands on her hips.

Martha and Curtis Purvis

That's when Martha and Curtis Purvis walked through the door, holding hands. They were from Harrison, north a ways near the Missouri border. They were driving to Greenville, Mississippi, to visit family, they told the baker. They'd read about the new bakery in their local paper and had popped in for some fresh bread to snack on while driving. Since Greenville was also where we had planned to rest our heads that night, I butted in and told them so.

Within minutes, we were telling them about our pie plight and Martha squealed. "I know *just* the place for Arkansas pie," she said in a voice sweeter than any pie we'd had thus far. "And it's on your way to Mississippi."

I wanted to kiss her.

"Pie is *the* dessert at Jones Café in Pine Bluff," she went on. "They make it from scratch, don't they, Curtis?" Martha and Curtis had been married for twenty-one years but you'd think it had been twenty-one hours by the way they clung to each other. Curtis, a sales contractor, agreed with her, of course, but he was quick to point out that no restaurant pie in the state could match Martha's.

"Martha can put a chocolate pie together in thirty minutes and then we'll sit down and eat the whole thing in one sitting," Curtis said, pulling Martha closer into him.

"Curtis makes a very good pecan pie himself," she countered, "his mama's recipe."

Then Curtis confessed that it was Martha's delicate ankles, not her pie, that won his heart.

Martha blushed.

She works at the cosmetics counter at Wal-Mart but she once dreamed of being a journalist, she said. She was crushed that we weren't going to drive through Missouri, because a restaurant there called The Sugar Shack had the most dizzying array of fresh-baked pies she'd ever seen.

"The first time we went there I ran back to the car to get my camera to take a picture, didn't I, Curtis?" she said. "Give me your address and I'll send you the picture."

The Purvises, who were driving a rambling baby-blue Ford pickup truck with a huge bugle horn on top of the cab, offered to lead the way to Pine Bluff, but we knew we'd be making some stops at antiques shops and fruit stands, and maybe even to walk a bit, so we declined.

Five hours later, after having done all of the above, we pulled into the Jones Café parking lot in the dark. We were making our way toward the front door when we heard a loud nasal honk coming from southbound Highway 65. Martha Purvis was hanging out her open window. "Yoo-hoo! Girls! Yoo-hoo! Enjoy your pie!"

You could have knocked us over with a pastry brush.

Ruby Jones was only 15 when she started cooking in Mrs. Walter Harper's boarding house—four boxcars pulled together at Stoudemire's lumber camp. The camp furnished the timber to the crew building railroad bridges. In 1925, at 23, she married Henry Jones, a Pine Bluff fireman. They opened the Central Grill right near the depot in town. She made from scratch dozens of pies, which she sold for 75 cents whole.

During World War II, Ruby fed lots of pie to the troops that pulled through town by train. When her husband retired, they bought a farm and Ruby opened the original Jones Café at nearby Noble Lake. All the fruit for the pies were grown at the farm. In 1985, the café moved to its current location, in Pine Bluff proper. When she was 90, Ruby would still turn up at the restaurant at 6 A.M., six days a week, to bake eighteen dozen rolls and make forty to fifty pies!

Ma Jones was 93 and living in a nearby nursing home when we dropped by the café, but her son W. R. "Wimp" Jones told us she was still calling daily "to make sure those pies are coming out just right," and that "those girls in the kitchen aren't using too much sugar and making that meringue weep" like those Arkansas willows we'd seen on our drive.

Several years ago Wimp convinced his mother to write a cookbook.

"It was really difficult to put it together because Ma's a *pinch* lady," he said. "You know, her recipes are full of a pinch of this and a pinch of that." Before she retired, Ruby passed on her baking secrets to Lizzie and Tootsie, the two gals in the kitchen.

Tootsie, 46, had just whipped up dinner for thirty, a party for a beloved teacher who was retiring from the Pine Bluff school district. The last customers in the house, we dined on broiled catfish, purple-hull peas, and corn bread. We left room, of course, for pie. The ten pies of the day were listed on a borderless blackboard hanging on the wall, with a piece of chalk tied to a string. Given the late hour, certain pies had already been scratched out—though not erased. We ordered a slice of lemon pecan and a slice of chocolate pudding pie.

How refreshing not to have to excavate through mounds of whipped cream or meringue to see the face of a pie, as we'd had to do in the last three states. The lemon pecan—predictably, another first for me—combined two of my favorite flavors and textures: a tart soft yellow filling capped with a sweet crunchy layer of pecan halves. Kris swooned over the chocolate silk, a smooth layer of milk-chocolate velvet pudding encased in a firm, no-nonsense crust.

Martha and Curtis Purvis were already spooning, ankles locked, in Greenville. No doubt our names came up that night. I wasn't sure why, but Martha Purvis got to me in some way. As naive as her airs were, she had one big secret over all of us, I'm convinced.

And it had nothing to do with chocolate pie or a well-turned ankle.

Tootsie came out of the kitchen to say hello after her shift.

"Miss Ruby taught me everything I know," said Tootsie, a big-boned gal with full lips, a beautiful smile, and ebony skin as dark and smooth as her silk pie. We asked her if she had any pie tips she could pass on to two novices like us.

"Make sure you work your dough real good just until you add the water," she said. "Real good." Hmmm. Kathy Duarte had told us she's careful not to overwork her dough, once she adds the milk. That's the thing with pie, we were learning. Everybody's got their own rules.

FIKE'S LEMON PECAN PIE
FROM THE JONES CAFÉ,
IN PINE BLUFF, ARKANSAS

(straight from *The Best of Ruby Jones* cookbook)

RUBY'S PIE CRUST

2 cups flour

½ teaspoon salt

⅔ cup shortening

6 tablespoons ice water or just enough to moisten and hold together

FILLING

3 whole eggs (unbeaten)

⅓ cup of melted margarine

1½ cups of sugar

¾ cup of pecan halves or pieces

1 teaspoon of lemon extract

juice of ½ lemon

a pinch of salt

Sift flour and salt. Do not measure flour until after it's been sifted. Mix shortening with flour mixture. Add ice water. (NEVER add more flour to mixture once water has been added, because pastry will become tough.) Makes 2 pie crusts.

Mix ingredients for the filling with fork. Do not use an electric mixer. Pour into unbaked pie shell. Bake at 300 degrees for 45 minutes.

BUFORD'S DAD'S
EGG CUSTARD PIE

CRUST
1 prebaked pie shell crust

FILLING
3 eggs
¼ cup sugar
a pinch of salt
1 cup whole milk
1 teaspoon vanilla
nutmeg to taste

Mix filling ingredients (except nutmeg) together in as pretty a bowl as you can find. Fill a prebaked pie shell with the mixture. Bake at 325 degrees for 45–50 minutes. Sprinkle nutmeg on top midway through cooking time.

π r round

Colonial women used round pans, literally, to cut corners and stretch out scant ingredients as much as they could. That's also why they baked shallow pies. Plump, juicy, deep-dish pies didn't emerge from

American kitchens until newly planted orchards and berry patches finally bore fruit.

By the turn of the twentieth century, it was not unusual for an American to eat a slice of pie daily. In 1902, when an Englishman suggested this was gluttony and that, perhaps, two slices a week would be plenty, the *New York Times* responded thusly:

> *"It is utterly insufficient . . . as anyone who knows the secret of our strength as a nation and the foundation of our industrial supremacy must admit. Pie is the American synonym of prosperity, and its varying contents the calendar of the changing seasons. PIE IS THE FOOD OF THE HEROIC. No pie-eating people can ever be vanquished."*

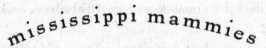

mississippi mammies

"Marriage pie is a pie made with two different types of fruit. In an ideal marriage pie, the fruit enhance one another while maintaining their respective flavors, textures and independence."

—PAT WILLARD, *PIE EVERY DAY*

I woke up in Greenville, Mississippi, wondering who had draped a wet blanket over me in the middle of the night.

I sat up, looked in the mirror across the bed, and shrieked at my Brillo-pad hair.

"It's the humidity," said Kris, who was already up and frantically searching for a scrunchie to tame her unruly curls.

Hair slicked down, we headed south on narrow State Route 1, toward Natchez. We had picked Natchez (pronounced Natch-issssssss) for our next pie stop, because it's the oldest settlement along the Mississippi River, and like pie, noble yet humble, it was full of contradictions.

Even though the cotton-rich city boasted the most millionaires and brass-button waistcoats per capita, Natchez was staunchly opposed to the Confederacy and Mississippi's secession from the Union. In its heyday, Natchez was as famous for its frilly antebellum mansions as for its steamy red-light district.

State Route 1 is a gangly road that slithers alongside the Mississippi River through spotty, forlorn towns where houses that had once stood proud are boarded up and left to the mercy of the oppressive, uncontrollable kudzu vine.

We passed lots of "shotgun" houses. From the road, you could see clear through the front-door screen to the barbecue smoker in the backyard.

The wet, taxing heat, the voracious vine, contributed to a sense of physical and psychic abandon in the air. For a change of scenery, we cut over to wider Highway 61 and saw our first fields of old King cotton, fields where the sweat and blood of blacks had paid for the fine filigree on those mansions still intact in Natchez.

Near Hollandale, a low-riding rusted-out Cadillac in front of us slowed way down. The driver opened his door and tossed the remains of his fast-food breakfast onto the highway. A foil wrapper flew onto my windshield and clung there to grease our disgust. After only a few days of driving, we were starting to feel a sense of ownership over these back roads.

At Vicksburg, we switched to the Natchez Trace Parkway, once a pre-Columbian Indian path, and that immediately lifted our spirits. The Trace, as it's called, was as forested and self-contained as Narnia: a shaded tunnel of kudzu vine, towering oaks, and Spanish moss. From the 1780s to the 1820s, the road was popular among farmers and craftspeople who would transport their goods downstream by raft and take the Trace home, watching for roving bands of thieves.

Natchez was ringed by the usual generic suspects: chain hotels and Jiffy-Lubes. But the generic quickly gave way to the genteel, when we drove into the old part of town, barely changed, it seemed, since before the Civil War.

In fact, Natchez, which sits on a high bluff, had been spared the ravages of the war, and when a boll-weevil infestation pillaged local crops in 1908, developers lost interest in the pretty town. Each garden was prettier and more fragrant than the next, brimming with azaleas, glossy-leafed camelias, jasmine, and dogwood.

We wanted to see the mighty Mississippi up close, so we made our way down to Natchez-Under-the-Hill, a spirited part of town with lots of restaurants and shops, which flanks the river. At an outdoor restaurant and bar we took in a Mississippi sunset and a mint julep.

A handsome married couple in shorts and flip-flops came to sit next to us. Braxton and Carol, both locals, both in the insurance business, said juleps by the river was a Friday-night ritual. They had lived in Natchez all their lives and they couldn't say enough about their hometown.

I had planned to ask one of the tour guides at the antebellum mansions where in Natchez to go for pie, but since neither Kris nor I wanted to leave this magical spot, we decided to stay put and ask Braxton and Carol instead.

"Mammy's Cupboard," they said without hesitation. "It's a restaurant shaped like an old black mammy and the dining room is inside her hoop skirt," they explained. "Doris, the owner, makes pies just like our grandmas did," said Carol. "We love the banana caramel."

A restaurant shaped like a mammy? Was that not considered insensitive, we asked. They laughed.

"Welcome to the South. . . . People don't get ruffled about things like that as much as they do in California," said Braxton. "But we all get along better than you think."

Just then, the *American Queen*, the largest paddlewheel steamboat in the country, crawled upriver, docking directly in front of the restaurant. With her delicate gingerbread filigree and two towering smokestacks, she looked like a floating wedding cake capped with a decorative bride and groom. Perhaps it was the julep working its mint-mash magic, but I half expected Mark Twain to come strolling down the gangplank, tamping his pipe.

When we stepped out under the canopy of stars, the paddleboat's thousand small lights beckoned. "They'll never let you on board without a passenger ticket," said Carol, who caught me eyeing the gangplank.

What Carol didn't know was that pie takes you places you never thought you'd go, from the artichoke patch at Duarte's in Pescadero to Elva Twitchell's living room to the king-sized bed Elvis slept on four times.

A grumpy guard at the top of the plank was about to prove me wrong, when an engineer named Mike, who just happened to be walking past, interjected.

"Did I hear correctly? You two ladies are driving across America looking for pie?" He unhooked the security rope to let us through.

We turned and waved good-bye to Braxton and Carol.

Mike had been an engineer for the touring steamboat company for years, and Natchez was his favorite stop along the Mississippi.

"Do you know *why*?" he asked. "Because there's a black mammy named Sophronia who sells delicious sweet-potato pies right on the lawn there," he said, pointing to the spot where, just moments earlier, we'd said good-bye to our new Natchez friends.

We asked him if he had heard of Mammy's Cupboard.

"Sophronia is the *only* mammy you need to know in Natchez," he said resolutely. Mike gave us a tour of the stately ship, from the turn-of-the-century opera house to the Mark Twain Gallery with its reading and writing nooks. Then he led us to the bow of the Texas Deck, where he invited us to sit on any one of an assortment of empty rocking chairs and porch swings.

"We call this 'the front porch of America.' Make yourselves at home," he said. "I'm going to go to my room and dream about that sweet-potato pie."

We sat quietly for a good hour on this "porch," watching the moon dance in the glossy licks of the river. I was 7 again, learning to jump rope on the front lawn of our Santa Monica duplex. With my arms shooting straight down either side of my body to keep my dress from rising up, I was chanting "M-I-SS-I-SS-I-PP-I."

Doris Kemp was about 7 years old when she got caught stealing an egg-custard pie from her aunt's windowsill.

"It was my cousin who put me up to it. We ate the whole thing to hide the evidence," she remembers.

"Children don't get caught stealing pies anymore, because there are no pies left on the sill to steal."

That's why they line up at Mammy's Cupboard on Saturday. Busy working people all longing for a slice of homemade pie. A slice of remember when. A slice of slow.

The sky-high café, truly shaped like a slim-waisted Aunt Jemima, is hard to miss. Mammy's head, adorned with hoop earrings and a knotted head scarf, towers above the oaks, themselves draped with scarves of Spanish moss.

The restaurant wasn't open yet, so we peeked through the front door and saw Doris, her white hair pinned in a loose bun, bringing her pies out of the kitchen one at a time until there were about fifteen on display. She carried each one with two hands and carefully placed it on a three-tier stand. Sometimes she'd take a step back to admire her handiwork. The coquettish tilt to her head suggested she was pleased. I felt guilty catching her in this moment of self-admiration.

The place filled up the moment Doris opened the door. First in line, we scored a table right next to the pies. We couldn't believe how many people ordered their pies at the same time as their lunch.

They didn't want Doris to run out of their favorite, they told the waitress.

Doris's pies were, hands down, the prettiest we'd seen so far, so we agreed to break our "share one slice" rule, just this once. Banana caramel sounded too sweet for this heat. Craving fruit, we both picked blueberry apple.

Some of my married friends tell me that they knew the moment they met their husbands that these were the men they were going to marry. I wouldn't know, but I can tell you that I looked down at the buckling slice of apple blueberry pointed directly at my heart, and I knew it was going to be the pie against which all others would be judged.

The tawny crust had a strong backbone but a tender touch. My fork slid through the filling but met only a touch of resistance at bottom crust, itself firm but pliable. The tart apples were rounded out by sweet, plump berries that managed to stay whole and independent in mind and in flavor. Doris had been gentle with the sugar, letting nature work its chemistry.

I took a bite, and it was one of those rare moments where substance and style come together with the grace of synchronized swimmers. It tasted deeply familiar and right. I shut my eyes to seal in the flavor and the feeling.

"You like it then," said a pleased Doris, pulling up a chair at our table. We asked how she had come upon this unlikely combination. And that's when she told us about her late husband who had died of cancer a few years earlier.

He started planting blueberry bushes right after the diagnosis, she said, "to keep his mind off how sick he was." He died before he got to see his blueberry bushes bear fruit. When she opened the café, she promised herself that she would have at least one special blueberry item on the menu each day, in his memory. Hence the tart-meets-sweet blueberry lemonade, which she serves in glass Mason jars.

One morning, she was making an apple pie and ran out of apples. It was only natural that she should grab for some blueberries to fill it out, meeting two challenges with one batch of berries.

"I tasted it and thought it was a real good combination, so I kept on making it," she said. "People love it."

We asked her what the secret is to making pie.

"Practice, practice, practice," she said. "When making the dough, don't stretch it. Don't work it too hard. Be gentle. That's the big trick. Be gentle."

Although most people like her meringues—Doris admits she's just a big showoff when it comes to getting her meringue as tall as a ship's prow—she has a soft spot for her fruit pies, especially blueberry.

"Next to mashed potatoes and gravy, I can't think of a better comfort food than pie, can you?" she said.

Doris learned to make pies from her mother, who learned to

". . . sweet potato, now that's Southern pie."

make pies from *her* mother. With working mothers on the run, and home-economics classes on the outs, who is teaching today's children to bake, she asked.

"It's not a judgment on working mothers," she hastened to add. Her own daughter has no time to bake with her children. "It's just the state of our society."

She was right. In every state so far, the pie trail had invariably led us to the kitchens of gray-haired women who feared that they were the end of the pie line.

Sophronia Dyson—Natchez's other pie mammy—was no exception.

Sophronia was leaning against an oak tree, making cardboard boxes from flats for her pies and candy, when we showed up about 12:30.

Sophronia's pies were tiny, but we could smell the nutmeg from ten feet away.

"You can get a cream pie anywhere, but sweet potato, now that's *Southern* pie," said Sophronia, who wore a blue bandanna scarf around her head. Some have argued that sweet potato—not apple—is the true American pie, and Sophronia would agree. Sophronia, who had the long, outstretched fingers of a cellist, used locally grown sweet potatoes.

It was impossible to put an age on Sophronia. Fifty? Seventy?

As for her beautiful name, "I always thought it was an old lady's name," she said. "But I've grown into it."

To sell her pies to tourists, she positions herself on a small folding chair, her back turned to the thick belt of churning water that is the Mississippi. She has mixed feelings about the river. River tourism butters her corn bread. But she was raised on haunting tales of ancestors being swallowed by its murky currents.

"I call it the baaaaaaad Mississippi River," she said, turning to face the river head-on, squinting like a crocodile coming up for air. I decided not to ask Sophronia for her recipe, much as I wanted it for my collection. Something told me she might take it the wrong way.

Some elderly tourists in seersucker shorts and crisp white polo shirts walked past, and Sophronia immediately switched currents: "Come try Sophronia's homemade sweet-potato pies," she said in a high-pitched and singsong voice. "It's homemade and it's so good, it comes with a money-back guarantee."

We took our sweet-potato pies on the road with us for the long drive toward Memphis, Tennessee. In deserted Tutwiler, the birthplace of the blues, we sat on the stoop of an abandoned junk store and inhaled Sophronia's sassy pies in three bites. A group of spindly girls in braids and hand-me-down dresses dreamed up a dance routine in front of a faded mural of B. B. King.

DORIS KEMP'S ACCIDENTAL
APPLE-BLUEBERRY PIE FROM
MAMMY'S CUPBOARD
IN NATCHEZ, MISSISSIPPI

CRUST

2 unbaked pie crusts

FILLING

2 cups of blueberries, preferably fresh, but frozen will work

3 Granny Smith apples, peeled and thinly sliced

1½ cups of sugar

½ cup of flour

1 tablespoon of lemon juice

½ teaspoon of nutmeg

1 teaspoon of cinnamon

2 tablespoons of butter

Combine the filling ingredients, except for the butter, in a mixing bowl and mix gently with a wooden spoon. Pour the mixture into a 9-inch pie pan lined with a basic pie crust. Cut butter over top of mixture. Cover with a top crust. Crimp edges together to seal. Cut slits into crust to allow steam to escape. Bake at 375 degrees for about 45 minutes.

salvation and a sax
in memphis

"I'm trying to get people to see that we are our brother's keeper,
I still work on it. Red, white, black, brown, yellow, rich, poor,
we all have the blues."

—B. B. KING

Our drive through the Mississippi Delta, birthplace of so many blues legends, had given us dancing feet, so, when we pulled into Memphis around 11 P.M., we freshened up and made a beeline for Beale Street.

We ducked for a late snack into the Southern Cultural Center where an old, thin black man with a salt-and-pepper, philandering beard wailed on a saxophone. When it was time for a break, he stepped outside to get some air back in those lordly lungs. I followed him and, after paying my humble respects, asked him if he could recommend a Memphis pie.

He didn't have much meat on his bones, but it was hard to imagine that good pie hadn't passed those amazing sax-blowing lips.

He smiled, massaged his beard, thought about it for a while.

"I gotta say Piccadilly over there on Elvis Presley Boulevard," he finally said. "Piccadilly has all kinds of good pie. Sweet potato. Custard. Cherry. That's where everyone goes for pie after church."

I was glad he brought church up, because Kris and I had a hankering for some live, soul-searing spirituals. Mr. Saxophone suggested the Greater Harvest Church of God in Christ Ministries for gospel, and then he shuffled back inside for another set. What's your name, I asked as he walked away.

"Fred Ford," he replied without turning back.

With our Sunday-morning strategy all squared away, Kris and I moved on to the B. B. King Blues Club up the street to shake a leg, or a pie thigh, as it were. We danced until closing, and when the last blues band was packing up, the keyboardist, who had to be 70 at least, stepped down from the raised stage to compliment Kris on her fine moves. He joined us for a drink and some reminiscing about the "old Beale Street." The keyboardist was touring the country and bound for New York City.

"Well, since we're going the same way, why don't I hitch a ride with you," he said. "I'm so sick of those damn buses and trains. I could use a stretch on the open road with the windows down."

Betty's backseat was loaded with mixing bowls.

He didn't mind, he said, he knew a thing or two about cramped spaces. He popped open his leather traveling case, battered like a thrift-shop shoe. All of its contents, razors, paperbacks, plastic combs, were disposable. We outlined our plans for Sunday: church for gospel, Piccadilly, and then Graceland. Was he up for it?

"Church?" he said, his voice cracking.

He grabbed his case, bade us farewell, and headed down Beale Street.

Greater Harvest is a futuristic church built like a modern fort. It has none of the charm of the intimate, whiteboard chapels we'd passed on some of the smaller country roads. The parking lot was packed with fancy cars.

We were late since we got lost getting there, but the two smiling ushers who greeted us at the door made us feel instantly at home as they showed us to the only vacant pew. From what I could tell, ours were the only white faces here on this sunny June morning. We'd missed most of the spirituals, but the impassioned sermon more than made up for it. It was all about "finding one's place" in the world, a tailor-made message for peripatetic pie seekers like us and, I thought, for a lonely, nomadic musician.

The crowd was pretty worked up. People burst out of their seats like geysers, shouting "Hallelujah! Amen! Uh-huh!" Then members of the deliverance team poured into the pews to seek out sinners. Naturally, they headed straight for the two redheads in the house. Minutes later, we were standing before the congregation, our heads buried in the salvation team's ample breasts, being saved for all to see.

As soon as the service ended, a group of women gathered around us and welcomed us to their church. They could not have been nicer. And we wondered how many churches with white congregations would be as welcoming to two new black faces in the pews. We told them we were just passing through, on a cross-country sojourn for pie. "Have you been to Piccadilly's yet?" they all asked.

"It's right near the house where Elvis lives," said a young lady in a flower-print dress. Her use of the present tense was sweet. The senior pastor stepped up and inquired about the commotion. Although ours wasn't the type of quest he was used to, he smiled. He dug in his pocket and pulled out a crisp twenty-dollar bill. "Have lunch at Piccadilly's on Greater Harvest," he said. Now, I haven't spent much time in church, but I did know this wasn't how things usually worked. We refused, but the pastor would not take no for an answer.

So, on divine orders, we headed for a free lunch at Piccadilly's, where we hoped to treat some locals to pie. The restaurant, one of 140 from coast to coast, was packed with families in their Sunday best, who had caravanned there from churches all over Memphis. Women in stylish plumed hats fanned themselves with church programs as they waited in the cafeteria line. Little girls with knobby knees and lemon-yellow tulle dresses stood on their patent-leather toes to glimpse pans of fried chicken and ribs and glistening sweet potatoes.

I scanned the room for someone who needed a piece of pie, and my eye fell on Sarah Webster—or, rather, her hat: a box-style black number with satin trim and two black feathers that shot straight up like a "peace" hand sign. She was sitting in the back of the room with three friends, gnawing on a chicken bone.

First, we complimented Sarah on her chapeau.

"This isn't my best," she said coolly. Sarah owns about fifty hats, we learned, one for nearly every sermon of the year. We asked Sarah if she wouldn't mind some company and conversation in exchange for some free God-given pie for her and her friends.

Her friends nodded, but Sarah looked us up and down, nostrils flared.

She'd been eating at Piccadilly every Sunday after church for twenty-five years. She thought she'd seen it all, she said.

We enlightened her about our quest, and it was obvious she deemed it frivolous. Pie was common, of the earth, almost heathen in its simple pleasure. It was not the noblest of grails. All this she said with the lift of an eyebrow. Still, Sarah did not say no to the slice of pecan pie I brought her back from my trip to the cafeteria line. And what a trip that was. There were at least eighty slices of pie stacked so close, the edges of their plates overlapped. It reminded me of that whimsical Wayne Thiebaud pie painting, though this display was messier and darker hued. These were working-class pies.

I held up the line for several minutes, trying to decide. I'd been dying to try a slice of custard pie since meeting Buford Smith, so I

Sarah Webster and Minister Wilburt Miller, Memphis, TN

grabbed one of those for myself and then an assortment for our new friends.

"Lord have mercy!" I heard someone say when I finally slid my tray forward. The custard was awfully eggy, and the soft, soggy crust spoke volumes about volume baking. I can't say the pies had any of that homespun richness of our Mississippi Mammy pies, but I looked around the room and people were enjoying their pie with relish. Even Sarah. They were eating for comfort, and what tasted better than custard pie after church with the family?

Uh-huh.

That's right.

Amen.

• • •

At Graceland, the kitchen was our favorite room in the house. All the appliances were avocado-green. On the counter sat a microwave as big as a '57 Chevy.

Bonnie Bale would have called it the perfect pie-baking kitchen.

bonnie bale—as in "hay"

"*I have always depended on the kindness of strangers.*"
—BLANCHE DUBOIS
TENNESSEE WILLIAMS, *A STREETCAR NAMED DESIRE*

We met Bonnie Bale the next day, on our drive to Lexington, Kentucky, where we hoped a horse trainer at the Kentucky Horse Park could point us toward some state chess pie or the famous Derby Pie™ we'd heard so much about.

In a town called Horse Cave, we stopped at a thrift shop and bought a stack of old pie tins from the 1940s for only $1 a piece. The owner of the store wondered if we were opening a pie shop. So we told her about our trip. She didn't have any suggestions on where to go for pie, but she gave us a Kentucky cookbook instead.

We pulled over to look for more pie paraphernalia at the Pumping Station Antiques Shop, about 20 miles or so north on the Jackson Highway.

The owner sat in a rocking chair, talking to a neighbor on the telephone. While we poked around, I saw her peel back the curtain and crane her neck to assess our license plate.

"You two ladies aren't from around here, are you?" she said after hanging up the phone.

"I'm Bonnie Bale," she said, extending her hand. "That's B-a-l-e, as in a bale of hay.

"What brings you to this sleepy part of Kentucky?" she asked.

"We're looking for pie," said Kris.

"Paaaaahhhhhhhhhhhhhh?" Bonnie said, raising her plucked eyebrows two inches and her voice two octaves. "I'm the BEST paaaahhhhhhhhhhhh baker in Kentucky. I'm famous in these parts for my butterscotch pie and—get this—(she leaned forward in her chair and whispered) I make it in a *mi-cro-wave!*"

She articulated every syllable of *mi-cro-wave*, the way people must have pronounced it when microwaves were still a novelty, back when Elvis bought his. Pie? In a microwave? We were skeptical and it showed.

"You don't believe me, do you?" she said, pushing herself out of her chair. "Do you have time to come my house so I can prove it? It won't take long . . . I can make it in less than twenty minutes—start to finish."

Bonnie put the CLOSED sign on the door and sent us down the road to get a carton of milk while she went and readied her kitchen for an audience. We met back at her home, which was set slightly back from the Jackson Highway, on a hill, in the hamlet of Canmer. Her house was filled with Early American furniture and her kitchen was Brady Bunch Kitsch.

She had already lined up on her kitchen island all the ingredients she would need: eggs, milk, margarine, brown sugar, salt, and corn-starch. And, of course, a store-bought pie shell she had been keeping in the freezer for just such an emergency.

She had also applied a fresh coat of persimmon lipstick and was raring to go.

"There's just no telling how many pies I've made in my lifetime," she said, mixing the ingredients for the filling. Kris was snapping pictures and Bonnie would often pause midsentence to flash a million-dollar smile. She always baked pies for church gatherings and other civic functions, she said, and when the nearby town of Edmonton was hit hard by a storm months back, she'd baked a slew of pies for the shelter.

"Y'all can't imagine how people like my pies around here."

With the ease of a television chef, Bonnie worked and talked simultaneously as we sat perched on kitchen stools. She talked about her recent thorny separation from her husband ("he was much younger than me") about her fiftieth high school reunion, which she had just hosted ("I was voted the *least* changed") and about her mother, who lived in a trailer in Bonnie's backyard ("we do need our privacy, you know").

She also talked about her constant battle with her weight.

She stopped to slip the filling mixture into the microwave. Pursing her lips for precision, she set the timer for eight minutes.

Then she turned to tell us about Earleen, the pastor in the next town over, who had, of late, become her best friend and confidant. The woman who had sold us the pie tin in Horse Cave had mentioned a son named Earleen who was a preacher. It had to be the same Earleen, so why hadn't the woman mentioned Bonnie's famous pies, we asked. Bonnie became as stiff as the egg whites she was whipping into meringue in her grandmother's aqua-green mixing bowl.

"Oh, women around these parts are very jealous when it comes to these kind of things," she said.

Then, with a forced smile, she switched topics. "You've got to be careful with meringue, you'll kill it if you're not absolutely gentle," she said, carefully stirring in the cornstarch.

For the fourth time, she opened the microwave door, eyed the filling like a sharpshooter, and gave it a good stir.

"You've got to keep control because otherwise it'll control you."

Once the filling was cooked, she poured it into her pie shell and layered her just-made meringue on top. She popped the pie in her oven and set a timer for fifteen minutes and ushered us into the living room where, from the comfort of her favorite velvet high-back armchair, she could tell us a little bit more about herself.

The small house was beginning to smell like a county fair.

"I was a Depression baby and my family was very, very poor," she began. "My parents were tenant farmers and they were very young when they had me. They were both sweet eaters. My mother would make nine pies a week and she'd cut them in fourths! She made her pie fillings in an iron skillet over a wood-burning stove . . ."

We talked about her high school reunion where her butterscotch pies were "a hit with the boys, let me tell you." Then, ding! The timer went off and Bonnie bounced out of her chair. We followed her into the kitchen where she yelped with joy when she saw that her meringue had turned a perfect golden brown.

"Now, ordinarily, I would let this sit and cool for a while so that the filling could harden, but since you girls are in a hurry, I'm going to cut you a piece right now." We promised we would not hold it against her as she sat us in the formal dining room.

We asked for small slices, since we were still recovering from our Piccadilly pig-out, but she cut the pie in fourths anyway. Old habits die hard. She wouldn't join us for a slice but she hovered over us to see what we thought.

"Weeeeellllllllllllll?" she asked, coyly pressing her palms together and leaning her head to one side.

Many months have passed since that first bite of butterscotch pie but I remember it well. I remember the hot, creamy puddle of honey-sweet caramel on my tongue balanced by a spiny meringue. I

"There's just no telling how many pies I've made in my lifetime."

don't remember the crust, just the filling: warm, soft, and puddingy.

We heaped on Bonnie the compliments she fully expected.

"Maybe I'll be famous someday," she said, walking us out to her deck. "I'm so glad you dropped by. This has turned out to be one fine day. Y'all have a safe trip, ya hear?"

We'd spent only an hour with Bonnie Bale but I felt I knew her. I knew how she'd behaved in high school and the wiles she relied upon to charm the boys at the dance. And, as we hoofed it toward horse country, I was sure Bonnie was sitting in her velvet chair, enjoying her slice of pie with guilty pleasure.

We still needed to find some chess or Derby Pie™ the state was known for. We drove past miles and miles of horse farms, all joined, it seemed, by one continuous white fence. Every farm had its weeping willow, and that seemed appropriate since most of the old barns in the area were painted mourning black.

The pretty young lady behind the information desk at the horse park listened intently as we explained what we were after: a horse trainer at the park who happened to also like pie. Did she have any suggestions?

"MY trainer," she said. "Every time we travel to a horse show somewhere, he always makes us stop to try different restaurants, and he always orders pie." She called him at home, and although he was busy getting twenty saddlebreds ready for a horse show in Ohio, he could take a few minutes to talk to us about pie. He lived in Richmond, about 45 miles due south.

We met Tommy Clouse inside his "office"—a horse stall festooned with dozens of first-place ribbons, with fluffed-out cat curled in the corner behind a bale of hay, a reminder of Bonnie.

American saddlebreds are known for their beauty and grace, Clouse told us. "They pick their feet up when they walk and know to keep their heads set and alert and their ears pointed forward." Clouse sat slumped in a chair, displaying none of the fine posture his horses are known for, but his warm, grinning eyes were filled with grace. He was 12 years old when he got his first horse—about the same age he discovered his love of pie. He had planned to become a doctor and was well on his way, but his unbridled passion for—and understanding of—horses led him on a different path. His second passion was dessert, pie specifically. He highly recommended the Boone Tavern Hotel in nearby Berea for their chess pie, a Southern favorite with a basic filling of sugar, butter, eggs, lemon, and a small amount of flour, that often invites sweet deviations.

"It's a pretty common-tasting pie," said Tommy, "but theirs stands out from the rest."

Just thinking of the pie made his eyes twinkle. If he hadn't been going to this horse show, he would have accompanied us to Berea, he said. Tommy wouldn't let us leave without introducing us to one of his favorite horses, a striking, albeit nervy, 3-year-old horse named Pablo. Pablo, who belonged to a local dentist, seemed perfectly aware that he had just won a blue ribbon in Knoxville, Tennessee.

Boone Tavern Hotel is affiliated with Berea College, a small, unique liberal arts-and-crafts college, which gleans 80 percent of its students from southern Appalachia and Kentucky. Students, who study anything from furniture-making to weaving, pay no tuition, but in exchange must work on the campus in one capacity or another.

Many work at the hotel, which was originally built in 1909 as a guest house for visitors to the college. Most of the hotel furnishings were handcrafted by Berea students.

Mark Williams, the chef at the hotel, was alone in the spotless kitchen when we arrived in the middle of the afternoon, between shifts. He told us, with some consternation, that the hotel's chess pie had recently gone back to its original name: Jefferson Davis pie, after the president of the Confederacy.

The previous dean of the college was a pacifist—the Dalai Lama has visited the campus on several occasions—so he had the name changed to chess pie. But, when he retired, the name was changed back to Jefferson Davis pie "because that's how locals remembered the pie best," said Mark, visibly bothered by the name himself.

We asked to try a slice of this Confederate pie. And though the dining room was closed, Mark gave us a table by the window and brought us each a slice decorated with bright orange nasturtium petals. The pie had a rich, bright, lemony taste. The crust was remarkably firm, with a posture as beautiful as Pablo's.

I enjoyed the pie, but I couldn't get past the notion of eating a pie named after a man who defended slavery. Call me crazy.

We asked to try a slice of Derby Pie™, which many consider Kentucky's state pie, and the chef was more than happy to bring out a slice of his version of the chocolate nut pie, so long as we didn't call it Derby Pie™.

The term "Derby Pie™" had been trademarked by Kern's Kitchen, the Louisville bakery that created the famous pie in 1954 in honor of the famous horse race, Mark said.

Still, restaurants continued to serve the Derby Pie™, and recipes for Derby Pie™ continued to appear in cookbooks across the country. Determined to protect their pie—and their bread and butter—the Kerns did what Americans do best: they started suing people left and right. They took on Bon Appetit and PBS for appropriating the name, and even Nestle (their own supplier!) for printing a Tollhouse Derby Pie™ recipe on the back of their chocolate-chip packages.

Since the pie is so popular, Kentucky restaurants have come up with alternative names for similar chocolate-nut concoctions: Racehorse pie, Winner's Circle pie, and Triple Crown pie are just a few examples of the Derby derivations. Boone Tavern's version is known as Race Day pie.

We liked Mark a lot, but all this negativity made us realize we really weren't hungry for a second piece of pie after all.

By the time we found a room at a hotel it was 9:30 P.M. We'd eaten nothing but racially insensitive pie all day and needed a square meal. Nothing was open at this hour on a Monday night in rural Kentucky. Nothing save for the Kentucky Fried Chicken where we had to beg the janitor to squeeze us in as they were closing. I had never eaten at a KFC before but Kentucky seemed like the best place to start.

I guess I was a little too effusive thanking the janitor, because as we left with our bucket of extra crispy, he proposed marriage and a new, better life for me in his native Bombay. We were four thousand miles and nineteen pies into the trip. Nothing fazed me anymore.

We set up our table in front of the television and poured ourselves a shot of Bourbon to go with our chicken. A *Brady Bunch* marathon was on Nick at Nite.

The gods were with us.

BONNIE BALE'S
BLINK-OF-AN-EYE
BUTTERSCOTCH PIE

CRUST

1 9-inch pie crust (Bonnie uses frozen)

FILLING

3 eggs

2½ cups of milk

1 cup brown sugar, firmly packed

½ cup of cornstarch, plus 1 heaping tablespoon

¼ teaspoon salt

½ stick butter or margarine

1 teaspoon vanilla

⅓ cup white sugar

Separate the eggs, being careful not to get any of the yolk into the whites. Using a whisk, beat the egg yolks in a mixing bowl. Add milk. Mix well. Stir in brown sugar, cornstarch, and salt. Mix well. Add the butter or margarine, in pieces. Cook the mixture on "high" in the microwave for about 8 minutes, pausing to stir every couple of minutes or so. Pour the cooked mixture into a ready-to-go pie crust and let it cool.

To make your meringue, make sure you use a bowl that is absolutely grease-free. Beat egg whites on a high speed with a hand-held mixer until they are very stiff. Gradually add ⅓ cup of white sugar while still beating, then add a heaping tablespoon of cornstarch and beat well. Spoon the meringue onto the pie, and bake in a pre-heated oven at 350 degrees until golden-brown, about 15 minutes.

JEFFERSON DAVIS PIE

CRUST

1 unbaked pie shell

FILLING

2 cups brown sugar

1 tablespoon sifted flour

½ teaspoon nutmeg

1 cup cream

4 eggs, lightly beaten

1 teaspoon lemon juice

½ teaspoon lemon rind, grated

¼ cup melted margarine

Sift sugar with flour and nutmeg. Add cream, mix well. Add eggs, mix well. Add lemon juice, lemon rind, and margarine. Mix well. Pour into pie shell. Bake at 375 degrees for 45 minutes. Cool and serve with whipped cream.

dutch treat

"Work and pray, live on hay
You'll get pie in the sky when you die."
—JOE HILL, "THE PREACHER AND THE SLAVE"
(AN OLD LABOR SONG)

By the time we got to Pennsylvania, about two and a half weeks into the trip, we became acutely aware of the passage of time. Not just how a hundred miles on the open road can seem like a thousand, but how time is measured.

Most of the pies we'd uncovered on this sweet treasure hunt could all be traced to the apron strings of white-haired women with calloused, rolling-pin palms. Grandmothers who took the time to bake pie because that was time well spent.

Who takes that kind of time anymore?

Over the last two weeks we'd been living on drawn-out time, the speed at which syrup slithers down a stack of hot cakes. From the long back-road stretches past lazy willows and tobacco barns, and the drip-drip-drip manner of talking in the South, to the meandering way people gave directions, this trip was as much about slowing down as it was about pie.

Slowing down long enough to talk to a stranger at a stoplight; to pick some flowers for the waitress at your local breakfast joint, to bake a pie for the new neighbor who just moved in down the road.

Today's pace isn't a pie pace.

Was that why we were finding so many cast-off mixing bowls and rolling pins in those roadside antiques shops?

In Lancaster, Pennsylvania, the contrast between old and new, fast and slow, hit us like a ton of pie weights.

We had hoped to arrive in Pennsylvania Dutch country early enough to scout out a women's quilting circle for local pie recommendations, but this time we were waylaid by a pair of twisters in Kentucky and West Virginia that had us holed up in tacky motels catching up on journaling and reading for a couple of days.

This part of Dutch country is a bundle of two-lane, unmarked roads dotted with 100-acre farms, each with its spartan oversized barns and quaint wood-frame houses with orderly vegetable patches. It was dusk, but many Amish farmers were plowing their fields with their teams of stocky horses, refusing to call it a day before the sun had.

Like that of most Americans, our exposure to the Amish culture was limited to the Harrison Ford movie *Witness*. So we read up on the Amish and Mennonite cultures in our West Virginia motel. As we drove through the small townships, we were struck by how visually accurate the movie had been. There were no cameras rolling, and yet these women riding alongside us on old-fashioned bicycles really were wearing white caps and dark peasant dresses with thick stockings, their hair parted as straight as the inner spine of a brand-new Bible.

We passed by several horse buggies with big spoked wheels, driven by stern-faced men with scraggly isosceles beards and wide black suspenders. In the backseat facing out, their boys in crisp periwinkle-blue shirts and drop-fall trousers grinned under the broad brims of their straw hats.

We did know that the Amish, also known as "the plain people," do not like to be photographed. We wanted, above all, to be respectful but we also wanted their advice on where to get good pie.

In the town of Intercourse, founded in 1754, we stopped at an educational center and asked the two young women in summer

dresses behind the counter if there was a proper way to approach the Amish and Mennonites without offending them.

The two young women looked at each other and giggled, coyly cupping their hands over their heart-shaped mouths.

"*We're* Mennonites, and you're talking to *us*," they said in unison. "We could recommend some good pie."

They were such a striking contrast to the white-capped buttoned-down women we'd seen on the road, we were confused.

"We're New Order Mennonites," explained Carol, the elder of the two. "Our guidelines aren't as strict."

Carol's mother made a wonderful shoofly pie, she said, but she wasn't too proud to go to the Bird-in-Hand Bakery in town for shoofly pie when time ran short. Carrie, her 19-year-old colleague, agreed that Bird-in-Hand made great shoofly. They called the bakery for us but it had already closed for the night, so we agreed to go to Bird-in-Hand, in the village of Bird-in-Hand, first thing in the morning. We asked if shoofly was something that was eaten only on special occasions or for the benefit of tourists, and they laughed again at our innocence.

"Oh no, we love shoofly and we eat it all the time," Carrie said. "Farmers like to eat it for breakfast before heading to the fields."

By then the last visitors had left the center, so the two young women, who weren't in a hurry to get home, sat with us in a circle on the carpet. Well past dark, we talked about what it was like, growing up Mennonite in '90s America.

They explained the vast differences in lifestyle between Old Order Mennonites and themselves. Yes, they watched television. Yes, they went to movies. Yes, they "dated," although that was something they were less comfortable talking about with strangers.

Carrie said her favorite TV show was *The Simpsons*.

"I think it's really funny, and they've had two episodes with Amish characters," said Carrie, who drives an '88 Dodge, not a horse-drawn buggy. They explained why the Amish disapproved of mirrors and rag dolls with faces sewn in. "Vanity is completely frowned upon," said Carrie, who, with her long, cornsilk-blond hair and pearled smile, would have every reason to be vain.

They admitted with visible relief that the Old World ways were disappearing in some families.

"My mother had to wear *black* shoes at her wedding," Carol said, eyes wide as pie. They told us how common it is for teenagers in their community to go through a rebellious phase. Boys often grow their hair long, drive souped-up cars, even get tattoos. Parents around here know better than to fight it, they said. Eventually, the rebels come back to the harbor that is their faith.

"What I like most about being a Mennonite is our emphasis on peace," said Carrie. "A lot of us have gotten away from that."

Indeed.

Throughout the trip, we'd often marveled at how different each state and region felt to us. The difference was sometimes as subtle as the way the air felt when we cupped our hand out the window, to the landmarks people chose when sketching us a map. Lancaster, we agreed, taking leave of Carrie and Carol, made us feel as though we had traveled through time as well as space.

We found a hotel run by an Amish family in Strasburg, a small town nearby. As late as it was, the purity of the air here, the absence of traffic, and a very bright moon called for a walk, our first on the trip so far. We followed the narrow road that led out of town, lit only by moonglow and fireflies (still following us since Oklahoma). Most of the Amish farmers were beneath handwashed cotton sheets by then, but a few of the homes were still lit by candlelight. When we would hear the clop, clop, clop of hooves, we'd jump out of the buggy lane and onto the shoulder, carefully avoiding pies of the inedible sort.

Shoofly pie is, in fact, the most popular dessert in Pennsylvania Dutch country, which says a lot, as the locals have always been big dessert-eaters. In an earlier time, the Pennsylvania Dutch ate pie up to three times a day, and pie was always served with the rest of the meal, not just for dessert. When a Pennsylvania Dutchman proposed to his wife, he gave her an elaborately carved rolling pin as an engagement gift.

Originally considered a filling breakfast pie for farmers, made with the workhorse ingredients left in the larder, shoofly pie has evolved into a fancier two-layer dessert with a gingerbread cake–like topping and a gooey molasses filling.

Some say the word shoofly comes from *choufleur,* the French word for cauliflower, because of its crumbly, creviced surface. Others, like food historian William Weaver, author of *Pennsylvania Dutch Country Cooking,* insists the pie was named after the Shoofly brand of molasses. That makes sense, since, after all, one of the main ingredients is molasses.

Carol and Carrie told us they thought the pie was so named

because Amish women were always shooing flies from the pies cooling on a windowsill.

I liked this interpretation best.

Either way, we were eager to try some shoofly for breakfast—farmer-style. On our drive to Bird-in-Hand, we stopped to take a picture of a vintage sign advertising shoofly pie, on the brick side of a country store somewhere on the old Lincoln Highway. Shopkeeper Wayne Meyers stepped out on the porch of his shop. Meyers was "English," like us (what the Amish and Mennonites call people outside their faith). He sells his own shoofly pie, which he buys from an elderly Amish woman in Paradise Township, who bakes in her basement kitchen at sunup using a recipe handed down by generations of baking women.

"I always look forward to picking up the pies at her kitchen," said Meyers, who was sorry he hadn't restocked since the weekend. "There are always a group of women baking together. They use large pizza ovens that are run by air compression."

Meyers was on his way to a produce auction in Ephrata to buy some strawberries, and invited us to come along. We hung back and watched as Old World Amish men craned their necks and stroked their beards in concentration to better hear the auctioneer's chant. Behind them, their demure wives, with five or six children in tow, waited patiently to help load up the buggies with crates of plump berries and rhubarb stalks that would most likely end up in jams or pies.

We would have liked to have gone to Paradise Township to meet his shoofly pie supplier, but Meyers didn't think that would be appropriate on such short notice and we respected that.

We met with the same reticence at the Bird-in-Hand Bakery, where the manager told us his pie baker was indeed in the kitchen but he doubted she would come out to talk to us.

"She's Old World Order Amish, you know, and they don't like to have their picture taken," he said, "but I'll ask her."

Becky, 25, who had been baking since before sunrise, invited us into her immaculate kitchen even though she was eager to get home. "I guess it's OK to have my picture taken as long as it's not going to appear in the local paper," she said, smiling. Then she insisted that her cobaker, Eva, an Old Order Mennonite, be in the picture as well. They adjusted their plain bonnets and straightened their aprons before posing by the pie rounder, each proudly holding a pie baked that morning. One was a shoofly; the other, a cherry pie with a lattice crust as delicate as the border trim on their aprons.

"Shoofly is not that difficult to make," said Becky, making up in humility, it seemed, for her brief lapse of vanity. "You mix the wet ingredients together and then you mix the dry ingredients together. Growing up Amish, you learn to make pie when you're real young."

And then the two young women looked at the time and excused themselves, as they had to go home "to do chores."

We bought a pie to go, grabbed two forks, and dug into it on our way out of town. It was jammy in texture and stuck to the roofs of our mouths, the way it must stick to a farmer's ribs.

As we drove out of town, wiping crumbs from our faces, we caught up with Becky and Amy walking briskly on the side of the road in their black, sensible shoes. They were chattering away. They were so young and yet so self-assured, inside the bakery and out.

I looked in the rearview mirror and pinched my cheeks, searching for some of their rosy spirit.

SHOOFLY PIE

Marcia Adams's Shoofly Pie, from *New Recipes from Quilt Country*, is the best I've tasted so far.

Pastry for a one-crust, 9-inch pie

FILLING

1 cup all purpose flour

⅔ cup light brown sugar, packed

1 rounded tablespoon cold butter

¼ teaspoon salt

1 egg

1 cup light molasses

¾ cup cold water

¼ cup hot water

1 tablespoon baking soda

Preheat oven to 350 degrees.

Roll out the pie pastry and line a 9-inch pie pan. Set aside.

In a food processor bowl, combine the flour, brown sugar, butter, and salt. Remove ½ cup of the mixture and set aside. Transfer the rest to a medium mixing bowl. In a small bowl, beat the egg lightly. Add the molasses and cold water, and blend but do not beat; you don't want bubbles in the batter. Set aside.

In a small bowl, mix the hot water with the baking soda and blend into the molasses mixture. Add to the flour mixture and mix well. Pour into the pie shell and top with the reserved crumbs. Bake for 35 minutes. The pie will appear quivery but will firm up as it cools. Transfer to a rack to cool completely before cutting.

connecticut

"Lux et Veritas" (Light and Truth)
—THE MOTTO FOR YALE UNIVERSITY

Never trust a man with a dead fox on his head.

With only two days left before I had to report to work in New York, Kris and I decided to squeeze in one last state. We made a beeline for Connecticut, on the advice of the biker we'd met on Route 66, at Lucille Hamons's gas station.

The bearded biker had recommended a "sweet, family bakery" in Hamden, the blue-collar town where he grew up. He'd scribbled the address on the back of a Route 66 postcard. *Best pie I ever had,* he wrote.

Only this biker forgot to mention one thing about this family bakery . . . it belonged to *his* family. They were expecting us, thought they might get some good press out of it. He should have at least mentioned it, Kris and I agreed. We might have been more forgiving if the pie had indeed been good. But I could tell it was Dumpster pie just by looking at it—not the pie note we wanted to end our journey on. Reluctantly, we turned around and headed for New York.

A stop at the Frisbie Pie Company in Bridgeport, Connecticut, would have been better. But that famous bakery closed its doors in 1958—exactly one year after the Frisbee toy, inspired by the bakery's lightweight pie tins, made its debut on beaches and lawns across America.

Students at Yale claim they were the first to discover the aerody-namics of the Frisbie pie tin in the early 1940s. But administrators from Middlebury College in Vermont credit *their* students with the discovery.

According to Middlebury lore, three undergraduates were driv-ing through Nebraska in 1939 when they got a flat tire. As two boys fixed the flat, a third wandered off alone and, in a cornfield, he stum-bled on a discarded pie tin from Frisbie's Pie Company. He picked it up and threw it in the air, and an American picnic tradition was born. In 1989, the college went so far as to erect a bronze statue of a dog jumping to catch a Frisbee, to commemorate the fiftieth anniversary of that pivotal roadside discovery.

It was Walter Frederick Morrison who took the campus game and turned it into a cool million. An inventor at heart, Morrison had flung a few pie tins and paint-can lids as a youth, and he wanted to capitalize on the nation's runaway obsession with unidentified flying objects.

He experimented with stainless steel discs to which he welded a steel ring inside the rim for stability. When that didn't work, he turned to plastic, America's new material wunderkind. Cheap, light, durable, and malleable, plastic was perfectly suited for America's new "use it, then lose it" culture driven by planned obsolescence.

Morrison called his plastic disc the Pluto Platter. A new California toy company called Wham-O, which had just hit it big with its Hula Hoop, bought the rights to Morrison's design. Once they learned about the college kids and Connecticut pie company that started the whole craze, Wham-O decided to call the disc a "Frisbee."

picture-perfect pie

*"The English are not an inventive people;
they don't eat enough pie."*
—THOMAS ALVA EDISON

Pies used to be part of every American holiday, so is it any wonder that George Eastman, the man who made holiday photos possible, was also a pie lover?

Eastman, who invented the first Kodak camera in 1888, even had a kitchenette attached to his darkroom so that he could whip up a pie on a whim.

"He was a regular Betty Crocker," says Kathy Connor, curator of the George Eastman House, the fifty-room colonial mansion in Rochester, New York, where Eastman and his mother lived.

Eastman loved to cook and bake. He planted fruit trees and a vegetable garden just so he could have the freshest ingredients available to him, she said. The man who toyed with gelatin emulsions in his mother's kitchen sink especially liked to tinker with recipes. Toward the end of his life, when he discovered Africa, he would often concoct dry-mix recipes for biscuits and pancakes to make his trips to the Dark Continent more enjoyable.

And while he may have called one of his most popular cameras "Brownie," Connor says it's plain that the entrepreneur was a sucker for lemon meringue pie, especially his own. It's not clear whether the recipe came from his mother or another close relative, Connor says, but, upon his death, a recipe for lemon meringue pie was found, scribbled in Eastman's own cursive script, in a box of personal correspondence.

Eastman, who liked to spice up a round of billiards by putting a case of champagne on the line, was extremely competitive when it came to pie.

That is painfully obvious in the following epistolary exchange between Eastman and a distinguished doctor in town named Edwin S. Ingress, launched after Eastman had tasted one of the doctor's pies.

April 7, 1927

My dear Ingress:

That lemon pie was absolutely top notch technically. I cannot hope to surpass it and will be satisfied if I am able to equal it. As to the recipe, however, I have got you beaten as I will show you at the first opportunity. As I did not originate it that will be no credit for me. All I am hoping for is to make the contest a draw.

With kindest regards, I am,

Yours very truly,
George Eastman

Five days later, Eastman received the following missive from the good doctor:

April 13, 1927

Dear Mr. Eastman:

In judging a lemon pie contest the decision should rest on an impartial consideration of the pie's component parts. Your crust was undoubtedly more flaky than mine. The two meringues were about on a par. In regard to the filling, I still maintain that there might be a difference of opinion.

However, I noticed that, when I asked for a second piece of your pie, I found that it had been entirely consumed, and, as I do not ever remember having had this happen so quickly to one of my pies, I feel that perhaps you are entitled to the decision.

Sincerely yours,
E. S. Ingress

GEORGE EASTMAN'S FAVORITE LEMON MERINGUE PIE, EXACTLY AS IT WAS WRITTEN, IN EASTMAN'S OWN HAND

FILLING
6 eggs. Beat yolks. Beat in 1 cup granulated sugar. Stir in grated rind
    and juice of two lemons. Cook in double boiler 15 minutes. When
    cooked and cooled, stir in beaten stiff whites of three eggs.

CRUST
1 cup flour
½ cup shortening
a little salt
sprinkle in water
make paste & roll [were it that easy!]

Connor says she once tried to make Eastman's pie for a charity event, but the filling did not quite fill out a standard nine-inch pie pan. "It looked like I was being chintzy," she said, "but they just used smaller pie pans back then." Connor wasn't quite sure how to fix the problem, not being a pie baker herself.

"I would love nothing more than to spend time baking with my daughter," she said, "but who has the time?"

new york

*"If children grew up according to early indications,
we should have nothing but geniuses."*

—GOETHE (1749–1832)

Kris rummaged in the backseat for the Frank Sinatra tunes her father had given us. She found the one with "New York, New York," popped it in the player, and, to the delight of the drivers on either side of us, we rolled down the windows and let it blare as we crossed the Hudson River, going west on the Tappan Zee Bridge.

To my left, I caught a glimpse of the Manhattan skyline, 20 miles downriver. From this vantage point, the city looked small and manageable, as if in a snow globe.

This was home now.

When I called my new editor to let her know I'd finally made it to New York, I asked her if she could recommend a good local pie to end the trip on. She suggested I pay a visit to Deborah Tyler, better known as the Pie Lady of Nyack. Tyler sells fresh fruit pies at the Nyack Farmers Market on Saturdays, my editor said, and from her back porch the rest of the week.

This being a Friday, we followed the handpainted signs for "homemade pie" leading to Tyler's home, not far from the spot on the Hudson where the shad fishermen gather every spring when the forsythia bloom.

Children's laundry and vintage kitchen towels hung, drying, on a line above potted pink geraniums and purple petunias.

Tyler had just returned from a trip to a Hudson Valley orchard, where she bought bushels of apples and peaches for pie. She looked harried. For the first time on this spontaneous adventure, I felt bad we hadn't called ahead to warn her of our visit. Reality was setting in.

The single, fortysomething mother finally eased up after she'd washed and stored the fruit. She'd started her business, a true cottage industry, she said, after a divorce left her and her three children financially crippled. She'd read an article in *Yankee* magazine about a woman selling blueberry pies from home and thought: "I can do that."

She had learned to bake as a child, and honed her skills while working at a college cafeteria in England. Until then, everything she'd heard or read in cookbooks about making pie "made it sound so traumatic and mysterious," Deborah said. "The secret is more in your attitude than in your technique."

In that regard, she said, pie-baking is a lot like child-rearing.

"You are the one in charge of that dough. Until you get that straight, it doesn't work. You have to be fearless.

"Children, by the way, are great pie bakers," she added, "precisely because they have no fear."

And then Deborah said something that gave us even more hope for the future of pie. Turned out, there was a boy in the neighborhood, Darrell, who wanted to become a professional pie baker when he grew up. The 12-year-old boy dropped by Deborah's house every day after school and tackled all sorts of pies, even some with lattice crusts.

"The hardest part at first was rolling out the dough," Darrell said when we spoke. "But I kept watching Deborah, the way she rolled hers back and forth, the way she patched up the cracks and made a perfect circle.

"I needed to watch someone before I could do it myself. Now it's pretty easy. And it tastes so much better than store-bought."

Like Elva Twitchell, Darrell said baking pie gave him "a real sense of accomplishment." He paused, lowered his voice: "It makes me feel like I have a talent."

What's the best advice he would give a novice pie baker, tackling crust for her first time?

"Take your time," he said. "You just can't rush a pie."

DEBORAH TYLER'S
APPLE PLUM PIE

CRUST

1 cup unsalted butter (8 oz)

3 cups unbleached all-purpose flour

½ teaspoon salt

¼ cup cold water

FILLING

6 oz sugar

¼ cup cornstarch

3 cups thinly sliced, peeled, cooking apples (about 1 lb)

3 cups quartered Italian plums

1 oz brown sugar

2 tablespoons butter

Cut butter into flour and salt until mixture is the consistency of cornmeal. Add water, turning mixture with a fork until it comes together in a ball. Wrap in plastic wrap and chill for one hour before rolling out, or roll out right away.

Combine sugar and cornstarch and add to prepared fruit. Fill a pastry-lined 9-inch pie plate with fruit mixture; sprinkle brown sugar on top; dot with butter. Adjust top crust. Seal and flute edges. Bake at 450 degrees for 10 minutes and at 350 degrees for 45–50 minutes more.

part two

"Nobody sees a flower—really—it is so small—
we haven't time—and to see takes time,
like to have a friend takes time."

—GEORGIA O'KEEFFE "ABOUT MYSELF"

rush

When you walk, just walk. When you eat, just eat.
—BUDDHA

One of the first things I learned about New Yorkers—and it nearly cost me my life—is that they don't know how to merge.

In California, merging onto the highway means patiently letting all cars pass until it is safe to proceed. In New York, merging means muscling your way into oncoming traffic.

Survival of the fastest.

It is this same fiercely urban instinct that causes pedestrians to rush the crosswalk even as the red light commands them not to. "The light's a challenge, not a warning," a friend and native tells me.

Californians praise multivitamins. Multitasking is the New Yorker's mantra. Sell a stock, a house, a manuscript, while on the treadmill, the subway, or in the colorist's chair.

In his book *Faster,* science writer James Gleick claims our society is plagued by "hurry sickness." Symptoms include standing in front of the microwave and instinctively pressing 8-8 instead of 9-0, to save a fraction of a millisecond. (Guilty!)

Studies show that advances in technology have gifted us with more leisure time than we've ever had before. To do what?

Grab an energy bar in the cafeteria. Eat it in the elevator or at your desk.

Balance makes a "lemon meringue"–flavored energy bar.

Only in New York can you eat a piece of pie on the fly.

Old-fashioned, sit-down pie seems antithetical to New York. Pie is soft in the middle, and New York is all about keeping your edge. Pie is about taking time, and New York is all about beating time.

I'm standing in line at Gourmet Garage on the Upper West Side, when a bright orange flyer on the community billboard catches my eye:

TOO BUSY TO LIVE YOUR LIFE? I CAN HELP.

WILL RUN ERRANDS FOR YOU.

EVEN FILL OUT YOUR DIARY FOR YOU.

CALL DAVE AT (212) . . .

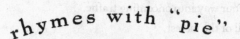

"A back road is so easy, it just rambles on and on
Take it or leave it as it rolls along
Drifts through things it cannot change and doesn't even try
Wouldn't that be something for you and I."

—KATE WOLF, "BACK ROADS"

There were two pieces of personal mail waiting for me when I arrived at my new home in New York.

The first was a letter from Harrison, Arkansas, home of Martha and Curtis Purvis.

"It was so much fun chatting with you girls in Leslie," it read. "I told Curtis that had we all been traveling north, instead of south, we would have taken you both home with us. We would have made some ice tea and swung on the gazebo up on the hill.

"Here's the photo of The Sugar Shack I promised. Did you ever make it there?"

Written in purple ink and curly script, the letter was signed, "a new friend, Martha P."

Attached was a blurred photograph of a truly decadent pie display.

The second piece of mail was a "card" with the lyrics to Kate Wolf's song "Back Roads" scribbled on the back.

Actually, it was a thick piece of cardboard that had been cut out in the shape of a large fish. All the postage stamps, at least thirty of them, were beautiful, carefully chosen, uncanceled stamps from the 1940s and '50s. The postmark told me the fish and I had left San Francisco on the very same day.

The fish was not signed, nor did it have a return address.

But I knew who it was from.

I'd met Ty a year earlier in San Francisco. He was just crawling out of a long-term relationship and I was contemplating settling down. Our timing could not have been worse. A dreamer and a drifter, Ty thought he had all the time in the world to become predictable. He was an oyster shucker today, but who knew where he'd be tomorrow? He liked to drive all the way to Santa Cruz to buy old stamps at a cluttered coin shop, because they made envelopes artful.

I was on the priority-mail track. There were things I wanted and I wanted them fast. We were driven by completely different engines.

Predictably, things got rocky. And when they did, and the New York job beckoned, there was no question I would make the move solo.

The plan was to not look back.

That was the plan. But he turned up. In my thoughts, in Elva

Twitchell's kitchen, and on the back roads of Kentucky. Then in my mailbox. Often.

Thanksgiving was approaching, and Ty hoped we could spend it together. A new beginning. Perhaps I should meet him in Colorado, where he grew up and where some of his dearest friends, who lived in a log house high on a hill, hosted a special "pie ritual" every year on Thanksgiving Day. They invited lots of friends, baked plenty of pies, and a "chosen" guest got to read a beautifully written ode to pie, out loud, before dessert.

"An ode to pie?" I asked.

The next day, the following Susan Bright essay from *Tirades and Evidence of Grace* came over the fax machine in the newsroom.

PIE

Ice water. Two silver knives to work through the flour and shortening, add salt. It is an old art. Do not work late into the night, with sleep nipping at your sleeves, you will fall off, wake up at 3 A.M. to a room full of smoke, two black disks in the oven, bad smell. Do not think about business, or the wave of darkness spreading through the Arts, do not think about depression looming on the horizon or the rhetoric and nonsense our leaders toss into its mouth, or the prospect of revolution in America. Zen. Concentrate on the art of pie. It is an old art. Ingredients spread through the house like a layer of snow, later people say: "O, Pie. Pie. We love pie." It is a good art. No one will say, "Make this pie with only one silver knife, or no ice, or make it with chalk instead of flour." Fill pie with ingredients at hand, cans of things, fresh fruit, cheese. Add it to a feast. Eat leftovers for breakfast the next day, the celebration begins again, pie filling the recesses of the body, exhilaration. Pie, it is an old art. If we lose it, infants will wither in their mothers' stomachs, writhe at sunken nipples, men will lose direction, U. S. Steel will manufacture rubber and the pillars of society will flop around like spangles on a half-mast flag. Pie, the planets are lined up—Saturn, Uranus, Mars, Jupiter pull earthquakes, pull poison from beneath the surface. Pie, cut through the mix gently, roll out on a layer of wood and flour, pie. Flute the edges, pour in apples and cinnamon and spices. Pie. Zen. Concentrate on the art of pie. The rites of passage pull us through the gates of depression and war. We shall make pie. Cannot resist. We shall celebrate Christmas, Thanksgiving, the Fourth of July; holidays shall find us traversing the continent in search of heritage. No one makes pie like Mother does. Pie. No one says one pie should represent all pies. Pie is like a thumbprint. Some are sour. Pie is silent, making only a light simmering noise as it bakes in the oven. It spreads scent gently into our hearts. There is ceremony as pie is lifted out of the heat. They gather. O, Pie. The clutter is swept away, space around pie is brought to sharp focus. Light pours down on pie. Concentrate. The art of pie is an old one. Try to imagine life without it. Like the unveiling of a great painting, breaking a champagne bottle over the bow of a ship going off to sea, the ceremony as a cornerstone is laid, pie. Do not roll the crust too thick, roll gently or the center will unfurl, rub extra flour on the rolling pin every fourth stroke, remember these things. Create pie often so the art is not lost. Do not forget temperature. Cold is essential, then heat. You must have an oven, cannot make pie over an open fire or in a barbecue pit. Be firm with those who insist pie can be made in a crockpot or on the

back window ledge of a Pontiac left out in August sunlight.
Respect the rules of pie.

Ty's invitation sounded tempting. But to go out West would be going back. I was going forward.

My parents weren't expecting me until Christmas and it felt right to spend the holiday East, where the glowing fall foliage spoke of cranberries and golden yams.

I'd always felt like such a fraud on this, the most *American* of holidays. Yes, my family served a token turkey with chestnut stuffing but we had none of the traditional trimmings. We started the meal with oysters on the half shell and a peppery *mignonette* sauce. Puree and haricots verts, yes, but never cranberries. *Iles flottantes* supplanted pie. No football, but the florid retelling of family stories after dinner.

Since the leaves had started to turn, I had gotten it into my head that spending Thanksgiving in the heart of New England, specifically Plymouth, might make up for so many holidays without pumpkin pie.

"Let me come with you," he said.

And I heard myself say "yes."

Because every relationship needs a road-trip test. And, if this confusion really was just homesickness I was feeling, as my well-meaning friends suggested, certainly a week on the road with Ty would let me know.

He flew in a few days later. He dropped his army duffel bag on the top stair of my attic apartment and, before taking off his coat, reached into the bag and pulled out a beautiful ceramic pie pan, jay bird–blue, which he'd wrapped in a favorite, scratchy wool sweater that no longer fit.

"I think we should make a pie together before we hit the road," he said.

I still had not made a pie since moving to New York. There had been no reason. No time. We'd never made a pie together, but I'd watched Ty make bread in San Francisco. Although the method for making bread dough is very different from that of making pie, I knew this: he had a way with dough.

"I'll make the filling," I said, not sure if I was ready to tackle my first crust. He smiled. "No pressure."

I had just bought some Macoun and Crispin apples while reporting a story on the Hudson Valley harvest. I still had blueberries in the freezer from a friend's trip to Maine. So it made sense to make the apple-blueberry pie from Mammy's Cupboard. Ty had read all about Doris Kemp's "accidental pie" in the series of newspaper articles I'd written about my cross-country journey.

We slipped a bowl in the refrigerator so that it would be cold by morning. When I woke up at dawn, Ty had already made the coffee and laid out all the ingredients. Otis the cat had perched himself on the radiator cover near the kitchen window to watch. A light snow had sugarcoated the fire escape.

Ty wore his Lucky Brand fleece and I asked him if lucky pajamas was the secret to a good pie crust.

"A good crust has nothing to do with luck," he said, sifting the flour over a yellow bowl. "It's all about feeling."

He used his bare hands to cut the shortening into the flour and massaged the two together with his ploughman's fingers until the mixture looked torn between sawdust and cornmeal. He poked a hole in the middle of the flour mound with his thumb, and to the hole he added water, one icy teaspoon at a time.

What scared me the most about going forward with Ty was his lack of direction or ambition. I had known I wanted to write since I was 12 years old. At 30, Ty was still aimless. But not with dough. With dough, he was rooted. Confident and in control. In his hands, at that very moment, nothing could go wrong. Babies could feel safe.

When he'd added enough water, Ty gathered the flour into his palms, and patted it into a rough ball. He plopped it on the flour-dusted counter.

"Perfect," he said, caressing the ball, smooth and slightly wet, though not slick. With the heel of his hand, he flattened it into a disk, then gently cloaked it in plastic wrap and placed it in the refrigerator to chill before rolling it out.

Respect the rules of pie.

"How did you know how much water to add?" I asked.

"You have to watch your dough, feel it, read it with all your senses," Ty said.

"It's hard to explain," he went on. "But you know it when it feels right.

"You just know."

pilgrimage pie

*"It is hard in this day in which the American tempo is so speeded up,
to sit back and be satisfied with what you have. It requires
education and culture to appreciate a quiet place,
but any fool can appreciate noise."*

—SINCLAIR LEWIS, ADDRESSING A VERMONT
ROTARY CLUB ON SEPTEMBER 23, 1929

Solo road trips are great for kneading thoughts. But a copilot offers another set of eyes. Same windshield, different landscape.

I saw gypsy flowers and funky mailboxes. Why so many tanning salons?

Kris spied roadkill and Dairy Queens (Oooh! Oooh! Can we stop? Please?).

Ty saw clouds, old trucks, and muscle cars.

"Check out the grille on that 1937 Willy's," or, "Did you hear the long-stroke engine on that '69 'cuda?"

I hadn't known the full extent of Ty's fascination with taillights, fins, and granny gears until we pulled onto the Taconic Parkway that gray fall morning, our bellies full with breakfast pie.

We were very pleased with our first joint-venture pie. Reluctantly, we left half of the pie on the kitchen table for the neighbor who would be feeding Otis in our absence.

Thanksgiving was three days away, and the plan was to slowly make our way to Plymouth, Massachusetts, to see, among other things, the rock where the pilgrims first set a buckled shoe onto the New World. And, of course, we hoped to experience a pretty traditional Thanksgiving meal in the part of the country where it was conceived.

Since we had some extra time, we decided to meander through Vermont first and get a feel for the Ben and Jerry state and for spending time together again.

Ty could identify every year and every make of every car that zoomed past slow-poke Betty. He could even list the cars his elementary-school teachers drove in Boulder.

When we crossed into Vermont, the glorious fall foliage was long gone, leaving only silver branches reaching skyward like giant whisks.

A colleague had mentioned some family friends, Don and Deb, who lived in Londonderry and made genuine Vermont maple syrup under the small Hell's Peak Farm label. Maybe they'd show us their sugarhouse, she said. She handed me their address, and with it came a gentle warning about how austere and intensely private Vermonters can be.

Driving through Vermont's rolling hills was like watching a silent movie. So quiet, yet so much drama. We drove across covered bridges with lattice woodwork sides, past proud barns that were sweater-green. Every porch, it seemed, was graced with pumpkins or bulbous hunter-green squash known as Hubbards. Road signs warned of wandering moose.

Ty wondered if we should call ahead to let Don and Deb know we were planning on dropping by, but spontaneity had worked so well for Kris and me on the pie trip, I suggested we didn't.

Not to worry, I said. We'd use pie as our calling card.

Hell's Peak Farm, on top of a hill at the end of Pitchfork Road, is nothing more than a gambrel house with cedar shingles, surrounded by sugar maples. The actual sugarhouse is down the hillside a ways, tucked in a thicket of trees.

Deb was washing dishes when we arrived. She wiped her hands on her apron as I mentioned our mutual acquaintance and, sensing a need for serious ice-breaking, I immediately brought up pie.

"I always make Hubbard squash pie this time of year," Deb said. "Made one last night. Don ate the last piece this morning, otherwise I'd offer you some."

Deb was shy but far from private. She was glad to show us around the farm and explain how the art of sugaring works. She threw on a thick cardigan sweater she took from a wooden peg, and then we followed her to the "sugarbush," or the stand of maple trees, closest to the house.

"Don's family has been sugaring for generations," she said, walking right up to a tree, and leaned into its silver-sage trunk. She pointed to where the tree had been tapped to extract the slightly sweet crystalline sap that flows through a sugar maple's veins.

Don and Deb tap six hundred trees a year to eke out about one hundred gallons of medium-amber syrup, which they sell in markets in and around Londonderry.

"The best yielders tend to be older trees," said Deb. How much sap a tree will surrender often can be predicted from the shape and fullness of its crown.

Deb led us down the hill to the wooden sugarhouse, which wouldn't come to steamy life until about four months later. It's in the sugarhouse that the sap is evaporated in large pans and boiled down. "Some people use oil for heat," she said, "but firewood makes the syrup richer in taste and in color."

Deb pointed to the funnel on the sugarhouse roof. When the sap boils, she said, it sends a fragrant billowing steam through the vents.

"When the air stops smelling sweet, you know the sugaring season's over."

Vermonters use maple syrup to sweeten just about everything, Deb said.

She added it to her baked beans, and most children dripped it onto their breakfast cereal. In fact, Deb said her children were incredulous the first time they saw someone sprinkle sugar on their cereal on a train.

Some bakers used syrup for their pie fillings, Deb said, but as often as she made pie, "we're better off selling the syrup." She did, however, use fresh cream from the dairy down the road for her fillings, whenever possible. And, like Duarte's in Pescadero, she used cold milk in her dough instead of water.

"My grandmother used to rub the top crust of her pies with milk to make them golden brown," she said.

A truck pulled up on Pitchfork Road. "There's Don," she said, and we climbed back up the hill to greet him. "Don isn't much of a talker," she warned. "He doesn't like to put himself out in the open."

Don said he'd answer any questions about sugaring so long as he could work on his truck at the same time. For the next twenty minutes, he spoke to us from the floorboard of his Dodge Ram, where he was, allegedly, installing a fuse. The truck door was ajar and his long legs hung out the side. And though we never had eye contact, he talked at length about the days when his family used a horse and sled to collect the sap buckets from tree to tree.

"The younger kids tapped and the older kids boiled," he said. He talked of the time the sugarhouse almost burned down when he got distracted and let the sap boil down to a sticky nothing.

"Hell's Peak Farm has had four sugarhouses in all," he said. "The original sugar shack dated back to the Civil War."

Don explained how Vermont Fancy is the queen of maple syrups. Drawn from the first sap of the season, which usually starts in March, it's considered much more delicate than the more robust syrups made with sap drawn later in spring. Sap drawn after the first budding tends to be bitter, he said.

Ty said he'd like to return to Hell's Peak Farm one day and help tap. We heard a grunt from the floorboard. Ty took that as a yes.

Over dinner that night at an inn in Dorset, Ty talked excitedly about spending six weeks in Vermont the following year.

Clearly, I thought, the drifter in him was alive and well and ready to jump the next train. Part of me was annoyed. Another part wanted to quit my job and learn to tap too.

Morning rose crisp, cold, and blue. We ate fat stacks of banana pancakes in amber syrup. At an antiques barn in town, I found a textured brown bowl with a pockmarked glaze. Ty emerged with a 1940 Ford Coupe Hot Wheels car that cost only 50 cents and put a million-dollar smile on his face.

"Aren't you a little old for these?" I asked, examining the tiny car.

Ty said nothing. I took the wheel for the next couple hundred miles and Ty played deejay, spinning everything from Ben Harper to Louis Armstrong.

"Did I ever tell you about the first road trip I took with Dennis?" he finally said.

I settled into the driver's seat sensing that Betty was about to become a confessional, as so often happens on long drives when the light and music and moment are right.

Dennis was Ty's adoptive father. Ty never knew his real dad, only remembered the sound of his motorcycle. He was only six when Dennis took him on a long drive from Colorado to Kansas to pick up a truck.

On the drive home, Ty was feeling cranky and Dennis stopped at a toy store to buy him two Hot Wheels.

"One was a Lincoln Continental," said Ty. "The other was a Ford Maverick."

Their first night home, Ty stuck his shiny new cars, which he'd clutched the whole drive home, under his mattress for safekeeping.

When he woke up, the cars had vanished.

"I never figured out what happened to them," said Ty, staring dead ahead. "When I go back home to visit, I still check the closets and look under beds hoping I'll find them."

Around 10 P.M., after heading north all day, we pulled off Route 91 in Wells River for a late-night snack at the the P & H truck stop. The full-service truck stop is one of the few that still offer showers, sleeping rooms, and a full-service restaurant decorated with Peterbilt wallpaper.

Understandably, it's a popular pit stop among long-haul truckers pulling rigs across New England and Canada. The twenty-four-hour café is also a favorite among local hunters and ramblers, like us, just looking for pie.

From our stools at the counter, we watched as truckers in thick red plaid shirts wandered in, slightly bowlegged. Some left their lumber trucks idling in the yard while they ducked in for coffee or a quick bowl of chowder. Those who planned to stay awhile took off their mesh caps, patted down their hair. Many of the truckers seemed to know one another by sight or name. Some truckers like to take their wives along on long drives, and at one corner table we saw one such couple saying grace over a bowl of cole slaw.

Nearly every trucker stepped up to the pie display to see what slice of home was on tap that day. The P & H usually offers ten pies daily. For the benefit of the Canadian truckers, they are listed in French on the menu, as well as in English.

There were several pies to choose from but maple cream pie was the obvious choice. They cut the pies in fourths at the P & H, so we asked to split a slice of the thick, caramel-custard pie.

"You're lucky," said Linda, our waitress, working the overnight shift. "We usually run out of that one pretty early.

"Truckers do love their pie. I can't tell you how many of them eat their pie before their eggs."

Nelson Baker, who owns the P & H, introduced himself. I'd watched him work the room at this late hour, sliding into booths to chat with regulars. In a prior life, Baker had been a criminal defense lawyer in Boston. He used to come to Vermont on weekends to unwind. One weekend, when he was going through a rough personal time, he picked up a realtor's brochure and saw that the truck stop was for sale. He stopped in on his way home that Sunday and made an offer.

Since chucking his ties and cuff links, he's become an expert on the trucking life, which, he admits, he tends to romanticize. "Truckers are the last American cowboys," says Baker, who is also fighting to preserve America's last few independent truck stops.

"They're all being swallowed up by the big chains," he said. "The independents are a vanishing breed."

Baker heads a national association of truck-stop operators, which took its message of preservation to Congress last year.

To drive their point home, they brought a fleet of truck-stop pies to Capitol Hill.

The Wednesday morning before Thanksgiving found us on Route 44, in Massachusetts, headed for the coast. We passed a turkey farm where people were lining under handpainted signs that said "A-M" and "N-Z," to pick up their fresh turkeys for the big day.

"I wonder where we'll be eating turkey tomorrow," I said to Ty. He squeezed my hand.

In Plymouth we saw a sign for a sandwich shop named Paulie's, and had to stop for lunch. Paulie's was where we'd had our first lunch date in San Francisco.

"Kismet," said Ty.

A cheery freckled woman in her 50s was sitting alone by the window, eating a sandwich and reading the *Patriot Ledger*. Occasionally, she'd look out the window and smile at all the tourists filing past on their way to Plimoth (sic) Plantation.

"This is one of the busiest weeks of the year in Plymouth," she said, sensing we were watching her. "What brings you here?"

I was about to explain about my Thanksgiving yearnings, when Ty jumped in:

"Pie," he said. "We're looking for good local pie. Any ideas?"

She chuckled. "My husband is the pie lover in the family," said the woman, who introduced herself as Ann Roach but sure looked like an Annie to me. "He makes a terrific strawberry rhubarb.

"Still, if you asked Rod, he'd tell you his best friend, Richie Brown, makes the best pumpkin chiffon pie in the world.

"Richie's a dentist in Cambridge," she went on. "He runs marathons, plays the mandolin, and bakes. He's a real Renaissance man.

"In fact," she said, "we're going to be eating some of his pie tomorrow."

In recent years, Thanksgiving was always at Rod's cousin's house, in Orleans, the crease in the elbow-shaped Cape. "Richie has a house in Chatham, nearby. He always brings the pie—and his mandolin, of course.

"Rod and Richie used to be in a bluegrass band called Stoney Lonesome," Ann said. "They always play some old fiddle tunes before and after turkey."

It sounded magical. And, oddly, deeply familiar.

Ann stretched her arms, then got up to leave.

"Well, it was nice chatting with you two," she said. "Good luck with your research."

I started to panic. Something deep inside me wanted to taste this Richie Brown pie, to sit next to Annie at the Thanksgiving table and hear myself say, "Will someone pass the cranberries, please." Somehow I knew the cranberries at Annie's table would not be the scarlet slinky stuff out of a can.

"What a coincidence," I heard myself say. "We'll be in Orleans tomorrow, too."

Ty kicked me under the table.

"Well, er, uh, maybe you can drop by and say hello and meet Richie," she stammered. "We'll be on Monument Road."

It wasn't exactly an invitation, but it was more than Don's grunt. It certainly was enough to warrant buying a bottle of wine for our hosts—just in case.

We wandered in an antiques shop to look for mixing bowls, but when we realized the store sold only big-ticket items, like rich mahogany armoires, we turned on our heels and headed for the door.

"Can I help you find something?" said a tall woman with a crisp British accent.

"Thanks, but we were looking for mixing bowls and rolling pins.

You know, pie stuff," said Ty as we opened the door, unleashing a clanging of little bells.

"What about pie birds?"

I closed the door again.

"What's a pie bird?"

She curled her finger and ushered us toward her office.

"I don't sell them here, but I collect them," she said, opening a catalog to show us.

Pie birds, also known as pie funnels, are small, open-mouthed ceramic figurines that double as steam vents in a pie, she said.

"Just like the vents on a sugarhouse roof," said Ty, who'd never heard of a pie bird either.

Since Victorian times, bakers in England have placed pie birds in the center of covered fruit and meat pies to prevent oven drippings and soggy bottom crusts, said the woman, who introduced herself as Jackie.

"My grandmother back in England used them all the time." Jackie had come to New England from Norfolk to work as a nanny when she was only 20. She fell in love with an American and stayed.

Traditionally, pie birds were always fashioned in the shape of a blackbird, she said, but eventually molds were designed in all shapes and characters.

"There's even one of Princess Diana," she said.

Jackie started collecting them twenty years ago, "long before they were all the rage on eBay." She owns about eight hundred figurines, which she finds at the same places I find my mixing bowls: church sales and flea markets.

"I just love the hunt," she said, eyes shining. "Usually, the people selling them have no clue what they are used for.

"It's a shame, really, because an apple pie isn't complete without a blackbird poking out of it," she sighed. "But then, nobody really bakes pies from scratch anymore, it seems."

Jackie belongs to an international group of pie-bird collectors. She said the "hot" pie bird of the moment, the one all connoisseurs coveted, was the rare Donald Duck funnel—worth a cool $1,500.

I took Jackie's card and promised to keep an eye out for Donald and other pie birds in my foraging. In exchange, could she recommend a place to stay for the night? She could.

Her friend Richard owned a B&B down the street, she said, right upstairs from his tea-and-curiosity shop. "It's across from the Mayflower Society Museum and just steps away from Plymouth Rock."

Richard, dressed like a pilgrim, was the biggest curiosity in his dark, cluttered shop which sold soaps, tea, pewter, and candles.

"How do you two know Jackie?" he asked. We explained how we'd bonded over parallel pie quests, and his face brightened.

"My great aunt in Portsmouth, New Hampshire, used to make the most delicious strawberry rhubarb pie," he said, stepping out from behind the counter.

"She grew the strawberries and rhubarb in her backyard and she'd shoo us all out of the kitchen when she baked," he recalled. "We'd wait in the garden and, when she was done, she'd rest the pie on the sill to cool.

"It was a regular Norman Rockwell painting."

His B&B, the Captain's Inn, had only one room, he said, "but it's an entire apartment and it was built in 1725."

It was available, so long as we promised to be out by noon, since he and his wife, Yoko, planned to serve their Thanksgiving supper there.

"You're free to come back for the meal," he said, "but we just need the space to cook in."

"Thank you," I said, "but we have plans on the Cape."

Our room had two fireplaces, creaky pine floors, and a window that looked out on Old North Street, one of the oldest streets in America. In the morning, we awoke to the musical sound of recorders, a "Pilgrim's Progress" procession headed straight for the Rock. We followed suit.

Like most first-time visitors, we were surprised by how small the Rock was in stature. Small and lumpy as misshapen dough. In the 1800s, it was common for visitors wanting a relic of the Rock to simply chisel away at it. In fact, de Tocqueville wrote about relics of the rock he encountered throughout his travels:

"Here is a stone which the feet of a few poor fugitives pressed for an instant, and this stone becomes famous . . . a fragment is prized as a relic," he wrote. "Does not this sufficiently show how all human power and greatness are entirely in the soul?"

Perhaps, but in the end, Americans got so greedy the Rock had to be enclosed by protective iron gates, like a lion at the zoo.

"Don't you feel kind of sorry for the Rock," I heard a woman say to her husband as we walked away. And I had to agree.

When we returned to our room, Richard had slipped our bill beneath the door. It read: "One night at the inn."

We headed south, toward the Cape, under a battering rain. At Ty's urging, we stopped at a phone booth on the side of the road to call Ann and Rod Roach (they were listed) to see if it was really OK for us to drop by and meet the illustrious Richie Brown—and to get the exact address on Monument Road.

There was no answer. We got the listing for a Richie Brown in Cambridge and tried that number, but got an answering machine. I was secretly pleased, because no answer was better than being turned down. I was determined to break bread with the bluegrass players.

I hung up the phone and noticed a soft kangaroo mouse, color of gravy, nestled against a rock, trying to find shelter from the rain.

When we got to Orleans, it was bigger than it appeared on the map. Monument Road was no narrow country lane. It was about three miles long, and houses were scattered on either side of the road from beginning to end.

Not only did we not have an exact address, but we didn't even know the name of Rod's cousins hosting the holiday dinner. We'd just have to try each house, one door at a time.

"Is this where the Roaches are having their Thanksgiving dinner?" I asked at the first house. That didn't sound right, and at the next house, I massaged my technique. But they had not heard of Ann Roach or of the famous Richie Brown, either. Neither had the next house or the house after that.

We'd covered about one third of the south side of Monument Road, when a gentleman who'd been watching us through his kitchen window for a while stepped out onto the side porch and signaled us over.

"Are you lost?" he asked, ushering us into the kitchen where the whole family was busy with last-minute preparations and barely noticed our intrusion. Wickedly handsome in a Hubbard-squash-green cashmere sweater, Steve Peno looked as though he'd just stepped out of a Ralph Lauren catalogue. As though everything in his visibly lush, terry-cloth life had come easy.

He knew just about everybody on this stretch of Monument Road, or so he thought, but he did not know their cousins or dentist friends who baked. If we had so much as a name, a phone number, an address, he'd take us there personally. Steve was a genuinely nice guy, and beneath all that WASP-y wool was a definite adventurous streak.

We pressed on, knocking on a least a dozen more doors. The rain had finally let up but too late for Ty, who was wearing a brown suede jacket that made him look a bit like that wet kangaroo mouse.

I sat on a curb, crushed and guilty for ruining Ty's Thanksgiving.

"Let's go back to Plymouth and find a nice restaurant for dinner," Ty said, pulling me to my feet. "Or we can go back to the inn and take Richard up on his offer."

"You're right," I said. "This was a crazy idea."

As we drove out of Orleans, we passed a sign for Chatham and that got me thinking. Didn't Richie Brown have a summer house in Chatham?

"If he's in charge of pie," I said, "shouldn't he be in Chatham baking just about now?"

Ty pulled over at the next phone booth and handed me a quarter.

Doc Brown was listed on the Cape and, while I dialed, I crossed the fingers on my free hand. Richie Brown picked up himself.

"Do you mind holding for one minute," he said, "I've got to pull a pie out of the oven."

I gave Ty the thumbs-up.

"How does it look?" I said when Richie returned to the phone.

"Not too bad," he said. "Who *is* this?"

I didn't want to scare him off with our convoluted story, so I stretched the truth a little, told him we were new friends of Ann Roach and she'd asked us to drop by so we could taste his pie, but we'd left the exact address at the hotel. Could he tell us where everyone was convening on Monument Road, and, er, the names of our hosts?

"I don't know the address," he said, "my car just goes there automatically once a year on Thanksgiving. It's a Cape-style house, I think, with gray shutters. Jim and Ellie's last name is Spainhour."

That was all we needed. This time, when we returned to Steve's house, we had something to work with. The Penos were just sitting down to eat in their formal dining room when we rapped on the kitchen window. Steve greeted us with a carving knife in one hand, a dishtowel in the other, as though we were old friends. "We have a name," Ty said. Steve grinned.

He put down the knife and paged through the small Orleans White Pages. I could hear an elderly relative ask: "Is it those wanderers from New York again?"

"What do you know," Steve said, dialing the number for us, "they're just a few houses away."

"Hey, neighbor," he said to Jim. "Happy Thanksgiving. Some of your dinner guests seem to be lost, but I'm sending them your way."

Steve followed us out to the car. "If it doesn't work out over there, you can always come back here for some food."

"Now we have two backup plans," Ty said.

A confounded Jim Spainhour was waiting on the lawn when we pulled up the drive. He had a nice broad face with a smile to match.

We were the first to arrive, which was good, because we had lots of explaining to do. But all we really had to say was that we were driving across New England researching good pies and that Ann had told us about Richie's pumpkin chiffon, and they were satisfied. Of course, they didn't know I had every hope of being invited for supper, too.

Jim lit a fire and opened some wine. He showed us some of the furniture he made by hand, including a beautiful Windsor chair that would have looked right at home at the Captain's Inn. By the time Ann and Rod arrived, we were looking pretty cozy in the living room, Boo and Clio, their two Labradors, at our feet. Ann nearly dropped her pan of braised leeks when she saw us on the couch. When Richie arrived with his pie and his wife, Margaret, we told the story all over again.

"I've got to hand it to you two for your stick-to-it-iveness," Richie said.

It didn't take long for Rod and Richie to bring out their instruments. Rod played a 1931 Gibson RB-6 Mastertone banjo. Richie's beautifully inlaid mandolin was also a Gibson, made in 1925.

They played classic fiddle tunes like "Soldier's Joy," "Gray Eagle," and, of course, "Turkey in the Straw."

They took a break, and Rod regaled us with tales of his wild years as a young banjo player in Bristol, Vermont, more than thirty years ago. Desperate to preserve a dying musical form, he and his friends would go into the woods to round up old fiddle players and bring them to bluegrass festivals, he said.

"We'd yank them right out of their cabins."

He told us about Fletch McIntyre, the fabled rambling fiddle player who knew nine hundred fiddle tunes. Fletch managed to get himself thrown in jail every year right after the first frost, just so he could have a warm bed and a roof over his head through those unforgiving Vermont winters.

"To thank the sheriff, Fletch would fashion orchestra figures out of tin cans," said Rod.

"Yeah, those old fiddle players are disappearing pretty fast."

Inevitably, talk of preserving traditions led us back to pie, specifically the one Richie Brown had placed on Ellie's sideboard.

The pie is an adaptation of Craig Claiborne's sour-cream pumpkin pie from the *New York Times Cookbook*, Richie said. It was his first wife's mother, Onnie, who first made the pie for him more than thirty years ago. He had to wait years before he could make it himself, he said, "because Onnie liked to think of herself as the only cook at the table."

When he finally was free to make it on his own, he tinkered with different crusts and settled on the buttery short crust from the *Vegetarian Epicure Cookbook*.

"They're never pretty and they're never uniform," he said, "but I'll admit, my pies are good." Lately he'd been experimenting with adding lemon to the crust.

"I don't know how you do it, Richie," Rod said, "but your pies get better and better every year."

Richie turned to me and Ty. "You'll have to tell me what you think."

An awkward silence filled the room and, though I don't blush easily, I felt my cheeks burn crimson. As cozy as we all were, and as much as the house was filling with irresistible smells, the fact was, no one had invited us to stay yet.

Ellie stepped out of the kitchen, where she'd been making the gravy, just in time. "Jim," she said, "will you get two more chairs for the dining room?"

Then she looked directly at me. "You *are* staying for dinner, aren't you?"

Ty ran to the car to get the wine and then we took our places in the dining room, around the cherrywood table, which Jim had also made.

Rod caught me eyeing the fresh cranberries. "I discovered a wild bog while taking a walk on the Cape the other day," he said. "I stuffed as many in my pockets as I possibly could for today."

Ellie set her famous yeast rolls on the table and, at that moment, all was right with the world.

We raised a glass to family and friends—the old and the very new.

HELL'S PEAK FARM
HUBBARD-SQUASH PIE

CRUST FOR ONE 9-INCH PIE SHELL

1 cup flour

⅔ stick of butter

3 tablespoons milk

FILLING

2 cups cooked squash (steamed or baked), mashed with a fork

¾ cup of sugar; use a little less if using refined maple sugar

1 teaspoon ground cinnamon

½ teaspoon salt

½ teaspoon ground ginger

½ teaspoon nutmeg

3 eggs

⅔ cup evaporated milk or ⅔ cup fresh cream

½ cup whole milk

Put the flour and butter in the food processor. Mix, then slowly add cold milk. Pulse. When it clumps together, take it out of the processor and roll it out.

Mix all filling ingredients together in a bowl. When thoroughly mixed, pour into a 9-inch pie shell and bake at 350 degrees for 50–55 minutes.

the pie siren

They took all the trees
and put them in a tree museum
And they charged all the people
a dollar and a half just to see 'em
Don't it always seem to go,
that you don't know what you got
Till it's gone
They paved paradise
And put up a parking lot

—JONI MITCHELL, "BIG YELLOW TAXI"

I came home from New England to a stack of unread newspapers piled at my front door. I scanned them briefly and was about to toss an obituary section in the recycling bin, when a headline caught my eye: SAXOPHONIST FRED FORD DIES AT 69.

Fred Ford . . . Why did I know that name? I read on:

"Saxophonist Fred Ford, a versatile jazz and rhythm and blues musician who recorded with B. B. King and Jerry Lee Lewis is dead after a battle with cancer. . . . A mainstay of the Memphis music scene . . . Ford was known for his baritone sax skills."

Of course. Ford was the Beale Street musician who'd recommended the Greater Harvest Church for gospel and Piccadilly's for pie.

Though he was a minor character in our pie adventure, news of his death distressed me, disproportionately so. I'd been thinking, you see, about how Elva Twitchell in Utah was getting on in years, as was her sister Beulah. Gloria and Ruby, both in nursing homes. So many veteran pie bakers who would soon be leaving us. And taking their rolling pins with them.

My favorite yoga teacher, Liz, walks us through meditation after each class. Focus on the inner light, she says. Surrender. Have no agenda. But no matter how hard I try to turn my mind to blank, a laundry list of "shoulds" and "whats" and "whys" struts before my eyes: I'm thinking of the mole on my arm that needs to be checked out; the names of the children I may or may not have.

But in the weeks that followed our Thanksgiving journey, I kept seeing the same singular image floating past my mind's eye during meditation: an infinite number of winged pies parading past me in assembly-line fashion, and then, one by one, floating upward and disappearing into the ether.

Ohm.

Then, my mother underwent emergency surgery for a cancerous tumor in her belly. Doctors warned us that the high-risk surgery would take eight hours, but if the cancer was too far gone, they would sew her up after two. My father and I spent the first two hours staring silently at the clock. And when two hours became three, then four, and the surgery continued well into the night, we bawled like children. When my mother finally came to, she reached for my father's hand to look at his watch.

I'd only been back from Los Angeles a week when Betty bit the dust. Not in the Ozarks, or the Nevada desert, as my parents had feared before I drove east, but in Peekskill, of all places. A young woman had ignored a stop sign and barreled straight into me. We were both fine, but Betty's front was pleated like a tart pan.

The collision was a logical culmination of my first year in New York, a crash course from start to finish. I was in the ambulance when it hit me. The epiphany, I mean, that I'd only scratched the surface of pie in those three weeks on the road, and that I needed to finish what I'd started.

My knees were scraped from hitting the dash but paramedics worried I'd also hit my head, because I kept asking about the piemobile.

"She can't die now," I said. "She's got miles and miles to go on the road to pie."

I called Kris in San Francisco the next day.

"How would you like to go back out on the road this summer and pick up where we left off?"

Silence. Then, "Can we bring our roller blades this time?"

Kris was in a funk herself. The advertising world was gnawing away at her now more than ever. In the year since the pie trip, she'd dived into photography as a hobby. She'd found a niche, taking artful black-and-white nudes of her pregnant friends. And they were all pregnant. I thought it was a ferociously brave and creative way to face her biological clock head-on. She wanted to quit the ad biz and pursue photography full-time, but found it hard to walk away from the money she made producing ads, no matter how stressful.

A soul-searching summer suspended in time was just what she needed.

I told her I wanted to stay out on the road longer this time, linger awhile. Rushing was antithetical to pie. I wanted to take this trip a little deeper. Besides, I was beginning to see the possibility of a book in this strange quest.

"Aren't you worried we'll run out of things to talk about?"

"Unlikely," I said. "Very unlikely."

Kris had a prior freelance job commitment for the end of the summer, so I'd have to find another pie traveler for part of the trip. Ty had turned out to be a great co-pie-lot. But, as he so rightly pointed out, "This is a chick trip."

I was glad he said it so I didn't have to. Besides, I was still unsure about us. He'd taken a gamble and moved to New York. I wavered. What if he wasn't the one? What if there was something shinier around the corner?

What if I took a leap of faith and fell?

What if I made a pie and the crust was tough as plaster?

Best to keep on driving.

I put out the call to my women friends to see who could join me on the road to pie. Teri was the first to call back. We'd met working at a newspaper in San Diego. We'd spent the year we turned 30 back-packing through India, Africa, and Europe together. Not only could she kill large pests with one swift blow of her Teva sandal, but she could read a map upside-down and roll with the punches and my ever-changing moods. Teri was also enrolled in film school at UCLA. Would it be all right if she brought along her video camera?

I felt it was my duty to remind Teri that she was getting married later that summer. Did she really want to drive around America eating pie three weeks before she had to squeeze into a wedding dress?

Bless her. She did.

My new New York City friend Nicole, a pastry chef, also answered the call. Food critics raved about her desserts, but Nicole was burnt out on the grueling hours. "I want a life," she said. "I WANT A LIFE."

Martha Stewart had offered her a job as pastry consultant on her television show, but Nicole fantasized about finding a small, honest bakery where she could Zen out and bake bread for a while. She was at the top of her game and wanted to sit out the season.

"Is there something wrong with me?" she said. I was the wrong person to ask, of course. I was finally working as a journalist in New York and all I really wanted to do was flee.

Four restless women in their 30s, all going through major life shifts. Four driven women in need of one long drive.

As with the first trip, pie-stop suggestions from friends, colleagues, readers of my newspaper column, poured in. I drew pie dots on the states I planned to hit, following a northwestern route from Michigan to Montana, straight down to New Mexico, then Texas and Louisiana. I'd feel my way slowly, through Alabama and the Carolinas and call it a trip in Washington, D.C.

I connected the dots and tried not to read too much into it when the outline looked just like a bat in flight.

my two betties

Fact: One of Jimmy Stewart's favorite co-stars was a horse named Pie. Together, they rode through seventeen westerns.

One cannot underestimate the bond between car and driver on an extended road trip. It's a relationship that requires lots of give and take.

You get me up this climb, and I promise I will check your oil at the next filling station—or at least within the next 1,000 miles.

Betty and I had that kind of bond. The teal-green 1988 sedan was my first serious car. I had bought it used, but it had power windows and locks and seat warmers—features that made me feel decidedly grown up and not a moment too soon, at 34.

On the pie trip, Betty cleared fifteen states without a hiccough. She did lose her antenna at a car wash near Berea, Kentucky, but that was entirely my fault for forgetting to retract it in my haste to pounce on a salty snack from the mini-mart. Through twisters and tread-melting heat, she'd kept her cool. Somehow, she always made room for one more mixing bowl, and always made it to the next filling station even when we were on fumes.

To filch my favorite Katharine Hepburn line from *The Philadelphia Story*, "My, she was *yar*."

So you can understand why I was so upset after the Peekskill crash. My New York mechanic, Tim, took one look at Betty and bit his lip: "Sorry," he said, "but Betty's gone on her last pie ride."

A friend at the paper sent me the following e-mail when she heard the news:

"I'm sorry about Betty, m'dear. She had a good run, served you well, and got to see a lot of fun places, listen in on some good talk. She had a better life than most and, now, she can rest in peace."

Ty surprised me by baking a Funeral Pie—a simple raisin pie that Mennonites and Amish traditionally bring to funeral services—the day a charity came to haul Betty away. (Just because you're in mourning doesn't mean you can't get a tax break.)

Replacing the piemobile proved a lot harder than lining up a new pie crew. Sure, buying a new car would have been easy. But it seemed inappropriate to drive across America seeking something old and handcrafted in a generic new Camry. No, the new piemobile would need a certain patina. Patina and personality.

Betty had been so loyal, it made sense to replace her with one of her own. Only this time, I'd look for a station wagon—more room for mixing bowls and vagabond musicians. A month before my late-June departure, I still hadn't found an old Volvo wagon and I was getting nervous. So nervous, I came this close to buying the 1951 Plymouth Cranbrook on the used-car lot in Croton-on-Hudson where I'd moved that spring, to a small cottage in the woods.

The car was mixing-bowl green with custard-cream whitewalls: pure automotive eye candy. On the test drive through Croton, the Cranbrook, which only gets nine miles to the gallon, cruised slow as molasses. The perfect speed for the kind of trip I was taking.

Just in time, gas prices shot up to $2 a gallon and the *Pennysaver* listed a 1990 navy-blue Volvo 240 station wagon in Bedford. Same as Betty, only bigger, newer, and bluer. I was immediately smitten with her retro chrome luggage rack and classy red pinstripe.

The salesman introduced himself as Ernest. Good sign, I thought. Then he slapped his card in my hand. "Ernest Wolf."

And what a wolf he turned out to be, pretending another couple on the lot was ready to buy the car and refusing to go down one penny on the price.

Driving her home, I decided to call her Betty Blue instead of Betty Two. To make it official, I decided to get some "IBRK4PIE" vanity plates, too.

My cynical New York colleagues worried this could be subject to misinterpretation—so, to make things perfectly clear, I attached a wooden rolling pin to her front grille and one to the rear handle.

There was *no* mistaking what this car was all about.

I picked Kris up at JFK airport on a humid day in June. "Meet Betty Blue," I said as she tossed her roller blades in the back.

We were still inside the terminal, stopped at a light, when the driver of a Holiday Inn shuttle bus honked for our attention.

"What's up with the rolling pin?" he shouted across two lanes.

"We're driving across America looking for pie," Kris shouted back.

"My mama makes the best blueberry pie you ever had," he said.

"That so?" said Kris. "Where does she live?"

The light turned green. Kris dug into her purse for a pen.

"Baton Rouge, Louisiana," the driver said before pulling away. He stuck his head out the window: "Her name's Madear. Madear Johnson. Euclid Avenue.

"Tell her her baby boy sent you . . ."

Kris jotted it all down in the palm of her hand.

It had been more than a year, but she hadn't lost her touch.

FUNERAL PIE

Adapted from the *Pennsylvania Dutch Cook Book—
Fine Old Recipes*, Culinary Arts Press, 1936

1 cup of raisins
2 cups of water
1½ cups of sugar
4 tablespoons flour
1 egg, well-beaten
juice of 1 lemon
2 tablespoons grated lemon rind
¼ teaspoon of salt

Wash raisins and soak in cold water for three hours. Drain. Combine 2 cups of water, raisins, sugar, and flour. Mix well. Add the salt, lemon juice and rind, and the egg and mix thoroughly. Cook the mixture over hot water for 15 minutes, stirring occasionally. Set aside and let cool. Pour mixture into a 9-inch pastry-lined pan. Cover with narrow strips of dough, criss-crossed, or lattice-style. Bake at 450 degrees for 10 minutes. Reduce heat to 350 degrees and bake another 30 minutes.

part three

"What is a man but all his connections?"

—ROBERT FROST

*"The everyday kindness of the backroads more than
makes up for the acts of greed in the headlines."*

—CHARLES KURALT
ON THE ROAD WITH CHARLES KURALT

oh-my-oh, ohio

"Slump? I ain't in no slump. I just ain't hitting."

—YOGI BERRA

We'd barely left the cottage when we came across a helmet in the middle of Furnace Dock Road.

A fist with eyes poked straight out one end of the khaki dome, and we realized this was a turtle. I swerved, and Kris jumped out of the car to carry it to safety.

A guy in a sportscar zoomed up behind us and started honking, flashing his lights, even though it was obvious we were on a rescue mission.

He was in a hurry. And he was wearing hospital scrubs.

We crossed the Hudson River, east to west, on the Bear Mountain Bridge. A giant American flag hung from one of the towers. I reminded Kris that Jack Kerouac had also begun his journey by crossing this very bridge, though in the opposite direction. Purely coincidental.

Since we'd already covered Pennsylvania on the first trip, we would zip through the Keystone State, then cut through Ohio to get to Michigan for some cherry pie.

I had no firm plans for Ohio, figured it would take me a day or two on the road anyway before I got my bearings. Other than my friend Jerry, who writes about food and travel at one of the nation's largest newspapers, I had never met anyone from Ohio.

I had lunch with Jerry at Picholine, near Lincoln Center, shortly before my departure, and asked him where he would go for pie in his home state.

Jerry, who grew up in Wooster, remembered picking tiny, tart purple elderberries for pie when he was a boy—but not fondly.

"It was a real pain in the ass. You'd have to pick about a million berries to make just one pie."

He could muster plenty of state pride for the Cleveland Indians, who were having a great season, but Ohio pie left him dry.

I'd read of a place called Henry's Sohio in West Jefferson. A flotilla of county- and state-fair blue ribbons was tacked to the pie display. They'd have good pie, *really* good pie, but that place was famous and I was hoping to find something fresh and original, particularly this early in the journey.

"We'll figure it out when we get there," I told Kris.

We lumbered onto US 6 and, judging from the map, we'd be staying on it for 700 miles or so, clear on to upper Ohio where we'd head north and let US 6 continue on without us to Indiana. There was something reassuring about knowing we'd follow the same two-lane road for such a long time.

About 200 miles into it, Kris had an epiphany.

"I think US 6 is probably the longest relationship I've ever had."

Like most relationships, US 6 has its ups and downs. At its best, it hugs the Susquehanna River and is lined with poppy-colored day lilies and quaint houses that face each other off across the thin highway like square dancers. At its worst, US 6 morphs into a tawdry four-laner, barreling through the grainy coal-mining northeastern part of Pennsylvania.

Talk of relationships led Kris to ask where things stood with Ty.

He'd been great on the road to pie, I told her, but I wasn't sure how we'd fare together on the road to life. He was the patient, sensitive soul I'd been seeking, and the best listener I could hope for, I said, but he had no set goals or ambitions. No five-year plan.

"Can I have children with a guy who thinks 401(k) is a breakfast cereal?" I said.

"Sounds like you want your filling and your crust, too," she said.

We stopped in Wellsboro for the night. We didn't want to kill ourselves the first day out and we'd spotted a cool, retro diner that would make for a fun breakfast stop. In keeping with our vow to exercise on this trip, we rose early and power-walked through the Wellsboro Cemetery. At least we tried, but we kept stopping to marvel at tilted tombstones from the mid-nineteenth century. Women's names were so dramatic back then: Isadora, Harriet, Matilda. So full of duty, purpose, and self-denial.

Harry was the name of the widowed dairy farmer we sat next to at the Wellsboro diner counter. He alternated between breakfasts at the 1939 diner and the McDonald's in town "because the coffee at McDonald's is a few cents cheaper and that adds up over time."

At the diner, the broad-backed waitresses all knew Harry by name, even knew how to get his goat by threatening to bring him tuna casserole. Still, to save only 30 cents or so a week, this lonely old man ate at McDonald's—where he was virtually anonymous—three times a week.

In Meadville, about 30 miles from the Ohio border we stopped in an antiques barn to look for a mixing bowl for good pie karma.

The owner, a crotchety old cricket, pointed to the rolling pin on my car and said: "You know what we call that in my business? A woman's best weapon!"

As we poked around the cavernous shop, the owner went on and on about Sharon Stone being Meadville's most famous resident. Personally, I thought Gideon Sundback, the guy who invented the zipper, had made more of an impact, but I let him blather on. I fell in love with a 1920s wicker table with great legs (OK, maybe not Sharon Stone–great, but whimsical great). A totally impractical purchase, but, as Kris pointed out, when they were passing out the practicality gene, I was out shopping for handwashables.

She started to talk me out of it, but knew better. And, to her credit, when the table slid back and forth on the luggage rack through the windswept plains of South Dakota, she kept her "I told you so"s to herself.

Oddly enough, from the moment we left Meadville, Betty Blue's glove compartment door started popping open at the slightest bump in the road.

Was she giving us a sign?

The state sign for Ohio was smaller than any I'd seen thus far. No motto. No sunset. No big-mouthed bass jumping out of Lake Erie. Just: OHIO. But then, who could top the Pennsylvania sign across the highway: AMERICA STARTS HERE.

Fiddling with the radio dial, we stumbled on a voice as smooth as Tootsie Price's chocolate silk pie in Pine Bluff, Arkansas. It belonged to Fitz, the host of the Fitz's Hour of Blues, on the local public radio affiliate.

The music was great and it got me thinking. Wasn't disc jockey Alan Freed, the guy who first coined the term "rock 'n' roll," from Cleveland? In the absence of anything more logical, my source for Ohio pie, then, would have to be affiliated with rock 'n' roll in some way. We'd head for the Rock 'n' Roll Hall of Fame Museum in Cleveland and take it from there.

We found a parking spot smack in front of the Rock 'n' Roll shrine and inches away from Lake Erie. Unfortunately, the Hall of Fame had just closed for the night. We were back at square one.

What about Fitz? Kris said.

I dialed up the station and Fitz answered the phone himself. "I'm a food writer from New York just passing through Cleveland and I was wondering if you had any suggestions where to go for pie around here."

"Excuse me?" he sneered. "Did you say *pie*?"

"Yes, pie. As in apple pie," I said, to distinguish it from the numerical pi.

"I don't eat pie," he growled. "Why are you asking me? Why don't you go ask a cop?"

"If I were looking for doughnuts, I might have asked a cop," I said. In as few words as possible, I tried to explain the treasure-hunt nature of my journey, the whole Alan Freed rock 'n' roll angle I was trying to weave into my story, which I hoped to turn into a book.

"What do *I* have to do with Alan Freed?" he barked. Then he hung up.

Was Fitz's behavior a harbinger of how this trip would go? Kris turned up the radio to see what Fitz would say, or play, next. And here is, roughly, what his Cleveland listeners heard late that warm Friday night in June:

"I've been in this business for 27 years and I've never, I mean never, gotten a call like the one that just came in. This lady from New York just called the station and said she was driving around America looking for pie. She's got a rolling pin on her car . . . Well, I don't know about you folks out there, but when I think of pie I don't think about apple or pumpkin. You know what I mean? She says she's thinking of writing a book about her journey. All I can say is: Good luck, sistah! This is going to be one helluva book!"

We laughed so hard, every walleye in Lake Erie must have

headed straight for Canadian waters. As we hightailed it out of Cleveland, Fitz continued to entertain us with his playlist. "Where Can I Get Some Cherry Pie?" was followed by a 1962 Bo Diddly tune called "Can't Judge a Book by Its Cover."

At least Fitz had found his sense of humor.

As late as it was, laughter had juiced us up, so we drove straight on to Sandusky to find a room for the night. We found some over-priced chain hotel where the nightshift hotel clerk was drunker (and smellier) than a skunk. I stared at the twinkly stucco ceiling for a long time, unable to sleep.

Instead of counting sheep, I calculated how many cups of coffee Harry could buy at the Wellsboro Diner with the money I'd spent on my wicker table.

cat in tree leads
to great pie

"Commonplaces never become tiresome. It is we who become tired when we cease to be curious and appreciative."
—NORMAN ROCKWELL
"COMMONPLACE," *THE AMERICAN MAGAZINE*

I learned to speak English when I was five, from my neighbor Marietta Smith and from watching reruns of *Leave It to Beaver* and *The Andy Griffith Show.*

Which is why, growing up, I felt secure in the notion that in small-town America cats never stayed stuck in trees long.

A stop in tiny Munith, Michigan, shattered that myth for good.

Our plan for mitten-shaped Michigan was to hit the National Cherry Festival in Traverse City, then head farther north to rugged Charlevoix.

On the way, I wanted to make a quick pit stop in Armada, just north of Detroit, in the thumb part of the state. A fellow food writer at the *Detroit News* had told me about Wendy Achatz, a young woman who baked luscious fruit pies in her creaky old home with her husband, Dave.

That sounded promising, so we drove through Detroit, Betty Blue feeling self-conscious, a "foreigner" among a sea of big American cars. Kris called the bakery for directions as we got closer and got a chirpy machine telling her the bakery was closed on Saturdays. Closed on Saturdays?!?

This threw us for a complete loop. Ohio had left a bad taste in my mouth and we needed to find some pie fast.

I pulled over in a Dairy Queen parking lot to plot the next move while Kris did some Pilates stretches on Betty Blue's hood. I remembered having a conversation once, with San Francisco chef Douglas Keane, a Michigan native, about an artisan bakery in Munith, near Ann Arbor, where his family owned a campground. He used to get pies there as a boy, and although he hadn't been to the bakery in years, he assured me that it was still open and worth any detour.

If central and lower Michigan were the palm of the mitten, then Munith would be where the life line and love line intersect, off of US 106, a short-lived two-laner that cuts right through the lush Waterloo Recreation Area.

Once in Munith, we needed only follow our noses and let the familiar scent of sour dough lead us to the Mill Pond Bakery at the end of the main street through town. The bakery looked plucked from a Marcel Pagnol novel. In one corner, an old bank vault next to the Blodgett Ovens serves as a reminder of the building's prior incarnation as the town bank. John, the owner, bought the bakery as a quality-of-life move. He forms the bread by hand, using flour from local mills. He waters down his bread with a garden hose.

People thought he was crazy to open a "yuppie" bakery in conservative Munith in the heart of Wonder Bread country.

Fortunately, enough restaurants opened up in Ann Arbor to keep the bakery busy and afloat. The bakery is considered so "alternative" that all the local youths want to work there in the summer as a rite of passage.

John had stayed up all night baking for a pack of seven hundred cross-country cyclists who had stopped in for some healthy carbo-loading that morning. He was exhausted when we dropped by seeking pie.

John said he did in fact make pies in the early years. "They weren't real big sellers back then because of the 'health food' craze," he said. Then, when the country went "gourmet," pies were dismissed as too pedestrian. But John was sensing a "back-to-basics movement" in America, he said, and he'd been talking to his wife about bringing pies back.

"Maybe your coming to Munith is a sign that we need to start making pies," he said. Maybe it was.

John had taped a quote from Calvin Coolidge on the wall, and I jotted it down in my journal while Kris bought some loaves for us for the road.

> *Press on: Nothing can take the place of persistence.*
> *Talent will not; nothing is more common than unsuccessful men*
>   *with talent.*
> *Genius will not; unrewarded genius is almost a proverb.*

Education will not; the world is full of educated derelicts.
Persistence and determination alone are omnipotent.

—Calvin Coolidge

Inspired by this humble little bakery, we went for a brisk walk along the road that connects Munith to the township of Waterloo. For a good hour, we walked along fields of chirping crickets and darting jackrabbits getting in their last kicks of the day.

We were on our way back to the car we'd left parked in grass behind the bakery when we noticed an older woman talking to a walnut tree in her backyard.

"You come on down now, kitty," she said. "You come on down here to Mama."

"Where's the fire department when you need it," I said, crossing the lawn to help. "Oh, they won't come out for a silly old cat," she said, laughing, "*even* in Munith."

She puckered her face and glared at a smug bruiser cat sitting in a patch of rhubarb also known as "pie plant." "See that tom? He's the one who chased my cat up the tree," she said. "That tom is nothing but trouble."

She was wearing loose cotton shorts and a matching top, and her dark hair was in tight Bette Davis curls. She was well into her 60s but there was something positively girlish about her and the way her exposed bony knees faced the world.

We took turns coaxing the cat who gingerly made his way down the trunk, like a skier on his first non-bunny slope. She picked him up, held him against her chest. "I'm Juanita," she said. "You two ladies getting your exercise?" she asked, as though we'd just met the week before at a church. We told her about pie.

"Well, isn't that too much?" she said. "I was just fixing to cut some rhubarb to make some pie. My feller is visiting for the weekend and so I thought I'd make a pie tomorrow morning."

"Feller" is a word you don't hear too often outside of America's pieways.

"Your *feller*?" I asked, to see what the word felt like.

Juanita said she'd been married once but now she preferred her independence. "I only date on the weekends. During the week I'm too busy, washing my car, working in my garden, puttering about."

I liked this woman enough already that I hoped she would offer to let us watch her make pie. And, I hoped, she'd do it fast, because mosquitoes were eating us alive. She must have read my mind, because she said, "Where are you ladies going to be in the morning?"

And so a plan was hatched that we would return first thing Sunday to bake pie with Juanita.

Juanita, the walk, the fact that my gut was back—all had conspired to put us in a great mood. The drive toward quaint Chelsea, where Juanita told us we could find a room for the night, could not have been prettier. The fireflies were out in full force and, again, the great DJ in the sky seemed to be keeping an eye out for us, because Gershwin's "Summertime" came on the radio.

Juanita was in her garden cutting giant stalks of rhubarb when we arrived. She seemed genuinely excited to see us. She'd carefully picked out her baking outfit and I particularly liked her fetching leopard-print apartment slippers. Such a coquette.

She had probably been up since dawn because, to my dismay, she'd already made her dough, rolled it out, and lined two pie pans. Most of the ingredients for two distinct pies, one rhubarb custard, one raspberry, were all laid out on her kitchen counter in perfect *mise en place*. Maybe the thought of making dough in front of two strangers made her nervous.

Juanita and her rhubarb

I realized that her kitchen window looked right out on Waterloo Road where Kris and I had enjoyed our walk the night before, and I envied her that serene view to wash dishes by.

"I love that window," she said, catching my gaze. "I've only used my dishwasher twice in eight years."

Her feller, Mike, stayed in the living room to watch sports on television and we sat at the kitchen table and watched Juanita work.

"Pie and coffee, it's a friendship thing, don't you think? If I go to somebody's house for dinner, I bring a pie. I often make a lemon pie for a lonely gentleman I know who lives in a nursing home. Last week, I made a pie for my neighbor who broke her arm in two places in a car accident. And the week before that, I made a coconut cream pie for my chiropractor's wife. Oh, and I paid the gentleman who cleaned my eaves in pie—and cookies—that I left on his porch. I just made a berry pie for the neighbor who helped me out when my well went dry."

She poured us more coffee.

"My late mother-in-law taught me to make pie," she said, chopping the fresh red rhubarb into inch-long segments.

"Not your mother?" I asked.

"My own mother gave me away when I was five," she said, not wasting any time to get personal. "My parents had divorced and my mother didn't want me, so I was sent to live with my aunt."

Juanita stopped chopping and smiled at us. "That's OK. I was strong, so I could take it.

"My aunt was strict and not very nice to me, but I never went wanting for clothes or material goods. I tell you though, I would have done anything to be the girl next door I used to give my clothes to. She didn't have much but she had *love*."

Juanita left her aunt's house at 17 to look for her mother in West Virginia, with the help of an uncle who thought they should finally meet again. "When we found her, I asked my mother if she wanted me, if I could stay awhile to finish high school.

"And she said, 'I want you, and I'll keep you forever.' "

I asked Juanita if she'd ever asked her mother why she'd sent her away in the first place and she shook her head no. "We never quite could talk about it." She dabbed her eyes with a kitchen towel. "I'm sorry," she said.

Don't be, we said. Pie, we'd found, often acted as a wooden spoon, stirring up the soul. Maybe it was the rhubarb, I said.

In ancient China, rhubarb was once cultivated and revered for its cathartic, purgative qualities.

"Every now and then all the sadness in my life just wells up on me," she said, "but I move on. I've learned to put my sadness on a shelf. It doesn't help to dwell on it or blame others for how you live your life."

She talked of how she met her husband, a dairy farmer, at a

Masonic Temple dance when she was barely 20. What she loved most about him, she said, was his extended family who treated her as though she were born into theirs.

"My mother-in-law, Opal, had hard, farmwife hands and she taught me how to do everything on the farm," she said. Every summer, Juanita followed her husband to the state fair in Detroit where his Black Angus cattle always snagged the blue ribbons. Eventually, she got to be such a good baker she worked up the courage to enter her pies and cookies at the fair competitions. She's garnered an impressive collection of blue ribbons herself.

"Baking was like an escape valve for me," said Juanita. Her husband was a drinker, it turned out. "He carried that burden to his grave and I stood by him," she said.

"You have to give more than you take in this life," she went on. "You'll be rewarded in ways that you don't always realize."

After her husband's death, she took care of her mother-in-law and when she died, Opal left Juanita almost everything.

Now, Juanita said, she's always looking for "any old excuse" to bake.

I asked her about the no-nonsense mixing bowl she held in the nook of her hip. "I've grown quite attached to it," she said. "I can't make pie without it.

"All bakers have their favorite little something they like in their kitchens. Opal had a favorite bowl she used to make her fudge in. She sold it at an auction. If I'd even looked at it cross-eyed she would have given it to me, but she didn't know how much I wanted it."

"I sure wish now I'd said something. It would mean a lot to me to have Opal's bowl," she said.

Ordinarily, Juanita would layer a meringue onto her rhubarb pie when it was almost baked, but she decided she'd leave this pie uncovered to save time.

While we waited for the pie to bake, she got to work on the second, raspberry pie made with berries picked by her friends near Chelsea.

Talk went from hair color to men. Juanita had just dyed her hair a shade or two too dark and, although she'd washed it three times since, could not lighten it up. Mike didn't seem to mind, she said. Juanita and Mike met nine years earlier and, she said, she was finally truly happy.

"He's a quiet sort and he lets me rattle on and on. When I was little, my aunt wouldn't let me talk much, so I guess I'm making up for lost time," she said. She was glad that they lived apart, because it's romantic to miss someone. "We send each other cards and letters when we get in a mood."

She called Mike in to join us when it was time to lay the lattice top crust on the raspberry pie. Mike had seen it done on television and picked it up "just like that," Juanita said.

One by one, he layered the thick bands of dough across the top, delicately lifting one to slide another beneath it. Juanita stood right by his elbow, watching and praising his every move.

The oven buzzer went off, indicating that the first pie was ready, and Juanita started looking for her glasses, which were pushed back in her curls.

She was nervous. She wanted this pie to be perfect. Technically, we should have waited for the quivering rhubarb custard pie to cool, but we needed to get back on the road so we could catch the cherry-pie eating contest in Traverse City, so she sliced it anyway.

The crust made with lard, just as Opal said, was among the flakiest I've ever had. I can still taste and feel the hot, sweet custard burning the roof of my mouth. Like Juanita's story, the filling was bittersweet.

She gave us the recipe and then made us peek at the raspberry pie in the oven before walking us to the car. This "feller" was a keeper: the lattice work was stunning.

Juanita took a minute to figure out my license plate and when she did, she clasped her hands together. "Thank you for coming," she said. "Let me know if you find another rhubarb custard pie on the road, all right? Safe trip."

And as we drove off, past the yucca plants and four-o'clocks lining her drive, Juanita waved slowly. Her cat was rubbing up against her leg and I realized we'd forgotten to ask its name.

What was it that made strangers want to open their hearts to us, Kris asked as we headed north to Traverse City.

"Maybe it's just like Juanita said," I replied. "Everyone needs to be listened to once in a while."

JUANITA'S RHUBARB CUSTARD PIE

CRUST

1 unbaked pie shell

FILLING

3 cups fresh rhubarb stalks, cut in cubes the size of your thumb
(preferably from a part of the garden where the toms don't go)

1½ cups sugar

2 tablespoons cornstarch

3 eggs (use 2 yolks and 1 whole egg and save 2 egg whites for meringue
topping—optional)

1 cup milk

½ teaspoon nutmeg

Line pie plate with pastry. Fill with rhubarb. In a favorite bowl, mix together sugar, cornstarch, eggs, and milk. Pour mixture over the rhubarb and sprinkle the whole with nutmeg. Bake at 375 degrees for

1 hour or until set. If you plan to add a meringue topping, remove the pie after 45 minutes, layer the meringue on top, and slide the pie in the broiler for another 15 minutes or until the meringue is golden brown.

the cherry states

"Years ago, manhood was an opportunity for achievement and now it's just a problem to be overcome. Guys who once might have painted the Sistine Chapel ceiling are now just trying to be Mr. O.K. All-Rite, the man who can bake a cherry pie, cry, be passionate in a skillful way, and yet also lift them bales and tote that barge."

—GARRISON KEILLOR,

THE BOOK OF GUYS

Turning 8 is a rite of passage for children growing up in and around Traverse City, Michigan. That's the pivotal age after which kids entering the pie-eating contest at the National Cherry Festival are no longer allowed to use their hands.

From ages 5 to 8, children keep their balled-up fists behind their backs until moderator Nancy Grin, known throughout Michigan as "The Pie Lady," tells them it's all right to use their hands—about a minute after the starting bell, or midway through the event.

That's when tiny arms, thin and malleable as a cherry stem, fly to the forefront and the shoving begins.

"Please remember to chew and swallow. CHEW AND SWALLOW!" shouted Grin through a bullhorn. "It's more important to chew than it is to win *any* contest."

Clearly, she was also addressing the frenzied parents who were crouched directly across from their children, screaming "Faster, *faster.*"

Grin, who has been moderating the pie-eating contest for 11 years, said critics of the event—which used to involve a whole pie rather than just one slice—claimed it encouraged gluttony. (And what exactly about American culture, from corporate raiding to jumbo-sized soft drinks

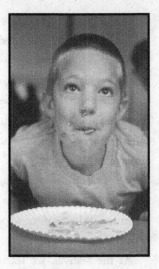

Pie-eating contest, Traverse, MI

and baseball players' pie-high salaries, doesn't?). So Grin kept reminding the audience that "seriously, folks, this is not something you want to practice at home."

"I've only had kids throw up on me three times," said Grin, who was decked out in festival-mandated maraschino red. As an extra precaution against gagging, young assistants stand behind the contestants, pulling back wayward pig- and ponytails.

That wasn't good enough for Kristy, a mom who snuck into the festival tent to hold her daughter Nicki's thick braids herself. Nicki captured first place in the 6-year-olds division. The tomboy blonde shot her arms straight up in the air when she was announced the clear winner after only one minute and forty-five seconds of scarfing that would put any truffling pig to shame.

Towheaded Cody, who later that morning took first place in the 9-year-olds division, told me he'd figured out the winning strategy:

"The more you wear, the less you have to eat," he said, before plunging his head in the designated water trough.

The pie-eating contest was a highlight of the weeklong Cherry Festival, which was celebrating its seventy-fourth anniversary when we breezed into town. The festival drew five hundred thousand visitors annually and started out as a simple ritual for cherry farmers calling on the agriculture and weather gods to protect their delicate crops each May.

The first "Blessing of the Blossoms" was held in 1925—about the time when local cherries started being produced in commercial quantities. Michigan now produces three quarters of the nation's annual sour-cherry crop.

At the festival, we learned that cherry juice can help relieve arthritis pain and that grinding the hulls of the seeds of cherry pits can help strip paint from heavy metals (but could it strip Cody's earlobes clean?).

With that in mind, I sure hoped someone came around to collect the hundreds of stray pits that were strewn about the long plastic tarp used for the cherry-pit spitting contest. The winner, a local guy with a pickle-barrel chest, had remarkable form. He would thrust his hips forward and his chest back, like a mating peacock, then pucker up and fire his pit. With a spitting distance of 48 feet, he left his competition in the dust and sideline observers freshly showered.

Each year during the festival, the elected Cherry Queen goes to the White House to offer an extra-large cherry pie to the president. I'm not sure if he was pulling my leg, but a spokesman for the event told me that after the Monica Lewinsky debacle, festival organizers decided they'd abstain from delivering a cherry pie to the White House that year.

At a brew pub in town, we met some locals who volunteered as festival "ambassadors" each year. When they heard about our trip, they graciously invited us to their home for barbecued pork chops the next day. We had plans to go to Charlevoix, farther north, for more pie research, but we'd be back in plenty of time for dinner and sure could use a home-cooked meal. Naturally, we offered to pick up a pie for dessert.

"Please," they said . . . "Anything but cherry."

I was having dinner with my friends Larry and Dorothea Smith one night before my departure, when Larry announced that his grand-mother, Mary Baumbach, was known in her day as "the best cherry-pie baker in the Wolverine State, hands down."

Now, I had been on this pie kick long enough to know that con-versations about pie invite hyperbole. But Larry, a former *New York Times* editor and the editor of *Parade* magazine, *had* to be objec-tive . . . didn't he?

"There's only two kinds of pie, my grandpa Rollie used to say: warm or cold," Larry said.

His grandparents were long deceased, but the two aunts who raised him as their son, Grace and Bessie, were still living in the Charlevoix area. They were both feisty, in their 80s, and *loved* to have visitors, he said. In fact, he'd just talked to Bessie that morning. She and Grace had gone to the Charlevoix cemetery. Bessie described the outing as "the half-dead visiting the short-dead and the long-dead."

I liked her turn of phrase, so I put a star next to Charlevoix on the map.

The widowed Bessie, the elder of the two, lived alone in an apart-ment in Elk Rapids. Her sister Grace, also widowed, lived on a dairy farm she still ran with her son, in Charlevoix proper. We'd arranged to pick Bessie up on our way to Grace's farmhouse where it might be more pleasant to chat.

About five miles before arriving at Bessie's, we pulled over near a cherry orchard to tidy up the car. After only four days out, she was crawling with cookie crumbs and sunflower seeds, and already smelled like a boys' gym locker.

Bessie was waiting patiently for us in her living room, her handbag at her feet. And two cherry pies made with local Montmorency cherries on the counter. I was delighted and surprised she'd bothered to bake at all. While I would have never admitted this to Larry, I had never had a slice of cherry pie. Not once, not ever. And I couldn't be happier that my first would be baked by the hands of a woman named Bessie in the heart of cherry country.

On the twenty-minute drive to Charlevoix, Kris sat in the back with one of the pies next to her on the seat, and Bessie sat up front, holding a cherry pie on her lap. I thought of my mother and her traveling floating-islands, and prayed that the glove-compartment door would behave just this once.

As we drove, Bessie explained how the old art of cherry picking had evolved over the years from simple, honest hand-picking to high-tech gadgetry.

Charlevoix sits on a scenic stretch of US 31 that hugs the shore between Traverse City and Petoskey. Once a lumbering community, it's now known mostly for its beaches and lakes.

"Tourism, T-shirts, and fudge, that's what Charlevoix is all about these days," harrumphed Bessie as we pulled into the dirt drive of her sister's farmhouse, a sturdy white house wrapped by a tidy, tended garden with a red milking barn out back. Grace, who has lived in that house since 1929, came out on the porch to greet us, and I noticed they were wearing the same exact blouse. We all sat around the table in the kitchen window, facing the barn. The kitchen was almost surgical it was so clean, spare, and white. The two warm cherry pies on the counter was as brightening as red lipstick on a geisha.

Unlike Juanita, Grace and Bessie were reserved and shy, at first. We spent a few minutes just staring at each other around the table, commenting on the glorious weather. Kris cleared her throat.

"So do you sisters always dress alike?" she asked to break the ice. As it turned out, they often went shopping for clothes together in Midland, about 200 miles away, and they had picked these blouses up on their last shopping expedition.

"So you are road trippers, too," I said.

We learned that both had taught in one-room schoolhouses. Both had been married and left widowed with one son. Kris and I had noticed that many of the women in Michigan had a certain masculine quality about them—broad shoulders, deep voices, and an undeniable strength. Grace and Bessie were no exception.

"There's a saying around here that goes 'all my sons are daughters,' " said Grace, who, at 82, still helped out with the milking and calving.

I asked them about Larry's claims regarding their mother's pie, and they shook their heads and smiled.

There had never been any official proclamation from the governor or anything like that, they said. But it was common knowledge among local folk how good Mary Baumbach's pies were. Everyone wanted to come help out during threshing season because a hard day's labor was always rewarded with a slice of Mary's cherry pie.

Their mother knew a thing or two about hard labor. She made her pies in a cast-iron skillet. She churned her own butter, did laundry by knuckle and washboard, and quilted, too. She still found time to cook three square meals a day for her husband and nine children, and on this Bessie and Grace agreed: those hearty meals in childhood were the reason for their longevity.

Was it intimidating to tackle pie when their mother's was so good, I asked. The sisters guffawed. As much as they admired their mother's baking skills, baking was not what either one of them wanted to be remembered for. These were educated women slightly ahead of our time, let alone theirs.

"I think it's puttery," Grace said about cooking in general. "Fools work, wise men eat."

Bessie glanced over at her sister quizzically. "I must be a fool then," she said, pointing to her two pies.

Sisters always seem to look at each other with a distinct set of eyes that alternate between judgment and admiration. Kris and I were witnessing "marvel," as though the two had never talked among themselves about the topics we broached that afternoon, or at least not in a long while.

No surprise, Kris and I had spent the first three days of this leg of our trip talking about relationships and why so many of our women friends were still single in their late 30s. In their day, an unmarried woman in her mid-30s was cause for alarm and pity, they said. But, as Bessie pointed out, women today really don't *need* to get married, or at least not for the same reasons women used to seek out a husband. The trouble with being so financially independent, we told them, is that it makes women too demanding.

"It's easier to find a man that can provide than it is to find one that can communicate," Kris said.

"You can never be too picky when it comes to that," Bessie said. "Isn't that right, Grace?"

"That's right, Bessie. You two girls just keep on doing what you're doing."

We hardly knew these women, yet at this very moment, their blessing meant the world to us.

We asked them how their parents, who married in 1900, had met, and neither one knew the answer.

"There are so many questions I wish I'd asked them when they were still alive," said Bessie. "I wish I'd asked my grandmother what toys she played with, who her friends were, what her house was like growing up. It just never occurred to me to ask."

One thing they did know for sure was that their mother made her pie crust with suet, the hard fat deposited around the kidneys and loins of cattle and sheep. Grace and Bessie used regular shortening to bake their own occasional pies. Like most Michigan homemakers, they used tapioca as a thickener for the cherry filling.

Before tasting the pie, Grace wanted to take us on a tour of the barn. We asked her to show us how to milk a cow, just so we could say we've done it. We snapped pictures of one another, each with a teat in hand, and among the stack of Polaroids from the trip I keep on my desk, my favorite is the one of Kris tugging on a teat, with an ear-to-ear grin, and Grace standing right next to her, her mouth open wide.

Bessie, who had a little trouble walking these days, had stayed back in the house and she was cutting into and serving the pie when we returned to the kitchen, still laughing.

Hers was a no-nonsense crust, as sensible as her Rockport shoes. Along the edges, rather than crimping, Bessie had drawn distinct slits, thin as the stripes in her seersucker shorts. She'd also cut in the middle of the top crust random steam valve slits that looked like a sandpiper's footprints on wet sand.

In her book *The Pie and Pastry Bible* Rose Levy Beranbaum says cherry filling (her favorite) should taste "like a cardinal singing." It's a sound I've gotten to know well since moving to my cottage in the Hudson Valley, where a pair of brazen orange-plumed cardinals serenades me most mornings.

Bessie's pie sounded more like a church bell. The taste was clear, but it had serious cherry depth. No glaze, no goo. Just cherry. Ruby-slipper red. Bessie had scooped vanilla ice cream on top and it was melting fast, slithering into a puddle of scarlet juice.

Grace was impressed, and so were we.

I confessed that this was my first cherry pie.

"Oh my," they both said simultaneously. I think Bessie was relieved I had nothing to compare it to.

We left feeling sated on so many levels. Bessie gave us a tour of Charlevoix—the old schoolhouse, the cemetery where "the half-dead go and visit the short-dead and the long-dead." When she slipped inside her apartment, we gave her a warm hug and thanked her again for her pies. Silently, we thanked both her and her sister for paving the way for independent women.

Then we thanked Betty Blue for keeping her glove compartment shut.

BESSIE'S ADAPTATION OF
HER MOTHER MARY'S
"BEST CHERRY PIE IN MICHIGAN"

CRUST

1 full cup (heaping) shortening
¾ cup of cold water
2 cups of flour
pinch of salt

FILLING

1 quart pitted sour cherries (Montmorency)
3 tablespoons tapioca (or flour or cornstarch)
1⅓ cups of sugar

Take the juice from the pitted cherries and mix it with the tapioca and sugar, then mix together with cherries in a bowl. Place the cherry mixture in an unbaked pie shell and bake for 30 minutes at 400 degrees and another 30 minutes at 350 degrees.

Serve with vanilla ice cream and eat in good company by a window that looks out on a bright red barn . . .

P.S. Cooking the cherries before baking the pie makes them lose their redness.

We stopped at one of the roadside fruit stands to buy fresh cherries to snack on and an apple pie for the barbecue. Our hosts turned out to be true ambassadors indeed, treating us to a fancy meal and late-night conversation under the stars on a private dock in the bay.

"I don't know too many people who would have taken in strangers for dinner," I said. "Certainly New Yorkers are far too jaded for that."

"I'm not familiar with that expression," said one of the gentlemen. "What does 'being jaded' mean exactly?"

"Being jaded means having seen so many cherries you can't see the beauty of just one," I said.

cherries redux

"Kindred Spirits aren't so scarce as I used to think."
—LUCY MAUD MONTGOMERY, *ANNE OF GREEN GABLES*

We left Traverse City the following morning, on the Fourth of July—a big day for pie-eating in America. Our plan was to take a car ferry to Wisconsin and then drive north to Door County, the windswept finger of land wedged between Green Bay and Lake Michigan's western shore, also famous for its sour cherries. Our dinner hosts had suggested we follow the Lake Michigan shoreline to get to the Ludington ferry dock and stop for a catnap near the Sleeping Bear Dunes. An isolated beach at the foot of Esch Road would impress even two jaded women like us. They were right.

A delicious swim put us behind schedule and we really had to rush to make the ferry. It would surprise none of my friends to know that we were the last car to board.

The ferry ride was four hours long, which meant we'd arrive in Wisconsin around 10 P.M.—too late to catch a fireworks display. We were disappointed, but no feat of pyrotechnics could rival the sunset that night. Even the bingo players came out on the deck to take it in. A tall man with a gaunt face took pictures of the sky. I offered to take one of him. He did the same for me and then small talk led to pie talk.

R., in his early 40s, had made his first pie in home-economics class in the seventh grade and hadn't stopped since. In fact, he had recently thrown a party for which he'd baked a panoply of pies, with lattice crusts and fancy crimps. He told me about a place in Randolph, Wisconsin, near his brother's house, where he was living temporarily that sold pie for $1.25 a slice on Thursdays! He handed me his card and asked us to give him a call if we were anywhere near that area.

It was starting to get cold out on the deck, so Kris and I retreated inside the cabin to write in our respective journals and study our maps. A professorial-looking gentleman leaned over and asked:

"Are you really looking for *pi*?"

We were not on the same oven rack.

Although many have described my quest as *irrational*, I told him, we were *not* looking for the irrational number by which the diameter of a circle must be multiplied to obtain the circumference.

A social worker, he was more interested, it seemed, in the spiritual virtue of pi than its mathematical significance.

"Many people believe that the answers to life's bigger questions lie in the numerical pi," he said. "Perhaps it's also true for the kind you bake."

I smiled. He didn't know how right he was.

In Two Rivers, not far from the landing, we found the quintessential shoreline motel complete with a view of the bay and a large freezer near the ice machine for traveling fishermen to drop off their catch. The owner of the motel lived right next door, and we paid for the room in his kitchen, which smelled of buttered popcorn. His undershirt was stretched so taut across his belly, it looked like an apple pie or a short-sheeted bed.

"Pie?" he said, when he saw me write my license-plate number on the motel registration card.

"Do you like rhubarb? That's my favorite." He leaned back in his chair, put his hands behind his head, revealing heavily forested armpits. I'm not sure, but I think he gave me some sort of "pie" discount, he said. When I pushed open the door to our room with my yoga mat, we gasped at how positively kitsch it was: vinyl wall paneling, a faux anchor above each bed, and an orange rug as shaggy as the owner.

Among the people we met on this trip, some stand out more than others, like characters in a pop-up storybook. In Mishicot, Wisconsin, our first stop the next morning, a thirtysomething woman named Lisa was a merry marker on the road to pie.

It was the "math guy" on the ferry, as Kris called him, who suggested we stop in charming Mishicot for lunch on our way to Door

County. The drive there was stunning. Barns in this part of the country are a soft, soldier blue, with minarets that pierce the sky.

On Main Street, we ducked into a store with vintage kitchenware in the shop window. It was a gallery and an antiques store, and Lisa was one of the artists who displayed her work there and occasionally worked the register.

Lisa was pleasingly plump, and I mention it only because her plumpness seemed inextricably tied to her personality, just as fuzz is to a peach. She had a distinct 1940s air about her, right down to the way she painted her lips.

A powder-blue bowl with an art-deco pattern in the back of the store caught my eye almost immediately. At $45, it was beyond the $35 cap I'd set for myself on bowl purchases. But I couldn't stop looking at it. Finally, I set it on the counter but told Lisa I hadn't made up my mind. If I was going to bend my rules, I had to at least put up a bit of a fight.

"It's so pretty," Lisa cooed. "But I understand having to limit yourself. I have a collection myself. I collect rolling pins."

Why, I asked, not wanting to let on quite yet that we were kindred collectors.

"I just love pie," she said, putting a hand on her heart.

Go on, I said.

"Pie is the last holdout of the Great American comfort foods," she said. "It's America's dessert darling.

"You eat pie when you're happy, don't you? That's because pie means somebody loves you," she said. "And all pie bakers are angels."

Maybe we should make room for Lisa in the car, I thought.

"Crust has a huge emotional content in my family," she said. For years, she and her mother were in a tiff over a difference of opinion on how to prevent a soggy bottom crust. I wanted to know more, but Lisa didn't want to go there. She was more interested in our trip. Where were we headed?

"Oh no! You're headed straight for 'Magazine Food' country," she said. "You know . . . *Ladies' Home Journal*, circa 1952. Everything is that same awful bland color and every recipe begins with cream-of-chicken soup."

Lisa's husband was a minister, and they'd just spent a few years living on the Plains, on the border between South Dakota and Minnesota. She was glad to be back in Wisconsin. Since she seemed to have a good grasp on the Midwest, we asked her to explain all the lawn gnomes and trolls we started seeing the moment we got off the ferry.

She rolled her eyes. We'd hit a nerve.

Turned out, she'd served on a regional arts board in Minnesota whose role it was to decide how to allocate public-art funds. A proposal came in to plant a 30-foot-tall troll in the middle of a small rural town. The entire committee thought it was grand, she said, "but I told them I'd rather burn at the stake than use public money to erect a 30-foot troll."

She put her hand on her hip so that she looked like a teapot: "I always was the turd in the punchbowl," she said.

I bought the bowl, of course.

We continued straight north on US 42 until we crossed into Door County. With its New England–style architecture and harbor towns, it felt quite different from the Wisconsin we'd left behind, as though we really had pushed through a door to get there.

People on the ferry had recommended Berry Best, an orchard and specialty-food market in Gill's Rock. The place was owned by the Teskies, an extended Door County fishing family with deep roots in Door. The Teskies' shop was known for its smoked chubs and its two-pound cherry pie.

At the Fourth of July parade, the Teskies and their seven children made pies on their float, tossing flour into the crowd.

The shop was already closed for the day when we pulled into the drive. Neil Teskie walked out to the car to tell us we were out of luck. Could we come back tomorrow? We explained that we weren't your typical tourists and that all we really wanted was to talk to the baker of the famous cherry pies.

"That's my wife, Fran, but she's had a long day and I doubt she'll want to talk to you," he said bluntly. "Fran usually goes for a run on the shore and then dives into Lake Michigan after a day of baking. I'm not sure if she's back yet."

Fran stepped out on the porch with a towel around her head, looking way too young and fit for a mother of seven kids, many of them full grown.

Fran warmed up pretty quick. She said she learned baking from her Belgian grandmother, an immigrant from Antwerp, who used to get up at 5 A.M. on Saturdays and bake until noon. Her grandparents were part of the flock of Belgians who moved to the Chicago area during World War I and joined the janitors' unions. For years, it was the same group of Belgians who banked the fires through the bone-chilling Chicago winter nights. "My grandmother would let me roll out the dough with her. It was fun, sort of like playing with Play-Doh."

When Fran and her husband became farmers, it made sense to the young newlyweds to turn the childhood memory into a bank-able hobby. With the variety of fruit from their own orchards, she experimented a lot. Now she taught a pie class in the summers, to young couples hoping to recoup what they missed out on as children, she said.

Making pie was like learning a language or learning to ski, she said. "It's best to learn young before the fear settles in." I thought of young Darrell back in New York.

Talk turned to fishing—Neil's area of expertise. We found out his tug was called *Betty,* just like the piemobile.

He had spent the day trimming down his fishing nets, a laborious task he used to dread. But only a few days earlier, something had happened to Neil. He'd had an epiphany.

"After 30 years of wondering if there was a right way to do it, I figured it out and it was like the sky just opened up before me," he said.

"Must be what it's like to finally figure out what pie dough is supposed to feel like in your hands," I said, looking at Fran. She nodded. And she wrapped her arm around her husband because she knew what a good feeling that could be.

They opened up the shop to give us for the road a cherry pie, which, we told her, we'd eagerly try once we'd had dinner.

"You *are* going to a fish boil tonight, aren't you?" Neil asked as we climbed back in the car.

Sure, if you tell us what it is, we said, slightly embarrassed by our Wisconsin ignorance. We'd seen the signs for "Fish Boils" all over the county but they'd left us clueless.

"It's a pretty dramatic fish-eating ritual unique to Door County," Neil said. He glanced at his watch. "If you hurry, you can still catch the boil at the Square Rigger, in Jacksonport. If you're not there by 8 P.M., you'll miss it."

What kind of restaurant—other than Alain Ducasse in New York—has only one seating per night?

"This isn't just for tourists, is it?" we asked.

"Nope. This is where Fran and I go whenever we are craving a good piece of boiled fish. And I *know* their fish is fresh, because I'm their main supplier."

It was already 7:30 P.M. and we had a good 30 miles or so to go, so I let Kris, aka leadfoot, take the wheel and I secured the pie on my lap. When we arrived at ten minutes past eight, the waitress ushered us straight to the outdoor deck where the other guests were already gathered, all eyes directed toward a huge kettle suspended over an oak-wood fire about 50 feet away, near the edge of Lake Michigan.

The restaurant's "master boilers" had lit the fire beneath the 22-gallon kettle about ninety minutes earlier. Once the water started to bubble, the two boilers tossed the baby red potatoes. Thirty minutes later, they added the peeled, sweet boiler onions. About twenty minutes after that, right when we got there, they'd dropped in the thick whitefish steaks, which must stay in the water exactly thirteen minutes to be cooked just right. All of the ingredients were dropped into the kettle in stainless steel baskets, easily removed once the kettle has boiled over.

The "boil over," we learned, was what made the event so dramatic. Right before the fish was done to a turn, the boilers doused kerosene onto the flames to make the preparation boil over—intentionally. This helped remove the scum and oil that came to the water's surface, and put out the fire in the process. But not before sending giant, roaring flames into the sky.

Despite the furious boiling method of cooking and the absence of any herbs or seasonings other than salt (15 pounds!), the fish was remarkably firm, flaky, and flavorful—(hmmm, all the traits of a perfect pie crust).

And, like pie, our waitress said, "there isn't a holiday or special event or church social that doesn't include a fish boil."

The table next to ours was celebrating a family reunion. Since we had Fran's pie in the car, I asked them to help us eat it, not knowing that cherry pie also came with dinner at the restaurant. Everyone ate two slices that night. Fran's pie tasted more dense, more deep than the restaurant pie.

It was good, but I still liked Bessie's best. I'd gone 36 years without tasting cherry pie and now I'd had three slices in 48 hours.

· · ·

We found a roadside motel in Algoma. The innkeeper had a funny accent I could not place. When she heard about our quest, she said "hmmmm" and then signed us in. The next morning, she came to find us as we loaded up the car. "You are going to try some Belgian pie, aren't you?" she asked.

The pies are a regional specialty in the heavily Belgian communities of Kewaunee and Brown counties just south of Door, she said. I had no idea so many Belgians were clustered in Wisconsin, so many, they even had their own pie.

I do love that about America: the fact that it's so vast, you could actually stumble on an entire subculture you didn't know existed, like finding a pair of never-worn shoes in the back of your closet. The woman wrote down the name of a polka musician who lived in Rosiere who could help us find good Belgian pie.

Since it looked like we might be having pie for breakfast, Kris suggested we go for a quick roller-blade. We found a fairly smooth stretch of paved road bordered by fields of tall grass and barns with gleaming silver silos. Kris took off ahead of me like a fish-boil fire. I sputtered behind, trying to remember if there was ever any mention of pie in the *Adventures of Tintin*.

Most of the older houses in Belgian Wisconsin were fashioned from "three little pigs" brick and had outdoor kitchens with large bake-off ovens.

We drove through a one–stop sign town called Duvall, closely named after a specialty Belgian beer I happened to be extremely fond of. A Duvel, or Belgian Chimay, sounded divine after roller-blading but it was early yet, and we were still on pie duty. So, when we stopped at a bar and grill, it really was in the hope of tracking down that polka musician.

Nancy the bartender was playing *cuyoo,* a Belgian card game, with two of her customers right on the bar top. "We've been playing *cuyoo* every Thursday for more than twenty years," said Joe, the eldest in the troika wearing a bolo tie and a bad toupee. Seeing Budweisers on the bar, I asked why no one was drinking Belgian beer. They look puzzled.

"Budweiser's our local beer. It's our biggest seller," said Nancy.

I didn't feel so bad for not knowing what a Belgian pie was.

Did *they* know what Belgian pie was?

"Oh sure," said Nancy, her eyes never leaving the cards. "Prune pie is as traditional Belgian as chicken *booyah*." Then, never tearing themselves away from the cards, the three argued over whether rice, raisin, or prune is the most traditional filling for Belgian pie.

Clearly, I needed an expert. The polka man could be that, they said, only he was away. Nancy scratched her head with the corner of a playing card. A woman at the bar said she'd just come from a funeral at the church across the street. "A lot of the locals and long-timers are there," she said. "You should be able to find someone in the bunch who can help you."

I had never been to a funeral, let alone crashed one, I told her.

"Don't worry," she said. "We're not so uppity here in Wisconsin."

Kris was happy to play reporter on this trip, but she drew the line at funerals. So, while she tried to learn the rules for *cuyoo*, I slinked over to the church parking lot and stood there among whispering mourners until somebody noticed me.

"Can we help you with something?" a woman with a kind face asked.

"Uh. Uh. I'm really sorry to barge in like this, and I'm truly sorry about your loss, but I'm trying to find someone local who knows a thing or two about Belgian pie," I said sheepishly.

"Oh. Too bad, you just missed some good Belgian pie in there," said a cousin of the deceased. "Is there any left?" asked another. "What about Emily Guilette? Has she gone home?"

There were echoes of agreement that Emily Guilette was defi-nitely the person I needed to see. "My cousin and I can take you to her house," said the woman with the kind face, Roxanne. "It's in Brussels. You can follow us there."

"I can't believe you got a pie tip at a funeral," said Kris as she settled up at the bar. I wasn't proud of it, I told her. But I got the distinct feeling that the distraction was welcome. Roxanne, our age, was clearly fond of Emily and welcomed any opportunity to visit with the old woman.

Emily, 91, was milling about in her kitchen when we knocked on the back door of her red brick house. She did not seem sad, and my guess was that, at her age, the best strategy was not to dwell on the losses. Her physique and nervous energy reminded me a lot of Granny Clampett—without the shotgun.

"So you're interested in Belgian pie," she said as she cleared some room on her kitchen table. "Too bad you came today instead of next week. I'm getting ready to make sixty of those pies for the Belgian Days Festival."

Belgian pies are small and so difficult to make, bakers rarely make fewer than three or four dozen at a time, she said.

The pie consists of a flat circle of raised sweet dough that is layered with a filling of sweet cooked rice, pureed prunes, or raisins. The pie is always topped with a sweetened cottage-cheese mixture. What makes it truly unique is that the sweet fluffy dough is made with *mashed potatoes*.

"There's no cutting corners with Belgian pie," Emily said. Who sells frozen Belgian-pie crusts?

Pie recipes floating around this part of Wisconsin "have not changed since the first Belgian grandmothers landed here in the mid-1850s," Emily said.

In those days, Belgian women would gather to make Belgian pies for the Kermiss—the annual harvest celebration. "For Belgian women, making pie was always a good excuse to get together among friends," she said.

Some say Belgian pies help new brides break the ice with their mothers-in-law. Emily, for example, learned to make the pies from her husband's mother who worried that her son might not get his Belgian pies with the regularity to which he was accustomed.

Though only 17 at the time, "I learned fast," Emily says, "in part because I had 'the baking hand.'"

"I've made thousands of pies, thousands," she said. "People tell me mine's the best Belgian pie around. I've never heard anyone say different."

Then Emily practically jumped out of her chair. She remembered having stuck a raisin Belgian pie in her freezer the last time she made a batch, for a friend who had threatened to visit unannounced.

She was so tickled that we would get to taste some of her pie after all, she popped it in the toaster oven. Even without the cottage-cheese topping, the pie was delicious. But it tasted more like danish to me than pie. Not that there's anything wrong with that.

Emily told us we really couldn't find Belgian pie anywhere outside this tight-knit Belgian community, so I was glad our Algoma innkeeper had been such a busybody.

"So you drove here from New York," Emily said, when she grew bored of talking about pie. "I've been to New York once. I just had to go and touch the Statue of Liberty with my own hands."

She disappeared into her bedroom and returned with lips that had been touched up. "I do love my lipstick," she said. "I put some on every morning, first thing, to take on the day."

Her current favorite was a "mood" lipstick, which looked green in the tube but changed color on her lips depending on her disposition.

I know Kris well enough to know that this was right up her alley.

Emily must have read our minds, because she leaned over and whispered in Kris's ear:

"They sell it at Wal-Mart."

. . .

As we approached Ripon, I realized we weren't too far from the home of R., the tall, gaunt pie fanatic we'd met on the ferry. We called to say hello and that we probably wouldn't have time for the café in Randolph. His family was having a party in honor of his brother's fiftieth birthday. "Come on over," he said. "We don't have a pie though. My sister made a cake."

So we found our way in this very rural section of southern Wisconsin to the old farmhouse where R.'s brother lived. Off a dirt road, the house sat near a creek and a patch of sunflowers. R's nieces and nephews were playing with sparklers and let us join in and get our yayas out.

His father, Art, a dead ringer for Jason Robards, was kind of an old coot. He didn't say much until the very end of the evening, when we were all gathered in the kitchen saying our good-byes.

Art sat alone at the kitchen table, taking it all in: his three sons and his daughter and his grandchildren all together, in one room. And then, I heard him say to no one in particular:

"All this happened because of me."

We found a motel in Ripon, the town that birthed the Republican party, or as my niece Natalie, 8, calls it, the Pelican Party.

In the morning, we filled up on gas before leaving town. The attendant was talking to a man with a shotgun in his hand. "Hey," he said, pointing to Betty Blue's grille.

"Did you know you hit a rolling pin?"

Astute, those pelicans. Very astute.

EMILY'S BELGIAN PRUNE PIE

THE POTATO CRUST

2 eggs (1 whole plus 1 yolk)

⅓ cup melted butter

¼ cup of sugar

¼ teaspoon of salt

½ cup of mashed potatoes

¼ can of condensed milk

1½ cups of flour (varies)

FILLING

1½ pounds of prunes, pitted

1 pint of applesauce (takes the tartness out of the prunes)

1 cup sugar, more if you like sweeter taste

a pinch of salt

CHEESE TOPPING

1 24-ounce tub of small-curd cottage cheese

4 egg yolks

½ cup of sugar

¼ cup of butter (4 tablespoons)

Boil the prunes in water until they are done (about 1 hour). Puree them in a blender or food processor, add applesauce, sugar, and salt. Set aside.

Put cheese through a food mill. Add the yolks, sugar, and melted butter. "Beat the hell out of it," says Emily, and then spread it over the face of your pie.

Mix crust ingredients and then let the dough rise until it doubles in size.

Prick the bottom with a fork. Put your prune filling in. Then add the cheese topping in a circle of a smaller circumference, about ¼- to ½-inch thick. Bake at 350 degrees for about 20 minutes. Can be eaten warm or cold.

iowa

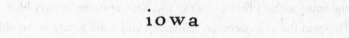

"SHOELESS" JOE JACKSON: "Is this heaven?"

RAY KINSELLA: "No, this is Iowa . . ."

—FIELD OF DREAMS, SCREENPLAY BY

W. P. KINSELLA AND PHIL ALDEN ROBINSON

Long after I'd moved to New York, I kept my expired California car-insurance card in my wallet. On the back of the card was scribbled a phone number, next to "Aunt Anne. Bernard, Iowa. Baked eight pies every Sunday for her eight children." Someone had drawn a big star next to her name.

I had no idea who this Aunt Anne was or who had given me her name, but even before I knew I'd go back out on the road to pie, something told me to keep it in my wallet.

I was glad I had, when we approached the Hawkeye State with no firm plans on where to find pie, other than a tentative lead on a natural hog farmer in Thornton.

As the crow flies, Bernard is only 20 miles southwest of

Dubuque, which we had to drive through anyway since we were coming from Wisconsin.

Driving across Dubuque, Kris and I shared a moment of silence in honor of her late grandpa Felix "Tubby" Leonard, a dapper clothier who for many years had managed the lingerie floor at the Zuckies department store. Tubby always sent Kris lingerie draped in tissue on her birthday. It was always elegant and aptly chosen. Still, I had a hard time imagining my French grandfather sending me teddies air-mail.

My Breton grandfather was an iodized fisherman who never left the house without his sailor's cap and *bleus de marin*, or navy blues. He spent the years between retirement and death sitting on an old stone wall in his village of Sainte Marine, watching the tides and the younger generation of fishermen slip out to sea.

On US 151, we passed the home of the New Melleray Abbey, a Trappist monastery founded in 1849, where thirty-five monks still live today supporting themselves by building wooden caskets entirely by hand from cutting down the trees to sewing the muslin lining.

Ironically, the monks shun caskets for personal use, preferring to be wrapped in robes in death.

With a population of 120, Bernard, only slightly bigger than a baseball field, was the smallest hamlet we'd visited so far. We stopped at Pearl's, the lone café in town, to ask a woman standing in the doorway if she knew who this "Aunt Anne" might be and where she lived. She stepped away from the shadows and pointed to the end of the road—and the end of Bernard, for that matter.

Anne's white clapboard house sat directly across a sprawling cornfield with stalks pushing six feet tall. All the window shades were drawn, which could have explained why there was no answer on the telephone when I'd tried to call from Ripon.

I knocked anyway, and was surprised to hear a "come on in."

Anne was sitting right in the middle of a very long white couch, almost in the dark. She apologized for the darkness.

"I can't let my African violets get too much sun," she said.

Anne seemed to be expecting us, or at least expecting something, the way she sat so tall and regal in the exact middle of her stretch couch, beneath framed photographs of her eight children when they were still toddlers.

Anne cleared up the mystery. I'd met her niece at a dinner party in San Francisco more than a year ago, when the subject of pies had come up. I immediately asked about the eight pies she used to bake on Sundays. She laughed.

"I only baked three at a time," she said, "*never eight.*"

Anne said she used to wake very early on Sundays to get to first mass and then come home and make her pies while the children went to a later mass.

"Kids are so fidgety in church," she said. "I liked to be there alone."

Anne, who had lived in this very house for forty-five years and in Bernard all of her life, still bakes a pie now and again for a special occasion, but since all the kids moved out, there hasn't been much incentive, she said. She learned to make pies from her mother, who baked up a storm, especially during threshing season. Anne remembered gathering berries with her siblings for her mother's pies.

"I was always so busy looking out for snakes, my bucket was rarely very full," she said. Anne still uses lard for her crust, mainly because "I never got good with that Crisco."

It was abundantly clear by the look on her face that Anne didn't want to dwell on the subject of pies.

India. Now there was something she wanted to talk about.

"My children bought me a trip to India as a present after my husband died," she said. "I was 70 years old, but I'd always wanted to go there."

Kris and I had a hard time imagining this flower petal of a woman maneuvering through India's crowded, dusty streets. I had spent a few months in India myself and knew firsthand how the sights, smells, and sounds of India assault the visitor at every turn. I also knew how India can change you. We talked about the saris, the color of saffron and mint, and the cows that amble through towns smugly asserting their sacredness. She remembered the women who wandered the streets carrying carved birdcages. Each cage carried a live sparrow, and locals paid hard-earned rupees for the privilege of setting a caged bird free.

"India was the highlight of my life," said Anne. "I have a little bit of an adventurous streak, you see. I still put my hair in pin curls."

Kris asked Anne if she ever went to Dubuque to shop and if, perhaps, she had known her grandpa Tubby, and Anne's face brightened. "I used to shop at Zuckies all the time. Your grandfather had a way with the ladies, didn't he?"

Kris blushed.

We asked Anne for a favorite pie recipe and she offered up her friend Pat Larkin's lemon meringue recipe from the St. Patrick's parish cookbook.

The introduction read as follows:

You are right in suspecting that the parish had a very Irish origin, however, the pastor for the first 15 years was French. Many of the pioneer names remain in the parish, and the grandsons and daughters of the pioneers enrich the bloodstream of the parish mingled with a sturdy influx of Germans and other nationalities. Intermarriages have mixed much of the blood of these five peoples, making us typically American and melting us into the mainstream of the 20th century, holding onto, we hope, the good from the old and the new.

The recipes in this book may not have been laboratory tested, but their merit has been established by church or civic groups and the most critical group of all: husbands and families . . .

Anne walked us to the door and I commented on the height of the corn across the street. She told us the crop alternated from hay to corn year to year.

"I like it when it's hay, best," she said. "With the corn, the heat just seems to close in on you."

On our way out of town, we drove the two miles along a narrow road to see the beautiful limestone church where Anne had spent so many Sundays in her own private world. The sun was a giant Sweet-Tart dropping into a cornfield. A white sheet on which someone had spray-painted "Congratulations Dan and Vera" hung from a tractor in a field where cows grazed. One cow had wandered away from the group, staking her independence in a patch of clover.

We headed northwest toward tiny Thornton, up near the Minnesota border in search of hog farmer Paul Willis. I had tasted one of his Willis's Niman-Ranch pork chops in a restaurant in New York, and it was hands-down the juiciest, sweetest pork chop I'd ever tasted. The chef said that was because Willis's hogs are allowed to roam free and are fed mostly organic foods. It stood to reason then that this farmer, who raised his pigs the old-fashioned way, would know a thing or two about old-fashioned pie.

Thornton was a one-stoplight town anchored by a gas station, a quaint corner church, and a seedy bar and grill. In a town so small (only slightly bigger than Bernard), how hard would it be to find a hog farm?

We stopped at the gas station first, where the woman at the mini-mart register said: "Make a right, then a left through town, and then, when you see a dirt road on your way out of town on your left, go *straight off*."

Huh? We stopped at the bar and grill and tried again. This time Kris did the asking and she came out shaking her head. "What the heck does *straight off* mean?"

We drove back through town and saw an elderly couple meticulously applying the black magnetic letters for the holy message of the week at the corner church. We'd chuckled at so many of these church ditties, but had never seen one being applied. We really were on a different pace.

The gentleman, a retired schoolteacher, told us that he and his wife had recently donated the church sign to the community and, consequently, got to select its first message.

They picked: "Jesus Calls Today, Come Follow Me—to the Park for a Picnic 7/9."

The sign had cost them a pretty penny but, he said, "if we can get just one new person to come to the church because of it, it'll be worth it."

We wondered if he could maybe buy a sign for Paul Willis's hog farm next, because we were having a hard time getting there. He laughed and gave us directions. And Kris and I high-fived each other when we finally stumbled on a Willis mailbox.

We turned into a long dirt drive that bordered an open muddy field with lots of pigs lolling in a pool of mud slush to stay cool. It didn't seem like a very big operation. The outbuildings were nothing fancy, to be sure, nor was the farmhouse framed by vines and wildflowers. We knocked, no one answered.

We wandered over to the farmhouse directly across the road, to ask a guy on a tractor where Paul Willis could be found.

"Try the Dream House," he said.

"The Dream House?" Kris and I looked at each other, puzzled.

"See that dirt road on the other side of the main road?" he said. "Just take that *straight off*, then make a left on the second paved road. The Dream House is the last house on your left."

Just as its name suggested, the Dream House was a pale yellow two-story house, with a side garden and a yawning back porch. It was the house of small-town novels. Several cars were parked on the dirt drive, so we figured Paul Willis was in our midst. But all the blinds and curtains were drawn, just like at Anne's, and no one answered our knocking or our bellows.

We were pulling out of the drive when we heard a woman's voice coming from the back porch:

"Do you two girls need some help . . . or do you just need some coffee?"

We backed up. The woman was tall and strong but with a soft, pudding face. "I'm Phyllis Willis . . . Come on inside."

Her husband Paul was sitting at the kitchen table, next to his sister Anne. Oscar, their father, was also there. They all looked up at us, waiting to hear what we'd come to sell.

Everyone looked a little groggy, as we'd just roused them all from their afternoon nap.

When we assured them we were doing research for a book, not witnessing Jehovah or selling vacuum cleaners door-to-door, they relaxed.

Before launching into pie, though, I was dying to know about the Dream House.

Phyllis leaned back in her chair and smiled. "We'd always wanted a vacation home, a place where we could get away from all the stresses of the farm and of daily living," she said. "But this was the house we fell in love with—less than a mile away from home." Since Phyllis didn't like to be away from her chickens and garden for too long, it made sense, they reckoned, to buy a vacation home in the neighborhood.

"What makes it a vacation or dream house is its spirit, not its location," said Phyllis.

Unlike their real house, *this* house didn't come replete with overflowing junk or project drawers. There were no piles of bills or paperwork that needed to be filed. Stress stayed on the porch, next to muddy shoes. The entire second floor was occupied by full-size beds—just like the dwarves' house in *Snow White*.

Napping was not only allowed, but encouraged.

"In fact, if you girls need a nap . . ." said Phyllis. It sounded tempting, but we did need to get back on the pie track.

We explained the loose rules of the pie trip and how it was that a fine pork chop had landed us here. Paul told us that his father had been among the first farmers in Iowa to shy away from the "factory" approach to raising livestock. Paul followed suit, taking it one step further. He manages thirty-five small hog farms in the area, where hogs are treated as humanely as possible.

"The whole point is to raise the hogs without any sort of trauma or pain," said Paul. "Even on their way to the slaughterhouse, we forbid the use of shockers to prod them."

We asked if they knew of a place around here that treated pie crust as lovingly as Paul treated his pigs. Paul, who'd just grabbed a piece of raspberry pie that morning at the farmer's market, said the best place for pie was a bakery-café that just opened in Sheffield, in a former Methodist church.

He offered to drive us there, since he had to take Oscar back to the retirement home in time for supper. Anne and Paul were torn up about recently moving their father to the home, but it needed to be done.

Anne was visiting from California, with her son, Casey. She'd come specifically to clear out Oscar's farmhouse—an emotional task, to be sure.

We had to fly, because the café closed early on Saturdays, Paul said. So, Kris, Oscar, Paul, Anne, and I all piled into Paul's truck. Phyllis stayed behind, alone—I suspect, to finish that languid nap.

Driving past cornfields "high as an elephant's eye," Paul told us the stalks had been growing about a foot a day in the last week. "You

Our Daily Bread

really have to watch those corn corners," he said, referring to the intersections where corn was high enough to obscure oncoming cars.

Sure enough, Sue Collins was locking up her bakery-café, Our Daily Bread, when we pulled up.

She let us inside for a quick peek. The pews had been replaced by flea-market tables draped in red-and-white checkered cloth. Still, the cathedral ceiling and the arched windows were unmistakably holy. Sadly, the pies had all been sold for the weekend, said Sue.

But she dug through her recipe box and pulled out a yellowed, grease-stained index card. "Here, you can have my mother's recipe for rhubarb pie," she said. "It's popular, and I know it by heart."

Paul and Anne took turns hugging Oscar in the parking lot at the retirement home. Paul slipped behind the steering wheel and was silent for a while.

"How would you two like to see some native Iowa prairie?" he said, perking himself right up.

When early explorers like Lewis and Clark crossed Iowa, they walked knee-deep in an endless sea of tall prairie grass. More than 85 percent of the state was covered in prairie, rich with hundreds of deep-rooted plant systems.

For years, roaming herds of buffalo and elk kept the prairie low and thriving by grazing smartly and selectively. But the Homestead Act, combined with the invention of the plow by John Deere in 1837, changed the prairie and Iowa forever. By the 1860s, most of Iowa prairie had been tilled for farming. Today, less than 1 percent of Iowa's original prairie land remains pure and unplowed. And a patch of that surviving prairie belongs to Paul's good friend Daryl.

It may be Daryl's land, but these 40 acres have become Paul's raison d'être. Although slightly blasé about the hog-farming revolution he helped stir, Paul became solemn as soon as we stepped onto the prairie—a privilege not granted to many, we gathered.

Paul and Daryl have been meticulously collecting seeds from the prairie as part of a statewide effort to restore prairie lands. Paul could identify every species of flower and weed on the hilly, vital terrain, from the purple coneflowers, on their last July bloom, to the thirteen types of milkweed, a favorite snack of monarch caterpillars.

I asked Paul about the tall, sunflower-like plant I had never seen before. "Oh, that's a compass plant," he said. The plant oriented its leaves to a north-south direction, away from the sun's heat, he went on. Early settlers often relied upon its guiding foliage on foggy days, when the sun and land forms could not be relied upon for direction. Every flower and plant on this land seemed to have sprouted with a purpose, and seemed to know exactly what that purpose was.

How lucky for them.

On the way back to Thornton, we stopped in a Sheffield watering

Paul Willis and his hogs

hole where Paul was sure we'd find Daryl, to thank him in person for sharing his prairie with us. I offered to buy a round of drinks, but Daryl refused. I insisted, and, eventually, we arm-wrestled for the honor. I lost. We toasted the prairie.

Daryl told us that the sheriff had been out to his house that day, because Daryl's pet ducks had been mysteriously vanishing, one by one, from his backyard. We'd noticed signs for duck races in the area, and he suspected there might be a connection.

When we returned to the Dream House, Phyllis had made the executive decision that we were staying for dinner: pork burgers and fresh vegetables from her garden, bouncy baby lettuces and deep-green Swiss chard. This was by far the healthiest meal we'd had on this trip. And to wash it all down? A tall glass of cold whole milk—something else I lived without, growing up French.

By the time dinner was over, it was past 9 P.M., and although Kris and I were game to hit the road for Minnesota, the Willises convinced us to stay the night. Anne and Casey had Oscar's big house all to themselves.

On our way to Oscar's funky farmhouse, Anne issued a warning. Her father, she said, had an obsession with contraptions, mainly metal. Indeed, in every room, metal rods, cables, and pulley systems hung from the ceiling and jutted out from walls, in a decor I could only describe as Rube Goldberg meets Chitty Chitty Bang Bang. Even the couch sat on a raised metal frame. Above the kitchen sink, an unwieldy contraption dispensed plastic wrap. In his bedroom, Oscar had even developed a pulley system to hang-dry his boxer shorts.

We slept in a set of twins in Anne's old room—happily contraption-free. As late as it was, it was still hot as a casserole, so we left the windows wide open. In the middle of the night, a racing wind blew the curtain sheers over my face. I dreamt of coneflower petals.

We all woke up early, took long showers, and drank good coffee. On one of the Sunday-morning news shows, ironically, the topic at hand was biogenetically engineered corn. Anne groaned and changed the channel.

Paul poked his head in the kitchen door, inviting us all to the "real" house for a Sunday-morning breakfast. This family was so easy to be around, it was hard to leave. Besides, I really wanted to see how the real house compared to the Dream House. One look, and it all made sense. Paul and Phyllis Willis were pack rats.

Daryl showed up, as did a friend of Phyllis's who brought a pineapple and carved it real fancy. We grilled up pork sausages and ate them with farm-fresh eggs. Life was good.

But the road to pie beckoned. Paul offered to tighten the ropes holding down the wicker table on Betty Blue's roof, and the rear rolling pin. Anne gave us the gift of an "itch stick" for mosquito bites and some portable plug-in contraption to boil water on the road. Like daughter like father, I said. She rolled her eyes.

Phyllis came out of the house with a stack of old *Kitchen-Klatter* magazines she'd been saving since the '70s.

"Now I know why I've been hanging on to them all these years," she said, tossing them in the car. We drove off—"straight off"— toward Minnesota.

On I-35, we passed the turnoff for the town of Britt, where, I'd read, hobos have been gathering for their annual convention since the 1930s. I thought of Norman Rockwell's famous illustration of a hobo running down the street with a stolen pie still steaming in his hands.

"Hey, we didn't have a single piece of pie in this state," Kris said. I hadn't even noticed.

PAT LARKIN'S LEMON MERINGUE PIE FROM THE ST. PATRICK'S PARISH COOKBOOK

CRUST
1 9-inch pie crust, prebaked

FILLING
1½ cups sugar
¼ cup cornstarch
dash of salt
1½ cups hot water

3 slightly beaten egg yolks
2 tablespoons milk
juice of 3 lemons
2 tablespoons butter

MERINGUE
2 egg whites
½ teaspoon of cream of tartar
½ teaspoon of salt
6 tablespoons of sugar

Mix 1½ cups of sugar, cornstarch, and salt. Gradually blend in water and bring to a boil, stirring constantly. Cook until clear. Remove from heat, add egg yolks and milk to hot mixture. Bring to a boil again, stirring constantly. Add lemon juice, reduce heat, and cook and stir for about 4 more minutes. Add butter, stir. Remove from heat and let cool for 10 minutes. Pour into a cooked pastry shell. (Use your favorite pie shell recipe and blind-bake it).

Beat 2 egg whites slightly. Add ½ teaspoon of cream of tartar and ½ teaspoon of salt. Continue beating until soft peaks form. Still beating, gradually add 6 tablespoons of sugar, one at a time. When egg whites form stiff peaks, spread meringue over the pie filling so that it touches the crust all around. Bake at 350 degrees until meringue turns golden brown—about 15–20 minutes.

SUE COLLINS'S MOM'S RECIPE
FOR RHUBARB PIE FROM
OUR DAILY BREAD IN SHEFFIELD, IOWA

CRUST

1½ cups of flour
½ teaspoon of sugar
½ teaspoon baking powder
¾ teaspoon of salt
½ cup of lard
4½ tablespoons of cold water

FILLING

4 cups fresh-cut rhubarb
4 tablespoons of flour
1¾ cups of sugar
2 beaten eggs

Mix one cup of the flour with the other dry ingredients, then add lard. Add water and remaining flour.

Mix filling ingredients well, pour into an unbaked pie shell and bake at 350 degrees for an hour.

PUMPKIN-APPLE PIE PLUCKED
FROM THE DECEMBER 1965 ISSUE
OF *KITCHEN-KLATTER* MAGAZINE

CRUST
Cider pastry for 1 single-crust pie

CIDER PASTRY
(MAKES TWO BOTTOM PIE CRUSTS)
2 cups flour
½ teaspoon salt
1 cup shortening
¼ cup cider

FILLING
4 large tart apples
2 tablespoons apple cider
¼ cup sugar
1 cup mashed pumpkin (canned or fresh)
¼ teaspoon salt
¼ cup light cream
1 egg, beaten
⅓ cup brown sugar
1 teaspoon cinnamon
½ teaspoon nutmeg
½ teaspoon ginger
¼ teaspoon cloves

Mix flour and salt. Cut in shortening. Mix lightly with cider to make
pastry. Roll out and fit into 2 pie pans.

Peel and slice apples; combine in a saucepan with cider, sugar, and salt. Cook 10 minutes at medium heat, or until just tender. Allow to cool. Line a 9-inch pie pan with half of the cider pastry. Let chill for at least an hour. Pour cooked apples into the pie shell. In a separate bowl, combine pumpkin, salt, cream, and egg. Add sugar and spices. Stir to blend well, then pour over apples. Bake pie at 425 degrees for about 45 minutes. Serve at room temperature.

braham (as in "graham cracker"), minnesota

"If I were asked to what the singular prosperity and growing strength of that people ought mainly to be attributed, I should reply to the superiority of their women."

—ALEXIS DE TOCQUEVILLE, *DEMOCRACY IN AMERICA*

The obvious destination in Minnesota would have been Betty's in Duluth, practically world-famous for its pies. But I'd heard of a little town called Braham in east-central Minnesota, which hosts an annual Pie Day and boasts a giant mural of a deep-dish pie in the center of town.

I was curious about this small town's love affair with pie.

We could have bypassed Minneapolis altogether, but since we were so close and had both been weaned on the *Mary Tyler Moore*

Show, we thought we should at least try to find the famous intersection where Mary Richards tossed her wool hat in the air, maybe even fling our baseball caps in solidarity.

City centers can be so stark and depressing on Sundays, and Minneapolis was no exception. We drove around in circles, recalling favorite episodes, and wondering why it was that Mary never stood up to Mr. Grant when she was in his office, or how Rhoda could fit all of that furniture in her tiny studio apartment. We finally gave up and headed for Braham.

Garrison Keillor kept us entertained on the drive north. We particularly enjoyed a sketch on the myriad uses for duct tape, having just borrowed some from Paul Willis that morning to strap that darn glove-compartment door shut.

Braham (pop. 1,300) is so small, we had no trouble finding the mural painted on the side of the Tusen Tack store right where Main Avenue hits Route 60.

We parked across the street from the mural, and leaned against

Betty Blue to admire it from a distance. It was a big pie, all right. Berry, judging from the purple-red drippings. Ribbons of steam billowed from the tawny top crust, its edges coarsely crimped. The mural was bordered with heavy ceramic coffee cups, giving it a real diner feel. The painting was so absorbing and comforting, we barely noticed the elderly woman slowly pedaling past us on her squeaky three-speed bike. I caught her cherry-red tennis shoes in the corner of my eye.

"Excuse me, do you know anything about this mural?" I shouted after her. She made a big circle in the empty street and rode back toward us. I don't know if she was tickled by out-of-towners ogling her hometown mural or if she was just plain happy to be alive and exercising at the end of a glorious summer day, but she was beaming.

She introduced herself as Jerrie Aune, and she wore her Scandinavian ancestry in her high cheekbones, her thin-lipped smile, and the slight tilt of the head.

"Well, you *do* know you're in the 'homemade pie' capital of Minnesota, *don't* you?"

"Braham? Really?"

She laughed demurely.

"It's *Bra*-ham, like the *gra*-ham cracker," she said. "Braaa-aaaam."

I had been mispronouncing Braham since we first saw it on the map, giving it a mystical twist—as in Brahman.

"For more than fifty years," she said, "people driving from Minneapolis to Duluth have been taking the shortcut through Braham and stopping for pie at the Park Café."

Of course, I pointed out, it's not much of a shortcut if you stopped and ate a slice of pie at the café.

"No, I guess not," she agreed.

She popped the kickstand on her bike and faced the mural as we did, her hands on her hips.

Her father opened the café in 1946. It had changed hands several times since, but the "hands" have always made the pies from scratch to keep the café's reputation intact.

The Park Café was already closed for the night, she said, "but if you want to come to my house, I have all sorts of information about the town and the Pie Day festival."

So we climbed back in the car and, at 10 miles per hour, followed Jerrie across Route 107 (called Pie Tin Alley as it goes through Braham) past the old railroad tracks and to her quiet, tree-lined neighborhood. Her husband, Herman, was reading the Sunday paper in the living room, and he didn't seem the least bit surprised that his wife could go out for her evening exercise and come back with two strangers. Jerrie poured us each a tall glass of cranberry juice and set out a tray of pecan-turtle cookies she kept in her freezer for surprise guests.

No sooner had we finished explaining our quest to the Aunes than Jerrie grabbed the phone and asked her friend Phyllis Londgren to come over.

"Phyllis is our own Barbara Walters," she explained. "She knows *everything* about Braham."

"But I have to warn you . . . she's *very* intense." I could hear Herman snicker from his recliner. "That Phyllis. She's something all right."

Herman had the most amazing way of looking at his wife. Miss Sweden could have walked into the living room in a bikini and stilettos, and Herman would barely notice. The two had met their senior year at Braham High School where Herman had gone on to become the music teacher and bandleader.

Herman knew what about Jerrie had caught his eye back in high school, but he wanted to know what had made us stop her on her bike.

"Those snappy red tennis shoes," I said. "If she hadn't been wearing them, we might have photographed the mural and forged on to South Dakota."

Herman crinkled his nose. "I really like those a lot, too," he said.

Then Herman excused himself to go find something he thought I might be interested in. He returned ten minutes (and three pecan turtles later) with the September 1956 issue of *Ideals* magazine, which contained the following Harriet Beecher Stowe excerpt on pie:

> *The pie is an English institution which planted on American soil forthwith ran rampant and burst forth into an untold variety of genera and species. Not merely the old traditional mince pie, but a thousand strictly American seedlings from that main stock, evinced the power of American housewives to adapt old institutions to new uses. Pumpkin pies, cranberry pies, huckleberry, cherry, green currant, peach, pear and plum, custard, apple, Marlborough pudding—pies with top crusts and pies without, pies adorned with all sorts of fanciful flutings and architectural strips laid across and around and otherwise varied, attested the boundless fertility of the feminine mind, when once let loose in a given direction.*
>
> *Fancy the heat and vigor of the great pan formation, when Aunt Lois and Aunt Keziah and my mother and grandmother all in ecstasies of creative inspiration, ran, bustled and hurried, mixing, rolling, tasting, consulting, alternately setting us children to work when anything could be made of us and then chasing us all out of the kitchen when our misinformed childhood ventured to take too many liberties with sacred mysteries. Then out we would all fly at the kitchen door, like sparks from a blacksmith's window.*

The doorbell rang and Phyllis Londgren blew in like a twister. Her arms were loaded down with history books, folders, pictures, and even official Braham pie tins—as though she had been preparing for this moment for years.

Careful to pronounce Braham correctly, I asked Phyllis how the town had earned the title of pie capital of the state, particularly when lutefisk eaters across Minnesota speak so highly of Betty's Pies, off of old Highway 61, in Duluth.

The mere mention of Betty's made Phyllis bristle.

"Betty's may have good pies, but *Braham* is the pie capital," she said, and, in one long uninterrupted breath that would have put Harry Houdini to shame, recounted the story.

It all started when state officials launched a "Celebrate Minnesota" campaign to promote tourism across the state. They encouraged smaller communities to "brighten themselves up a little," put their best foot forward, even host an annual celebration of some sort. Since Braham had long been known for its Park Café pies, Phyllis suggested at a civic meeting that the town host an annual Pie Day. The first festival was held on July 20, 1990. All the church ladies of Braham made pies by the dozen. There was a pie-eating contest for the kids. "It was all very garden-variety," Phyllis said.

About a year later, then-governor Rudy Perpich stopped into the Park Café unannounced, with his wife, after visiting a local rodeo. Perpich had made a campaign stop at the café once, and he'd remembered the pies.

Phyllis heard that the governor was in the house, as it were, and she raced over to the Park Café. "I grabbed a pot of coffee and refilled his cup and then I sat down right next to him in the booth," she said.

"And that's when I told him, 'Governor, you should name Braham the Homemade Pie Capital of Minnesota!' "

Phyllis pounded her fist on the table so hard that both Herman and the pecan turtles jumped. Phyllis popped one in her mouth.

"Jerrie, you're a regular Perle Mesta!" she said.

Because no one ever says no to Phyllis, the governor's official proclamation arrived in the mail within days and was immediately hung in the main dining room of the Park Café. Bolstered by its official status, the town's annual Pie Day just grew and grew until it finally required a committee to make preparations year-round.

A group of women named the Peach Ladies—all in their 70s and 80s—are called in to peel and slice buckets of peaches for the event. Entertainers are flown in from Sweden, and competitive pie bakers travel from as far as Maine to participate in the various contests.

"It's gotten totally out of control," said Phyllis, beaming. Of course, with expansion have come problems.

A few years ago, the committee approved a "cow pie" contest, in which festivalgoers had to guess in which section of an open pasture a Holstein would leave, ahem, a *cow* pie.

"The Swansons would bring in a couple of their heifers, and then you'd have to wait all day for those cows to crap," Phyllis said, rolling her eyes. The event was shelved after three years. Herman snickered.

Pie Day has even had its first political scandal.

To celebrate and cement its new identity as the "pie capital," the people of Braham decided to put out a cookbook of prize-winning pie recipes in 1993. They solicited pie recipes from all over the state to compete in a number of categories. The clear winner in the custard-and-cream pie category was the creamy peach pie "family" recipe submitted by a certain state senator. None of the judges noticed that the creamy peach pie, made with Jell-O, ice cream, and instant-pudding mix, was, in fact, absolutely peachless. The local press had a field day. What's more, the state senator's "family" recipe had, in fact, come from the back of a General Foods package. The scandal erupted the same week said governor had been slapped with a paternity suit.

Phyllis insisted we meet with the pie committee at the Park Café early in the morning before leaving town. She would make sure Gary, the high school media center director, would be there. Gary was in charge of the pie-baking contest, she said, and "he's a *very* eligible bachelor." She winked at each of us.

Phyllis snapped a picture of us in front of our license plate. Then she handed me a soft-cover book the size of *Webster's Dictionary*, on the history of Braham—a little something she threw together for Braham's centennial.

Our heads were spinning when we got in the car. As much as we loved Phyllis, we thought of calling up Garrison Keillor and suggesting another use for duct tape.

There were still about thirty minutes of daylight left, so, as soon as we got to the dreary Cambridge Imperial Motel about 12 miles away, we put on our roller blades and headed toward the local high school, where we bladed in circles in the newly paved parking lot to work off our day's intake of calories: pork sausage and pecan turtles.

I stayed up far too late reading about the history of Braham, with characters straight out of Lake Wobegon.

My favorite was J. Wallace Rock, an undertaker and fireman who also served as city clerk for thirty-four years. Rock always did his books in the mortuary or the fire hall. I learned that the "pooper-scooper" was invented in Braham, and that Braham was also the birthplace of the first handheld egg beater.

I stayed up so late reading that I managed to sleep right through the alarm. The committee was waiting for us at the café, tapping pencils, at a U-shaped table when we came screeching in, without our morning coffee, "like sparks from a blacksmith's window."

We were surprised at how serious everyone was about Pie Day, especially Gary the Bachelor, a real stickler about the entry rules for the contest. The event was only a couple of weeks away, and, clearly, nerves were a tad frayed.

What's more, the committee was on pins and needles, waiting to hear if their request to have a highway sign posted on Route 107 promoting Braham as Minnesota's pie capital had been approved.

No one was more serious than pie baker Lola Nebel. Though not on the committee herself, Lola had gotten a call from Phyllis late the night before, urging her to attend our breakfast meeting.

Lola had been the first-prize winner at the very first pie-baking contest at the first Pie Day in 1990. She had since gone on to win several state-fair sweepstakes and had even recently been a finalist in the Pillsbury bake-off held in San Francisco.

"I guess I've always been kind of competitive," she said, her hands resting on her stack of winning recipes.

Marilyn McGriff, a local historian and librarian, was much more low-key, even though she is the one who is ultimately responsible for getting five hundred pies baked for Pie Day each year.

"Basically, we've got it down to a science now," said Marilyn. "As long as you're breathing, you can volunteer to help make pies for Pie Day."

The pies are prepared over a three-day period, with volunteers working three shifts a day, mixing the dough, then pressing the crust in tins, then filling the shells and layering them with a top crust. The pies are baked off in the high school cafeteria—about eighty at a time. Most of the pies are fruit: rhubarb, raspberry, cranberry, and apple, and many combinations thereof, she said, because the local health inspector, rightly, had "issues" with cream pies being sold on the sidewalk unrefrigerated.

Pies are so integral to the identity of Braham that when Marilyn visits local schools on Community Day, she always brings a just-baked pie to illustrate the meaning of community.

"I tell the children that every community needs a good foundation and infrastructure—*that's* the crust," she said. "The filling is made up of churches, businesses, banks, and schools—all the things that make a community work.

"The fluted or crimped edges are more decorative than essential," she went on. "They are the trees on Main Avenue, the gazebo in Freedom Park. They are what makes a community a much more pleasant place to live."

The banana cream pie at the Park Café is what makes Braham such a nice place to live, a customer at the counter chimed in. "We never go without it," said owner Ellie Grell.

Kris and I ordered a slice of fresh rhubarb with a Dutch-crumb topping instead. It looked healthier, and maybe we needed some tartness to transition back to the real world.

When I returned to New York, there were two pieces of mail with a Braham postmark waiting for me. One was Lola Nobel's recipe for Rosy Raspberry Pear pie, which follows. The other was a copy of the July 22 issue of the *Star,* Braham's local newspaper, with the words "See Page 4" scribbled on the front page.

I turned to Page 4 and saw this screaming headline:

"Pie Book Author to Include Braham in U.S. Pie Book."

Beneath the headline was a very large picture of Kris and me, standing next to Betty Blue, in the Aunes' driveway. Jerrie and Herman are standing close together, on their lawn, off to the side. Oddly enough, the setting sun is hitting the IBRK4PIE license plate in such a way that is glows.

"Your license plate looks like a halo," Phyllis Londgren had scribbled on a Post-it note affixed to the article, which was, I'm guessing, written by her, although it had no byline.

The article related our visit—blow-by-blow—and ended with this paragraph:

> *By the time they left Braham, around noon, they had a vast*
> *amount of information regarding the role pie plays in east cen-*

tral Minnesota. There are many in Braham who are looking forward to the book. The author had not arrived at a title yet, but
Braham hopes to be one of the first communities to know when
the book is available as well as its title . . .

You betcha, Phyllis.

LOLA NEBEL'S
ROSY RASPBERRY PEAR PIE

CRUST

1 15 oz. package Pillsbury Refrigerated Pie Crust, softened as
   directed on package

FILLING

3 firm ripe pears, peeled and cut into ½ inch slices

1 tablespoon lemon juice

½ teaspoon almond extract

¾ cup sugar

3 tablespoons all-purpose or unbleached flour

1 cup fresh or frozen whole raspberries without syrup, partially
   thawed

1 tablespoon butter or margarine, melted

1 tablespoon sugar

Heat the oven to 400 degrees. Prepare pie crusts as directed on the
package for one-crust filled pie using 9-inch pie pan. Reserve second
crust for cutouts.

In a large bowl, combine pears, lemon juice, and almond extract;
toss to coat. Add ¾ cup sugar and flour; mix well. Spoon about half

of pear mixture into crust-lined pan. Top with raspberries. Spoon remaining pear mixture over raspberries. With 2½-inch floured round cookie cutter, cut 9 rounds from second pie crust. Brush each with melted butter. Place 8 rounds, butter side up, in a circle on the outer edge of fruit, overlapping as necessary. Place one round in center. Sprinkle rounds with 1 tablespoon sugar.

Bake at 400 degrees for 40–50 minutes, or until the crust is golden brown and the filling is bubbly. If necessary, cover the edge of crust with strips of foil after 15–20 minutes of baking to prevent excessive browning. Cool 3 hours, or until completely cooled. If desired, serve with vanilla ice cream.

political pie

Bachelor Pie: it's what cowboys ate on the wagon trail . . . basically a quick biscuit dough filled with whatever filling was handy or available, such as prairie oysters (bull testicles) sliced thin and fried in bacon grease.

My rough plan for the camel-skin plains of South Dakota was to get invited to one of those weeknight church socials. I hear they are big in the Mount Rushmore state. And they almost *always* serve pie.

Shortly before leaving New York, I met a fashion photographer named Sean who was from Aberdeen, South Dakota, a hog's breath away from the North Dakota border.

Sean was feeling homesick. Pining for the one diner in Aberdeen that served good pie. I told him that maybe I'd check it out when I got to South Dakota.

In the following week, I received a barrage of e-mails from Sean. He had telephoned all of his relatives in and around Aberdeen to tell them we might be coming through. Even Mel, a friend of the family who lives in Eureka and still roasts fresh pumpkins for his pie, had been put on pie alert.

Sean had made it so easy.

Perhaps—on the heels of sugar-coated Braham and in a state known for its harshness—*too* easy.

So when Betty Blue crossed over into South Dakota from Minnesota, I told Kris we were bagging Aberdeen and heading south, instead of north, straight for the Badlands.

"Huh?"

I pointed to my gut.

She switched lanes.

. . .

It was almost dark, and our plan was to drive as far west as we could manage that night so that we could make it to the Badlands, clear across the plains, by the following afternoon.

Route 14 was dark as a bat cave, for long stretches at a time. We drove through De Smet, where Laura Ingalls Wilder and her family homesteaded.

I took in a deep breath and got a faint whiff of those thick Wilder books I used to borrow from the Santa Monica public library.

It was my father who taught me to smell books. Every September, when my sister and I would get our new batch of textbooks, my father, his own schooling halted by war, would crack them open and sniff.

"This," he would say, "is the smell of knowledge."

In Huron, I smelled trouble. Lots of hotels, not a vacancy sign in sight. "Sorry, ladies. Truckers keep us booked solid 365 nights a year," said hotel clerk after hotel clerk. "You won't find anything until Pierre."

Pierre was a long, dark, and lonely hour away.

Kris handed me the keys. "We'd have found pie and gone to bed already if we'd stuck with the plan and gone to Aberdeen."

She passed out as soon as she buckled in. What kept me awake was a gas gauge close to bone dry.

I was never so happy to see a blinking neon vacancy sign, right at the entrance of Pierre.

Mike, the owner, was remarkably perky at this late hour—about 2 A.M.

"We have a really nice pool," he said as I signed the credit card slip. He was curious about the license plate and rolling pins. I gave him the abridged version of the quest, and then we retired to our rooms and collapsed ourselves.

In the morning, we got up early enough to swim laps and work off some crankiness. At lap forty, I stopped to catch my breath and felt a light tap on my swim cap. I looked up, and there was Mike, chipper as ever.

"I've been thinking about your pie adventure," he said. "Did you know that pie is a political force in South Dakota?"

I shook my head from side to side, to clear water from my ears.

"There was a big scandal a couple of years back. Something about voters being bribed with pie during elections."

OK. This was good. Worth getting out of the water for. He handed me a towel. His details were sketchy, but he suggested that we walk on over to the Capitol building and talk to the governor. "He'll fill you in."

"We're just going to waltz right into the governor's office?" Kris said, as we crossed the Capitol building's beautiful gardens thirty minutes later, our hair still wet.

"Apparently so," I said. The black domed Capitol building was exquisite and so clean, we could have rolled out a pie dough right there on the rotunda's shiny marble floor.

"We're here to talk to the governor about pie," I said to a man who looked fairly official standing in a doorway.

The man whisked us into his office. His name was Larry Long and he was the deputy attorney general. He said it was actually his boss, Mark Barnett, the attorney general, who was behind l'affaire pie. Barnett, who just happened to be eyeing the governor's seat, was not in the office that day, but Long would happily fill us in.

It all started when Attorney General Barnett decided to clamp down on an age-old law barring enticements on Election Day. The law had been on the books since 1891, but it had resurfaced in 1994 with reports that Democrats had been serving lunch to voters on local Indian reservations on Election Day.

Barnett, a Republican, drafted a letter describing the law's intent and sent it, as a gentle reminder, to all political parties and election officials in every town and South Dakota municipality.

It just so happens that for more than eighty years, the little old ladies of Wasta (pop. 70) had been baking pies from scratch, to serve and sell on Election Day. Since Wasta, a former cattle town, is made up largely of ranchers, the Election Day pie social provided just the right incentive for farmers to hang up their overalls for the day and come to town. For many, it was the only socializing they did all year. Sure, it was a bribe. A bribe to get farmers to come out and vote, though for whom, it did not matter.

So you can imagine how upset the people of Wasta were when they found out that their sweet tradition, which had also helped them raise money for their church and community center, was now illegal.

Wasta's indignation and outrage made the local newspapers. And, on Election Day that year, only 49 percent of the 109 eligible voters turned out in Wasta, down almost 20 percent from the last nonpresidential election in 1994.

Commentator Charles Osgood read a little ditty about the scandal on the air.

No fool, Barnett fired off a poem of his own to prove that he wasn't antipie:

> There was a town called Wasta
> where they fed the voters pie.
> The people came from miles around
> To vote and nibble, eye to eye

It was fine tradition
These hot apple pies from Mom
Until the prosecutors
dropped a legal bomb
The law, you see, is very clear . . .
No pie, no steak, not even beer!
The Legislature's spoken,
The tradition must be broken.
Said one hungry rancher:
"Who will make this nightmare right?
We hardly get a turnout
If there isn't food in sight."
"I can't help you with your problem,"
Said the General on his horse . . .
"If it's pie that is the trouble
I will buy you some, of course!
"Come ye to the Capitol
To see the Christmas trees . . .
A week before the Lord is born,
Is when we plan to please
"Have your pie and eat it too . . .
On the 19th of December
We'll bring the food and hope you have
A Christmas to remember!"

And so, a bus came to Wasta on the 19th of December to whisk its residents to Pierre for pie. Only twenty-eight Wasta residents forgave the attorney general enough to attend. They ate deer salami on the bus ride to the capitol and brought Barnett a cow-pie clock to show there were no hard feelings.

We were heading for Wasta.

·   ·   ·

After days of gazing at endless silos, in South Dakota our gaze rose to the dramatic sky, which seemed higher than it had been until now.

We stopped to take pictures of a wild horse on a ridge and it started to canter along the ridgeline, mane flying, the moment we approached. It was easy to see why Kevin Costner had come to the dramatic Dakotas to film his epic *Dances with Wolves*. We stopped in Philip for gas and strawberry popsicles, which tasted divine in this heat, even if they made our tongues vixen-red.

In the middle of nowhere we stumbled on a small pioneer museum where we learned that cowboys used to call the chuck wagon "the pie box," because pie could always be counted on after a day of cattle rustling *and* it was the warmest spot on the cattle spread.

In Badlands National Park, we took a quick walk through the moonscape. I felt like Frank Lloyd Wright who, upon seeing the Dakota Badlands for the first time, said: "I was totally unprepared for the revelation called the Dakota Badlands . . . What I saw gave me an indescribable sense of mysterious elsewhere—a distant architecture, ethereal . . . an endless supernatural world more spiritual than earth but created out of it."

Nothing could yank us further from this spiritual beauty than the garish signs for Wall Drug.

It would have been un-American, I guess, not to stop at the famous drugstore. Besides, we'd been brainwashed by the hundreds of arrogant road signs advertising the store since we crossed into South Dakota from Wisconsin. For endless miles of crew-cut prairie on either side of the highway (quite different from the prairie Paul the Hog Farmer had shown us in Iowa), the only splashes of color were painted Wall Drug signs: WALL DRUG OR BUST, ONLY 5 CENTS COFFEE, WALL DRUG.

Ted and Dorothy Hustead moved to Wall from Canover, South Dakota, in 1931, hoping to make a living in this impoverished town of 326. Their family thought they were crazy. Not only was the drugstore in the center of nowhere, but the Depression and drought had made the residents, mostly ranchers, dirt poor.

The Husteads, who lived with their young son in a room behind the Main Street shop, took in only $360 the first month. They gave themselves five years to make a go of it. Six months shy of their do-or-die deadline, business was still slow as diner ketchup.

One particularly hot afternoon in July, Dorothy went home for a nap. The rumbling of the jalopies on Highway 16 kept her awake. What could they do to persuade these drivers to pull off the highway and visit the drugstore, she asked herself, staring up at the ceiling. And then she got an idea: what if they put out on the highway a sign advertising free ice water—something any driver would go out of his way for on a scorching day.

Her husband was skeptical at first, but he and their 9-year-old son planted a wooden sign on the highway that read: GET A SODA/GET ROOT BEER/TURN NEXT CORNER/JUST AS NEAR/TO HIGHWAY 16 AND 14/FREE ICE WATER/WALL DRUG."

It wasn't Wordsworth, Ted Hustead quipped years later, but it worked. By the time they returned to the drugstore, it was crowded with customers. They came for the water, yes, but many left with a piece of toffee candy, or an ice cream cone. The following summer, the Husteads added more signs and the store got so busy they put behind the counter salesgirls in candy cane–striped A-line dresses. Within a few years, the place with the free ice water had evolved into what many call "The Mother of All Tourist Attractions."

Since they'd worked so well for him, Ted Hustead became obsessed with the painted-wood road signs, planting them in every state in the union. The signs have since come down because of Lady

Bird Johnson's Highway Beautification Act, which was passed by a pressured Congress in 1965. Fortunately, Hustead got himself appointed to the South Dakota Transportation Commission to protect the signs in his state. In time, Hustead was spending about $300,000 annually on road signs. Some cropped up on London buses, near the Taj Mahal, and in the train stations of Kenya. Many of the signs still visible in Germany, Korea, and Vietnam were placed there by homesick GIs from South Dakota.

On a good day in summer, about twenty thousand visitors visit the 75,000-square-foot Wall Drug, which stretches across several city blocks and takes in $10 million in sales a year. For the busy summer months, the Husteads hire a fleet of eager workers, from senior citizens to European exchange students, to handle the crowds.

In the fudge shop (kitty corner from the Travelers Chapel and the Apothecary Shoppe) we met a young woman named Luciana who was visiting for the summer from Slovakia. Her English was limited; still, she managed to convey that she had already gained two kilos in the two weeks.

We told Luciana we could relate. We explained all about our road trip, and she was envious of how much of the country we were seeing—since she was confined to the drugstore for the summer. She'd learned about Rocky Road and marshmallows but she was curious about the "pie."

We told her she'd have to have a slice of pie before heading home, because as fond as Americans are of fudge, pie is the quintessential American dessert. Luciana thanked us for the tip.

We couldn't wait to get out of this crazy crowded place, and we were about to make a clean break when we noticed a sign for home-made pie, pointing to the cafeteria.

We bought one slice for us for later, and one for Luciana. She was sweeping the shop when we returned. She happily accepted our slice

of pie, which she gobbled right in front of us. With every bite, she nodded approvingly, heaping us and the wedge of America in her hand with compliments.

Feeling righteous about our good deed, we headed toward Wasta, about 20 miles away, in pitch darkness. Fortunately, the town motel with the pink neon sign had a room for us. Esther, the motel owner, was really friendly and chortled when she laughed, like a chipmunk. She'd always dreamed of owning a vintage motel. After putting in forty years in the office of a trucking company in Minneapolis, she heard this one in Wasta was for sale and she started a new grand-plains life for herself.

We poured ourselves some bourbon in plastic cups and sat in the tomato-red vintage chairs outside our motel-room door, going over our day. I brought out our slice of Wall Drug pie to eat in the moon-light. It was truly a perfect moment. Then we took a bite of the pie. It was foul. Chemical-tasting. This pie was about as far removed from an apple tree or a flour-dusted rolling pin as Luciana was from home.

Poor Luciana! To think she would go back to Central Europe thinking that she'd tasted the quintessential American dessert!

"I feel like I've contributed to the delinquency of a minor," I told Kris.

We managed to fall asleep anyway, like Dorothy Hustead, to the rumble of trucks on I-90.

In the morning, we told Esther we were looking for some of the pie-baking ladies of Wasta. Esther suggested we talk to Lloyd and Margee, first. The couple was renovating a turn-of-the-century buttercup-yellow hotel around the corner. "They know everyone in Wasta."

Lloyd and Margee, who had moved to Wasta a couple of years earlier from Los Angeles, were in spackling mode when we knocked on the door. Esther had called ahead, so they were expecting us and invited us into their living room for a chat.

Both had gone to school in the Rapid City area, then went their separate ways and, coincidentally, ended up out west, she as a sheep farmer in Utah, he as a computer consultant just outside of Los Angeles. They reconnected at a high school reunion in 1988. Both were going through a divorce at the time, and so they made a date for five days later. They'd been together ever since.

"There's a unique trust and friendship that develops when you've known someone since you were a child," said Margee. "There is much to be said about where you come from. The thing about Lloyd is that he knows the little things about growing up in

South Dakota. He knows that you always bring a pumpkin pie and a lemon meringue pie to a funeral. That's a South Dakota thing."

What they also both knew was that they were not cut out for life in Los Angeles and both wanted to go home, to their prairie roots. They found this old hotel that needed some care. Margee would like to turn it into some sort of artists' retreat or a cozy hideaway for family reunions. They seemed happy in their new surroundings.

"It's not Wasta per se that makes the experience, it's the people," said Lloyd. "Here, they don't know about plastics, or the Bloods and the Crips. But they know about the stars and the price of hogs and when it's time to cut the corn. They know how to treat people, that's what they know."

Since their arrival, Lloyd and Margee have plunged themselves into local politics. In addition to trying to get their hotel, which was built around 1906, listed as a historical monument, Margee was trying to get the community center a sorely needed face-lift. Barnett's pie party aside, she said, the pie scandal created deep fractures in the community.

She suggested we talk to Ruth Bruce, a longtime Wasta resident who had been making pies for Election Day since the 1940s. Ruth and her husband, Charles, had recently moved to an assisted-living facility in Rapid City, due to his failing health.

We thanked Lloyd and Margee, told them we might be back some day, maybe to rent a room for the summer to work on a book, and then we headed for Rapid City.

Ruth came to Wasta to teach in the new schoolhouse in 1941. Six months later, she met Charles, who delivered gas to farmers for Standard Oil. He'd asked permission from the town doctor to take her out on a date. They'd been married fifty-five years. With her husband as sick as he was, shy Ruth seemed like a doe caught in the headlights.

She made it clear she didn't want to make waves about what happened in Wasta. Didn't want to stir up any more trouble.

"I just think those folks in the capital misunderstood what the pie was all about," Ruth said. "It was all social, not political. The bachelor ranchers would buy whole pies to take home, and we'd make a little extra money for the church."

"Sometimes politics gets in the way of common sense," she said, "don't you agree?"

We asked Ruth if there was one pie that was particularly popular in Wasta, and Ruth didn't skip a beat: "Mildred Snook's Sour Cream Raisin pie," she said. "I once saw a woman on the elections board eat three pieces in one sitting."

Mildred lived on a cattle-and-wheat ranch with her husband. "She was a real hardworking ranch lady. They didn't have children but they were active in the community and she was a member of the Rebecca Lodge," Ruth said, still visibly impressed by Mildred's flair, so many years after her death.

Ruth had been making Mildred's pie for years.

"I got the recipe from Mildred herself. There are some people in Wasta who won't share their recipes. There was one lady in particular who would tell only part of the recipe but keep a part of it to herself, so that it never came out right."

Ruth dug through her recipe file and brought out a yellowed sheet of paper with Mildred's recipe.

"The meringue's tricky," she said, looking it over. "You better hope nothing comes to distract you or it will burn."

Charles, who'd barely said a word, except to agree that Mildred's pie was best, shuffled with his walker into the bedroom, in search of something to show us, too. He returned flashing his Black Hills Ordnance Unit Badge.

Ruth said she learned to make pies just by watching her mother. Eventually, without any fanfare or ceremony, the roles were switched in the kitchen and Ruth's mother started watching her. The roles of this sweet couple had also been reversed, it seemed.

Kris wanted to take a portrait of Ruth and Charles on the couch, below an old, framed aerial photograph of Wasta taken in the middle of last century. Charles reached over and put his arm around Ruth's shoulder, sneaky-like, as though he were 14 again, stealing a grab at the picture show. Ruth put her hand on his thigh.

We left the retirement home and smiled at the dinner menu posted in the lobby. Dessert was pumpkin pie.

MILDRED SNOOK'S
SOUR CREAM RAISIN PIE

CRUST:

1 9-inch baked pie crust

FILLING

1 cup raisins

¼ cup water

1 cup sugar

1 cup sour cream

2 egg yolks, lightly beaten

2 tablespoons flour or cornstarch as a thickener

1 teaspoon vanilla

MERINGUE

2 egg whites

½ teaspoon of cream of tartar

½ teaspoon of salt

6 tablespoons of sugar

Put raisins in a pot and cover with ¼ cup of water. Simmer gently until tender, about 20 minutes. Add remaining filling ingredients and simmer, stirring often, until thick. Cool slightly and pour into pie shell.

Beat egg whites slightly. Add cream of tartar and salt. Continue beating until soft peaks form. Still beating, gradually add sugar, one tablespoon at a time. When egg whites form stiff peaks, spread meringue over the pie filling so that it touches the crust all around. Bake at 350 degrees until meringue turns golden brown—about 15–20 minutes.

more political pie

"Maybe seeing the (Dakota) Plains is like seeing an icon:
what seems stern and almost empty is merely open,
a door into some simple and holy state."
—KATHLEEN NORRIS, *DAKOTA: A SPIRITUAL GEOGRAPHY*

When the plan to carve the likenesses of four presidents into the craggy granite rock of Mount Rushmore was first announced in the mid-1920s, there were protests. Early-day environmentalists argued that the natural beauty of the rock had been designed by a higher authority and should not be defaced—or re-faced, as it were.

Had the project been completed today, no doubt protesters would have thrown a pie in sculptor Gutzon Borglum's face.

Pie throwing is the latest nonviolent form of protest in vogue among antiestablishment groups seeking spotlights on their cause.

In the last few years, victims of "pie smooshing" have included San Francisco mayor Willie Brown, Bill Gates, and fur-loving fashion designer Michael Kors.

The most notorious pie thrower is Noel Godin, of Belgium, who also goes by Georges Le Gloupier. It was Godin who masterminded the pie-pelting of Gates in Brussels in 1998. For that highly publicized ambush, more than thirty activists—all members of Godin's International Patisserie Brigade—hid pies under their coats and in camera bags.

Godin told the *New York Times* that he'd targeted the Microsoft mogul for the simple reason that "he chooses to function in the service of the capitalist status quo without really using his intelligence or his imagination."

Not that a pie in the face is very original.

Buster Keaton elevated pie throwing to an art form in the 1940s. Keaton developed all sorts of slinging styles ranging from "the catcher's pie throw" to the "Roman discus pie throw."

The first time he flung a pie was in the 1939 movie *Hollywood Cavalcade*. Alice Faye was his target, and Keaton practiced by throwing a wooden plate at a wall on which he'd drawn, with chalk, a circle the approximate size of Faye's head. Keaton even drove nails into the plate to make it as heavy as the real custard pie he would actually toss. He learned the hard way that a double-bottom crust was essential to prevent the pie from crumbling midflight.

If he was pieing a blonde, Keaton liked to use a chocolate, strawberry, or blackberry filling for contrast. For brunettes, lighter lemon meringue was the flavor of choice.

Most of the young, radical pie throwers these days use vegan or organic pies made with a tofu custard. As much as I support many of their causes, I cannot endorse any pie made with tofu.

That, I'm afraid, is as serious an offense as a capitalist lack of imagination.

montana,

the mother lode

*"Every blade of grass has its angel that
bends over it and whispers, 'Grow, grow.' "*
—THE TALMUD

I've always admired doctors who can engage in small talk in the examination room. My doctor in San Francisco was unusually chatty and during my last physical, before I drove to my new life in New York, he talked at length about huckleberry pie.

"You can't drive across America and not go to Montana for huckleberry pie," he said. His in-laws were from Montana and "ever since I tasted huckleberry pie there . . . say AAAAHHHHH . . . *no* pie has compared."

Unfortunately, I wasn't taking a northern route on that trip. But when I set out for the second trek, I put Montana at the top of my list.

I'd only been to Montana once, briefly, for the wedding of my friends Doug and Susann. They were living in Los Angeles at the time, but the ceremony was held high on a wind-kissed ridge near Livingston, where their log home would soon be built.

I didn't try any huckleberry pie that weekend, but I did get a dizzying dose of that stretched blue canvas that passes for sky there and knew I wanted more.

Kris and I entered the state from the bottom southeast corner on a hot morning in late July. Route 212 showed us nothing but flat river valley for a long time. We passed a slew of small, two-bit towns with abandoned homesteads and the occasional gas station. Betty Blue's windows were open, and the air outside felt hollow and quiet, like the ripping silence of a hawk circling its prey. We stopped in Broadus to get some gas. I pumped and Kris went to forage for some snacks in the mini-mart.

"Nice license plate."

I turned and saw a lanky man sitting—his back against the gas-station brick wall, one knee bent—in the shadow of his Harley. He had helmet hair, wore dark shades, and was eating Oreos.

"Yours isn't so bad either," I said, noticing the "My Honi" plate on his '98 Road King.

Tom worked in a plant that made aerosol cans, in Wisconsin. A high-pressure job, he said, in more ways than one. His favorite escape was a long, winding ride on his bike, alone or with his bike club, the Fairbault chapter of HOG (Harley Owners Group). I asked if they were anything like the Hell's Angels.

"Naaa. We're much more family-oriented," he said. "The highlight of most rides is stopping for ice cream at a Dairy Queen . . . . Unless we're in Duluth, then we stop at Betty's, of course, for pie."

Phyllis Londgren's ears were ringing for sure.

Tom said he used to have a drinking problem and since he turned in the bottle, he'd developed a craving for sweets that just wouldn't quit.

"I know it sounds weird, but now I get my kicks out of sugar. I've got this thing for chocolate silk and peanut butter pies."

He was heading toward Billings, though his route was a little fuzzy. Tom had sketched out a detailed itinerary for his two-week solo ride, but had left his map on the kitchen table at home.

"Accidentally?" I asked. He shrugged.

Today he was going to visit the historic site of the battle of Little

Big Horn but tomorrow was a question mark. He liked not knowing where he'd be from one day to the next. Not knowing the next can would roll off that assembly line as sure as the odometer would click over at the next mile and every one after that.

Tom seemed lonely, but he also seemed to know he still had a few demons left to conquer before he could let anybody else ride on that bike with him.

We left the gas station at the same time. It was understood that Betty Blue would fall in behind Honi. For the next 150 miles or so, we followed his one-note silhouette on the highway. He leaned far back on his banana seat, the scenery yielding like an open book before him. He rode like someone who knew exactly where he was going.

We passed rivers with funny names like Pumpkin, Rosebud, and Tongue, and then we honked and waved good-bye to Tom as he turned off to the site where Custer met his doom.

We had planned to spend the night at Doug and Susann's newly completed home, Sky Ranch, west of Livingston. Our plan was to track down Dave, the bear trapper and pie baker in Choteau, but I also hoped to find a horseman or maybe even a horse whisperer, to tell me where to go for huckleberry pie in cowboy country.

I didn't think there was a native American tribe that considered pie a traditional food, but thought I should at least inquire, while in Montana, just to make sure I wasn't missing anything. Near where US 212 T-bones into I-90, I saw a sign for Crow Agency and, figuring it was some sort of agency representing the Crow Indians, I took the exit. Crow Agency, in fact, was the name of a town, not a bureaucracy. I ducked into a corner market to inquire about pie but was greeted with such steely stares, I turned right around and walked across the street to the post office. I approached a woman with soft, doe skin, and posed my pie question.

She took a full minute to absorb my request. "We eat Juneberry pie," she said tentatively. "You need to talk to Alma Snell out on the reservation. She's in Yellowtail. She's the expert on Juneberry pie and all traditional foods and herbs."

I called information for Alma Snell's number and was surprised that she was listed. Her voice on the line was like a bird on a branch. She just happened to be preparing a traditional Crow feast for a lecture she was giving at Montana State University the next day. She was getting ready to make a Juneberry pie, in fact. "But you better hurry if you want to watch because I'm going to make it very soon."

"She's making a pie? Now?" said Kris. She'd been looking forward to a nice relaxing glass of wine and a meal on Doug and Susann's deck after so many days of dining on soy nuts. It was an hour's drive to the Crow Reservation on US 313, a desolate stretch of highway at the foot of the Big Horn mountains.

We got held up by road work. A long stretch of US 313 was being tarred, and we had to wait ten minutes in the broiling sun for the pilot truck to come get us. Two Crow men pulled alongside us in their pickup. "Are you two going for a swim?" they asked. That was usually the reason white folk went to the reservation. "No, we're going to visit Alma Snell," I said, "for advice on Juneberry pie."

"That's my grandmother," said the younger of the two. "She makes good pie." And they drove off. Since it was one of the hottest days on record—105 degrees, according to radio reports—I stupidly left the air-conditioning on while we idled and, sure enough, Betty Blue overheated.

The young, cheerful Crow woman, who stood in the middle of the freshly paved road holding a STOP sign without breaking a sweat, chirped into her walkie-talkie: "I have two white girls here who are having car trouble. Can you send someone?" We were back on the road within a few minutes, but we'd lost so much time, I feared Alma would be finished with her pie.

Alma's house was nestled in the crook of a hill, in a part of the reservation that is called Windblowing Place. It was a modern, modular home with a cozy living room and large, updated kitchen. Alma was standing at the stove when we knocked on the door. "Come on in," she said. "Door's open."

Strangers drop in on Alma Snell all the time. They come from as far away as Australia, Africa, and Germany, to the tune of two or three a day. "I don't always know how they find me," she said. "But they come."

She grew up during the 1920s and '30s, as part of the second generation of Crows to be born into reservation life. It was her grandmother, Pretty Shield medicine woman, who taught Alma about all things Crow. Pretty Shield was a deeply spiritual woman who led her life by nature's rules and forces. If an otter touched you while you were swimming, for example, that meant grave illness or death, and a cleansing was in order. Alma, too, spent her days digging for roots, communing with birds, and conversing with creeks. She had devoted her golden years to passing on these customs and traditions. That's why the people came.

"I'm trying to stay as authentic as I can," she said, pointing to the ingredients lining the kitchen counters. She'd even rendered some buffalo bone marrow to use as butter. We'd taken so long, she'd already made her dough and was letting it chill in the refrigerator. She was stirring the Juneberries in a large soup pot on the stove. When she finally looked up from her pot, showed us her round-moon face, Kris and I both tripped on our breath at her radiance.

Alma was once known as Lady that Searches for Rocks with Holes in Them, but, to her delight, Pretty Shield changed her name, when Alma was only eight, to "Well-Known Woman," a name she clearly has lived up to.

The Juneberry, a native of the Northern Great Plains, also answers to many names, including saskatoon or Rocky Mountain blueberry.

Alma explained that her great ancestors didn't eat pie, in the tra-

*"We all need one another to get along
and survive in the universe."*

ditional sense, but they did eat pie filling. After a day spent hunting
and foraging in the aspens, they would gather around the fire to eat
and tell stories.

First, they'd pass the smoke pipe around, she said. And then
they'd pass around the cooked Juneberries, which they'd eat with a
round piece of push bread made with turnip or cattail flour.

Eventually, the push bread evolved into pie crust.

She lay her disk of dough on the counter and, with a smallish
rolling pin, began to stroke it with slow, gentle, deliberate move-
ments. She raised the pin after each stroke, and, after two strokes,
she'd lift the disk and give it a quarter spin. Gentle. Always gentle.

She lay the crust in her pie pan as though it were a shroud, and
filled the shell with the purple berries, one spoonful at a time.

Then, in the same way she had turned her dough, Alma turned the conversation onto something else, something bigger than berries and pie.

She told us about the birds that come into her yard each morning, which she quietly observes from her window.

"Some of the birds have red spots and some of them have yellow spots," she said, speaking slowly. "Some have white spots. I watch them, these birds with different colored spots, gather in the morning and talk together. I watch them communicate. And, after a while, they stop talking and each group goes its separate way."

Then she stopped and looked at us both with those pools of wisdom that passed for her eyes.

"Nature is trying to tell us something, don't you think?"

She moved in closer and her words began to take flight.

"The white people, like you, they are the people of the sky," she said, raising her hands into the air. "They are the stars in the universe, they are the light and are always reaching for the light. The red people, the Indians, like me, they are the people of the earth. They draw from the earth for their medicine. If a red person has a bellyache, she lays down, presses her body against the earth."

She pressed her hand against my belly.

"The yellow people, Asians, they are quiet and powerful, like the wind in the air. They are like a whisper. They make things *bend*. The black people are fiery and magnificent like the jewels and minerals that live beneath the earth. They entertain us with their fire and their beauty.

"We all need one another to get along and to survive in the universe," she said, shrugging her broad shoulders slightly.

Bill, her husband, walked into the kitchen. With his shock of white hair set against deep eyes of coal, he looked like a winter white rabbit. He smiled. How many times had he watched strangers get drunk on his wife's words?

Instead of a recipe, Alma gave us a copy of her autobiography, *Grandmother's Grandchild, My Crow Indian Life*. She signed mine thus:

"May the great spirit lead you in paths of love wherever you may go."

It was 11 P.M. by the time we got to Billings, and we still had an hour's drive to get to Doug and Susann's Sky Ranch. We offered to take a hotel in Billings, but they insisted we drive up anyway; the buffalo steaks were ready to toss on the grill.

"Betty's feeling a little sluggish in this mountain air, but we'll get there as fast as we can."

"Who's Betty?" asked Susann. "Should we put another steak on for her?"

We laughed and set her straight.

We ate our steaks and salad at midnight on their deck, and it was 3 A.M. before I finally hit the pillow in a loft with windows to the stars.

While helping Susann feed their infant twins the next morning, I mentioned that I had a tip on a bear trapper in Choteau who baked pie, but I also hoped to find a true horseman to point me toward some good Montana pie.

One of their neighbors on the pass just happened to be a horse whisperer (though he dislikes that term). "I'm not sure how Bill Devine feels about pie," Susann said, "but he's amazing with colts."

In Montana lore, horse charmers, men who could cajole wild horses into submission, were once considered charlatans. Skeptics believed the root of the asafetida herb—not personal magnetism—was the horse charmer's secret weapon. Charmers allegedly rubbed the dried root powder all over their clothes to render horses docile as dormice.

It took about five minutes around Bill to find out that he smelled of clean cotton and soft leather, *not* asafetida, and there was nothing crooked about him, except the way he walked—with a tilt—from a riding accident that left him partially paralyzed.

A shy sort, Bill was happy to talk to me about pie, so long as we could talk while he worked. He was busy "breaking" three colts for a local rancher. Only three days earlier the horses, about three years old, were running wild on the range. "Breaking" is an ill-fitting term to describe the method Bill used to get the horses to respond to him. Everything about his manner was gentle, soft, and subtle, like Alma with her dough.

"Horses aren't mean by nature," he explained as he stood in the center of the pen. "Horses have always seen us as predators, and they've survived all these years by being hypervigilant." He had tied a rope around the colt and, as he spoke, he moved around the ring, trying to get the scared and confused horse to face him from every angle. The horse's inclination was to turn away, show Bill his hind-quarters, but Bill kept asking for the face.

"That's 'a give,' " he'd say every time the horse would turn a quarter step in his direction. "If you get angry with a horse, you've lost its trust. Then you become part of the problem."

Devine knows about losing trust. After returning from Vietnam, he said, he felt the nation had turned its hindquarters on him. He formed a veterans' group where other men could gather in confidence and talk about how the war and the country had played tricks on them. It was about that time that he decided to get back into riding horses. He'd heard about the horseman Ray Hunt who had a uniquely humane and caring way of training horses. After studying Hunt's technique, he started breaking colts professionally himself.

One day in 1986, a wily horse he was breaking on Crazy Mountain got spooked and bucked him. Bill landed on the corral floor with a broken neck. It was months before he could move, let alone walk again. For a long time, Bill wore a metal contraption that circled his head and was held up by four rods bolted to his skull. One morning, he was at a local coffee shop when Rachella, a petite red-headed woman, approached him on the line and asked him about his "halo." They've been together ever since.

Although doctors told him he could never mount a horse again, Bill has found an ingenious way to get back in the saddle. He shimmies himself up against the inside railing of the ring and has trained his beloved palomino, Sweetheart, to press herself against his legs, so that all he has to do is fall back into the seat.

And if Bill can do that, anyone can make a crust.

I asked Bill if there was any connection between making pie and breaking horses. "Only that when Rachella makes me a pie, my ears twitch," Bill said, and his belly shook with laughter.

Actually, there are a lot of similarities, I realized as we drove across the vast Montana prairie to meet Dave, the bear trapper. The goal, Bill says, is to be "so present" with your horse, that eventually there is no separation between the two of you. "What happens then," says Bill, "transcends the physical senses and evolves into a higher, spiritual union with the horse."

I remembered what Ty had said that November morning I watched him make pie in his Lucky Brand pajamas in my apartment in New York.

"You have to watch your dough, feel it, read it with all your senses," he'd said. "You have to become one with your dough."

Our talk with Dave lasted well into the night. Like Bill, Dave had turned to animals at his most vulnerable and reaped the benefits of this union on a daily basis. The matchmaker in me couldn't help thinking there was a Rachella out there for Dave, too. And I hoped she would spot his halo soon.

On Sunday morning, we headed north, toward Glacier National Park, to find some huckleberry pie. Dave had mentioned a town called Hungry Horse, near the West Glacier entrance, where we were sure to find huckleberry pie at a restaurant called the Huckleberry Patch.

The drive up was stunning. Purple and yellow wildflowers rustled to either side of us and the sky was so generous, I felt I could never repay it.

As we approached Glacier National Park, we started noticing roadside shacks selling buffalo and venison jerky and fresh huckleberries. We went straight to the Huckleberry Patch and Gift Shop. Oh, they had pie all right: served à la mode with a crass scoop of commercialism. It's one of the things I hate most about this country, this knee-jerk tendency to take something precious and market the hell out of it so that it loses all its preciousness in the process. The Huckleberry Patch sold *everything* huckleberry from T-shirts to key chains to baseball caps and coffee mugs. This was *not* the huckleberry experience we were hoping for, so we turned on our heels and walked directly across the street, where a flimsy wooden shack on the side of the road advertised fresh huckleberries—just picked.

Henry David Thoreau once said that only the grizzly and the hunter ever get to truly taste a huckleberry, because a huckleberry loses its intensity of flavor the moment it leaves the woods. Clearly, Thoreau had never met Marc, an aging French hippie and huckleberry-picker in hot pants.

Marc, who wore a long gray beard, a black beret, and itsy-bitsy denim shorts, had spent years working in restaurants in Los Angeles before moving to Montana for a change of pace.

We asked him if there was any particular art to picking huckleberries, which were going for $10 a pound.

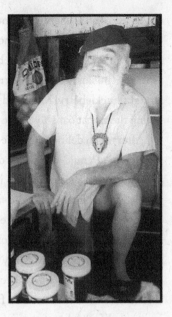

"The only secret," he said, "is that once you find a patch, you cannot tell a soul." Marc said that, shortly after moving to West Glacier, he'd been lucky enough to stumble on a glorious 50-yard patch at about 4,500 feet elevation. Every summer he held his breath when he returned and "so far," he said, knocking on the wooden beam of his shack, "no one else has discovered it."

Not even the bears? Marc, who wore a lion's-head necklace, said the bears were the least of his concern. Much more worrisome were the greedy pickers who came from nearby Idaho and Wyoming armed with tennis racket–like contraptions to beat the hucks out of the bush.

Being French, Marc did not make pie with his huckleberries. He prefered to soak them in lemon juice, sugar, and brandy. Nor did he feel qualified to send us anywhere local for pie.

"*Je ne mange pas de pie [I do not eat pie],*" he said, shrugging his shoulders, as though it should be obvious to me and . . . didn't I feel a bit like a traitor?

"But I do know that a lot of the locals like the Spruce Park Diner in nearby Coram and I've heard them mention how good the pie is there. *Bonne chance!*"

We had to double back to find the Spruce Park Diner, which was tucked behind an Esso gas station. The proximity to the gas pumps made me a little skeptical about finding homemade pie there. We ordered some huckleberry lemonade and then wandered over to the pie case to examine the goods: huckleberry peach, huckleberry marionberry, huckleberry raspberry, and for hard-core huck lovers—straight huckleberry. Most had lattice crusts, only four strips across, giving them that oafishly rustic look.

After much deliberation, we decided to split a slice of huckleberry peach, and I could not think of a happier combination. The firm, just-ripe peach slices stood up in texture and flavor to the wild-and-woolly huckleberries. And the sure, flaked crust was bold and buttery without being bossy. We clinked our lemonade glasses. "Here's to a Frenchman pointing us to one of the best pies in America," Kris said.

The café belonged to Mary Lou Covey and Laura Hansen, two women in their 40s, who'd been friends for twenty-five years, ever since Laura drove to Montana from Illinois in a '66 Dodge van seeking a new life. "A lot of men in suits tried to talk us out of going into business together," said Laura, a former mail carrier. "They said we'd ruin our friendship and lose a lot of money."

But ten years later, their business and their friendship were as solid as ever. She credited the pies, which had the locals talking from the get-go.

And, one local in particular, had a large audience.

George Ostrom, a local radio personality and a member of a seniors' hiking club called the Over the Hill Gang, discovered the pies at Spruce Park one afternoon after a long hike in Glacier. After that, the elderly hikers made it a habit of stopping in for pie after their weekly hikes. George would always wax lyrical about the slice he'd had—and later dreamed about—the next day on the radio.

"Pie has talking powers," said Laura. "It speaks to people in the middle of the night.

"People tell me they wake up in the middle of the night in their campgrounds thinking about pie."

One gentleman came in every single day for a slice of pie and he accused Laura of being a "temptress." Another regular was convinced that the secret to Laura's flaky crust was bear fat. (Laura thought that particularly funny, because she uses the very tame crust recipe that is the back of the Crisco can).

The divorced mother of two said she hadn't gotten any marriage proposals—yet—but a handsome Italian man was so taken by her huckleberry pies that he asked her to come to Italy and bake for him. She was considering it. If only we could roll back the tape and give Luciana a taste of Laura's pie instead of the disastrous Wall Drugs apple, I told Kris.

Bringing so much joy to people on a daily basis made it hard for Laura to imagine doing anything else for a living. Two years ago, when she was diagnosed with multiple sclerosis, she worried she might have to, particularly since the pain from the disease had, curiously, lodged itself in her hands. Oddly enough, she said, the pain went away whenever she was making pies.

"There are mornings when I wake up in so much pain, I think, there's no way I'll be able to use my fingers today. Then I'll get my hands on a rolling pin and the pain will disappear."

When people tell her they could never roll out a pie crust, she says "hooey." "I've made a thousand pies in the last three months, in this tiny hallway of a kitchen," she said. "I just made fifteen this morning.

"You try it. Be FEARLESS. It won't be such a mystery after you've done it a couple of times."

She admitted she was lucky to have a Polish grandmother who baked and got her "over the fear of the rolling pin at a very young age." Although they made apricot klatchkes, *not* pie, Laura had her own mini–rolling pin and got used to having her fingers in dough, and flour on her cheeks.

Laura took photographs as a hobby and she was considering

entering a National Geographic photo competition calling for photos of subjects that were uniquely American.

"I've been thinking about this for a while now," she said. "And I really want to photograph a slice of huckleberry pie."

We bought one whole huckleberry peach pie for Doug and Susann, who, once again, were waiting up for us. At least this time, we were armed with pie—possibly the best on the entire trip.

We got to the bottom of Elk Ridge road, a winding dirt-and-gravel stretch that climbed straight up almost one vertical mile to their ranch, around 11 P.M. Two big brown bears appeared in our headlights about 100 feet ahead of us. We both screamed.

"Are the doors locked?" Kris asked.

We did, after all, have a huckleberry pie in the car.

For reasons I can't explain, I developed a completely irrational fear of bears when I hit thirty. When my parents used to take us camping in Yosemite, bears ran rampant through the campgrounds at night. They'd poke their big heads inside the old aluminum trash cans that are no longer allowed under the bear management program, and, inevitably, their heads would get stuck and they'd stand on their hind legs and shake their heads until the can popped loose and went rattling down the road. We'd peel back the tent flap and watch, more excited than afraid. Now, the idea of being this close to a bear made me limp with fear.

We stayed in stare-down mode for a good ten minutes.

"Just be fearless," I said, repeating Laura's mantra for crust, as I drove toward the bears. They lumbered out of our way.

Inside, by a crackling fire, Doug poured us a much-needed bourbon, and we dug into the unharmed pie. We told them about how good Montana, the Treasure State, had been to us.

Then, not too loud, because the twins were asleep, Doug broke out into a jazzy rendition of "If I knew you were coming I'd have baked you a PIE."

"Well, it sure seems like you've got a pie angel pointing you on your path," Susann told me after she'd walked me to the room with the stars.

An angel. A reliable gut.

And lots of fancy footwork—courtesy, I'm sure, of Mr. Poulet's rabbits.

LAURA HANSEN'S RUSTIC HUCKLEBERRY PEACH PIE

use a deep, 9-inch pie pan

CRUST

1 9-inch double-crust:
(Laura uses the recipe on the back of the Crisco can)

FILLING

3 cups of huckleberries (fresh or frozen)
2 cups of peaches, sliced and peeled (fresh or frozen)
1 cup sugar
3 tablespoons of tapioca

Pick your huckleberries clean of stems and leaves. If you plan on freezing them, do not wash them as they will release too much juice when they cook.

In your favorite mixing bowl, gently toss huckleberries, peaches, and sugar together. Add tapioca, mix well but gently. Score bottom crust with a fork.

Pour fruit mixture in your deep-dish pie tin lined with your favorite crust recipe.

Cut the remaining dough into four wide bands, interlay them on top of the pie to create a weave effect. Sprinkle top with 1 tablespoon of sugar.

Bake at 350 degrees for 75 to 90 minutes. Top crust should be golden brown.

Eat with your best friend.

roadkill

"Words are holy. Treat them with respect, there's power there."
—PRETTY SHIELD MEDICINE WOMAN

In my fifteen years as a journalist, I've interviewed hundreds of people, from child molesters to government spies to truffle hunters and high-ranking politicians.

But Pat Dahl—beauty queen turned naturalist—will always stand out from the pack.

Pat Dahl lived for roadkill.

From the basement of the Museum of Natural History in San Diego's Balboa Park, Dahl ran the "stuffed-animal lending library," a place where teachers in search of wildlife teaching tools could borrow a stuffed fox, hawk, or raccoon for their classroom.

A flattened-out badger on the side of the road wasn't merely roadkill to Dahl. It had the potential of becoming one inner-city child's pivotal first encounter with wildlife.

So, whenever she drove around her rural Poway neighborhood,

she'd be on the lookout for dead animals on the road. A leggy doe-eyed blonde right out of Raymond Chandler's imagination, Dahl would slam on the brakes for a fur flat that wasn't too mangled. Using a shovel, she'd scoop up it into the necropsy bags she always kept in her trunk, then give the animal a mortician's makeover.

Pat Dahl would have had a field day on this trip, though we probably wouldn't have made it far.

Like pie—yes, there is a connection—roadkill changes from state to state.

The brittle roads of Texas are paved with dead armadillos. There is nothing quite so peaceful as a dead armadillo, flat on its armored back, tender yellow legs sticking straight up, candles in a birthday cake. Near Roswell, New Mexico, we saw lots of dead cows—more on these later. Michigan was riddled with rigor-mortis raccoons. Once, we came upon an entire family of them—a mother and her five pups in tow—still in a row, dead on the road. The Montana River Valley gave us more dead rabbits than *Watership Down*.

One piece of New York roadkill really threw us for a loop. We had just stopped to rescue the turtle parked in the middle of the road and were feeling righteous, when we saw a bloody red mess splayed across the yellow line just ahead. I winced and looked away and let Kris ID the poor critter.

"Eeeewwwww! Pepperoni pie."

I systematically recoiled at roadkill. Kris whipped her head around to get a better look. "Visualization helps me process," she said after I caught her staring.

"Visualization makes me gag."

As the trip progressed, Kris became more and more obsessed with roadkill. The attraction was philosophical, not grisly.

"I just don't understand," she'd say each time we passed a bloodied fur flat, countless times a day. "Why do they cross the road? They see cars coming. Why do they cross anyway? Why?"

This rhetorical line of questioning would go on for about ten minutes. At first, I thought it was sweet, how Kris failed to recognize the distinction between the peanut-sized brain of a roving raccoon and that of, say, a thirtysomething college-educated woman. But after a few weeks, it became as annoying as her tirades about the "ego-driven, shallow, soulless" world of advertising from which she couldn't tear herself away.

Of course, *she* had to listen to my endless questions about Ty.

"He's such a good listener, he's so communicative, so supportive . . . but why couldn't he have a job with benefits? A five-year plan? A matching pair of socks?"

Everything came to a head on our way to pick up Teri in New Mexico. In the late afternoon, when we came upon a freshly killed doe. She lay on her side, and her graceful legs were stacked, front and back, one on top of the other, hooves touching. Five chicken hawks were lining up for happy hour.

This one really set Kris off.

"WHY DID SHE CROSS? IT'S SO DANGEROUS! WHY DO THEY KEEP GOING BACK?!?!? WHY?"

"Maybe all these animals are wondering the exact same thing about you," I said. "Why do *you* keep going back—to advertising?"

Kris was silent for a good 10 miles.

"No," she finally said, staring dead ahead. "They're too busy wondering why you're always searching for something better around the next bend."

She switched on the radio, and it was my turn to say nothing.

a slice of heaven

humble pie: 1. *a popular 17th-century English dish for servants in which deer innards (heart, liver, kidney) were mixed with apples, sugar, and currants. While the rich dined on succulent venison, the servants ate "humble" pie. 2. to eat humble pie is to take back one's words or deeds.*

I'm not a bumper sticker kind of gal. Never have liked those narrow strips of vehicular vanity and have always found a voting booth a more effective place to make a political statement than a car bumper.

Though essential, the "IBRK4PIE" vanity plate was embarrassing enough. Now, Betty Blue also sports a bright purple bumper sticker in her rear window that reads: "Pie Town, New Mexico, *A Little Slice of Heaven.*"

I smile every time I see it.

They call New Mexico the "Land of Enchantment," and, having been bewitched by tiny Pie Town (pop. 70 or so), I see why. "Town" is a generous term for the funky cluster of run-down houses and trailers, two churches, seven sleeping dogs, and post office that make up Pie Town, located along a tumbleweed, rolling-pin stretch of US 60.

You'd think a place named Pie Town would be famous. But I never heard of it until the tip of my finger landed on it while skating across the map of New Mexico. Was this a joke? Had someone rigged my atlas? There it was, in legitimate type, and in sprawling Catron County, quite possibly "pie Mecca" at 8,000 feet above sea level. Nestled between the Gallo (rooster) and Gallina (hen) Mountains, it appeared within spitting distance of the Continental Divide, although hard to tell on which side.

I drew a fat pie dot on Pie Town with a straight line above it, so that it looked like an exclamation point.

In the early 1920s, Pie Town was known simply as "Norman's Place"—after Clyde Norman who had filed a 40-acre gold-and-silver mining claim there. But the mining venture turned out to be a bust, and Clyde went broke. Since US 60 was a coast-to-coast road, and America was discovering road tripping, Clyde opened up a gas station. For extra flourish and cash, he started selling fresh-baked pies and doughnuts he bought from a small baker in Datil, a few miles east. When the baker found out he was selling *her* pies for profit, she nearly clocked him with her rolling pin and told him to bake his own. And so he did, using dried fruit for filling, as well as pinto beans—the only sustainable crop in this parched part of the country. Turned out, Clyde had a real knack for pie. His pies were so delicious, everyone started calling the pit stop on US 60 "Pie Town." Eventually, the gas station became a pie shop and, together, they became a town and a natural place for homesteaders to end up.

The history of Pie Town had been relatively easy to pin down, but it was much harder to find anything current about the place, and I was a little worried about what we might find, or not find, there.

Teri, who was going to be relieving Kris through Texas and Louisiana, was curious about Pie Town, so she flew into Albuquerque a couple of days early. Kris and Teri would "overlap" in New Mexico and Texas, at which point Kris would fly back home and Teri and I would carry on to Louisiana together.

I took it for granted that Kris and Teri would get along, although, looking back, it was probably foolish to introduce two of my girlfriends this way, confining them to a station wagon for three days in a 100-plus-degree heat. Things had been a little tense since our road-kill spat, and I, for one, was grateful for the infusion of new energy.

Teri's camera was rolling the moment we pulled up outside baggage claim—late, of course. She panned from the rolling pin and license plate straight to the tarp and table on the luggage rack.

"Oh, my God! What on earth is that?"

We stopped for gas near the airport, and the guy waiting for the pump across the island noticed my "IBRK4PIE" license plate and the bug-covered rolling pin on my grille. "Going to Pie Town?" he asked. He was a reporter for the Associated Press, based in Albuquerque, and had once, years before, written a feature article on Pie Town.

"There isn't much left in Pie Town," he went on to say. "Not much at all."

"But there is *pie*, right?" I asked.

The man winced. "There *used* to be a café in town, but I think that shut down years ago."

Teri refused to believe such a thing.

"Oh, come on. If you can't find pie in Pie Town, just where are you going to find it?"

We pulled onto I-25 toward Socorro, after which the more intimate two-lane new US 60 would carry us through Catron County, the largest county in New Mexico and one where the elk population easily outnumbers humans.

"I promise not to read all the road signs aloud, like my mother used to do," Teri announced, and then she demonstrated by reading every billboard in sight: "Tom's Taxidermy . . . The Owl Bar . . . Brownbilt's Western Wear . . ."

In Socorro, we stopped for lunch at a *taqueria* where, predictably, there was *no* pie but where we enjoyed some spicy, soft chicken tacos with fresh tomato-and-chipotle salsa.

Teri looked at her watch, and in her lovable, uniquely dramatic style said:

"I've been on this trip for two hours now and I haven't had a slice of *pie* yet. What kind of *pie* trip is this?"

Was this the same person who had made me promise she would not gain an ounce on this trip, scheduled three weeks before her wedding?

Truth be told, the gold shantung-silk wedding dress—with its empire waist—was relatively forgiving. Teri was more concerned about maintaining a tortilla-flat tummy for the clingy, garnet, beaded number she planned to wear at her twentieth high school reunion in New York, where she was headed directly after her stint on America's pieways.

When we returned to the car, she pulled the skimpy number out of her suitcase and held it out in front of her to show us. Two cowboys walking by whistled. Kris and I hadn't seen a steamed or fresh vegetable in weeks. We traded a knowing glance and said nothing.

Once we hit the open range on US 60, Teri hung out of the passenger seat and gasped in amazement at everything she saw. Even mole hills. For the past two years, she'd been commuting from her job in Santa Ana to the UCLA campus in West Los Angeles along the dreaded I-5 corridor. Scenic it's not. Comparatively, I guess even New Mexico roadkill had its cachet.

"Who lives out here? I would love to live right in that house," she said, pointing to a bone-bare adobe dwelling complete with rusty, red, crinkled Ford pickup out back. Teri's unbridled appreciation for everything from vultures to barbed wire made me realize how road-jaded I'd become. Those long stretches through South Dakota had numbed me, and I was grateful for the wake-up call. I love the mountain roads but the bareback desert did have a haunting beauty I could learn to appreciate.

As we drove west in the hot afternoon, Teri regaled us with stories from the outside world. Kris and I hadn't read a serious newspaper since we'd left New York, and, although it was liberating, we did feel out of touch. Was it true that Meg Ryan and Dennis Quaid had called it quits?

Teri had worked quite late on a story the night before, trying to track down the mystery man from Microsoft who had given a $20,000 tip to a limousine driver for driving him from Disneyland, in Anaheim, California, to Seattle in one straight shot.

"I bet the guy would have thrown in an extra ten grand if the chauffeur had stopped in Pescadero for some olallieberry pie," I said.

"God, that was good pie," Kris agreed. We seemed to be back on track.

We stopped to stretch our legs in tiny Magdalena, not far from the Navajo Indian Reservation, and about 60 miles east of Pie Town. An eclectic used-book store caught Teri's eye. A power outage had forced her to pack in the dark, and she'd left the book she meant to read at home. We knew she would have no time to read on this peripatetic journey, but we pulled over nonetheless.

The book selection was decidedly unfrontier-like: Simone de Beauvoir's *Second Sex,* Ayn Rand, and Oscar Wilde. The owner was a recent transplant from Algoma, Wisconsin, where, he said, "I never really fit in."

I thought of Lisa, our Wisconsin rolling-pin collector who always felt like "the turd in the punchbowl."

He was an avid appreciator of pie, but diabetes had forced him to edit pie from his life completely. This was particularly hard for him, since he'd been raised on a dairy farm, where he had churned his own butter for pie crust. A graphic artist by training, he said his absolute favorite illustration was J. C. Leyendecker's portrait of a mother holding an unbaked pie out in front of her, using a paring knife to trim the overlapping edges of dough.

"The dough is just coming down in curls, like an apple peel, and there's a little boy standing by her side, watching the crust come tumbling down," he said. "I always thought that little boy was me."

Life seemed pretty unfair at that moment, I thought.

To avoid temptation, he had never gone to Pie Town. But he thought there was a café in town that still served pie. He wasn't sure.

I was getting nervous that Pie Town would turn out to be a complete bust. But it was hard not to be hopeful here in the heart of Catron County, with piñon and juniper trees rising from the brush, in the shadow of mountains the color of eggplant. The juniper made us think of gin, which made us long for a gin-and-tonic.

We passed through tiny Datil, "date" in Spanish, so named by the first Spanish settlers who mistook the dark seedpods of the native yucca plant for dates. Talk of Spanish settlers led right into a graphic discussion about Antonio Banderas (Kris had just had a vivid dream about him) and what his wife, Melanie Griffith, had done to her lips to make them stick out like a grouper's. This was clearly a bonding moment for Kris and Teri, and one so riveting that I actually missed the sign for Pie Town.

In fact, we almost missed Pie Town altogether. Easy to do.

The only evidence of a "town" on the highway are the adobe Pie Town post office, with its apricot window frames and hand-painted sign, and a phantom gas station. The residences are all clustered together, east of the highway, along the original Route 60, which branches off from its replacement in a spit of gravel and dust.

The town was perfectly still, save for a light breeze that made the sage brush shiver. I slowed down to a crawl and wanted to roll down my window and shout: "Anybody home?"

Then I noticed a woman pedaling jauntily on a rusty bike toward the residential part of town. She had long brown hair and wore a sage-green summer dress splashed with a field of daisies. I thought of the bicycle scene in *Butch Cassidy and the Sundance Kid*.

"Excuse me, do you know where a person could find some pie in this town?" I cried out through the open window, dust filling the car.

The woman turned around and caught a glimpse of Betty Blue's license plate. She pedaled toward us, then stopped and straddled the bike inches away from my door.

"Aloha!" she said, leaning into the car and flirting with Teri's camera—rolling, of course, and pointed right at her. "Welcome to paradise. Welcome to the Pacific side of the Divide."

Well, that answered one of my questions about Pie Town. This woman looked so deliriously happy, I thought at first that she'd dipped into some peyote. But, by the end of our afternoon in Pie Town, it was clear that Nita, a Southern California transplant, was simply high on small-town life in high ranch country.

"I make pies for the café over there," she said, pointing to the Pie-O-Neer Café, right across the highway, which all three of us had somehow missed. "I'll take you there. Follow me!"

She pedaled across the highway to the Pie-O-Neer, where she propped her bike across the porch and burst through the café screen door like a kid with a great report card. "Kathy, we've got some visitors looking for pie. You gotta check out their license plate!" The three of us hung back on the wide-open porch, under a string of red chile pepper lights, to read the sign by the door.

> Due to the stragetic [sic.] location of our town, folks have always found it a pleasant place to stop, rest and—refresh. The first merchant in town had such a demand for some home-made pies and they were of such quality that they became justly famous . . . Local folks as well as travelers began to refer to the community as "Pie Town."

Kathy, the owner, stepped out of the kitchen, wiping her hands on her apron. She had been cooking pinto beans for the next day's blue-plate special, green chile burgers, and was flushed.

Before I had a chance to tell them about my quest, Nita had already slapped on the counter two large pieces of pie with three forks. One was an apricot cream pie made with sweet, fleshy apricots from a neighbor's tree and a basic cream filling Kathy's grandmother, Rosie, liked to use as a pie base. The glazed apricots formed a circle slightly smaller than the actual pie shell, revealing a yellow-white custardy cream filling so that it looked like a large egg fried sunny side up. The oatmeal date pie made no bones about being a cookie parading as a pie. They were both delicious.

While we dug our forks into our two pies at the counter, the two women shared a little Pie Town and personal history. Clyde's pies may have given the town its name, they said, but it was Russell Lee who put Pie Town on the map in the 1940s. Lee was a photographer for the Farm Security Administration, who had been sent out west to document social problems as a way to bolster support for federal assistance programs.

Drawn by its name, he landed in Pie Town, where he found two hundred homesteading families. Each had been given a second chance—320 acres to plant and build a home on.

"Pie Town was a real boomtown back then," said Nita, "nothing like it is now."

Nita was born in Hawaii but raised in Malibu, and moved here more than twenty years ago, when her husband got a job fighting fires for the Bureau of Land Management. She had vowed to herself that she would raise her children in a town that was "at least 100 miles away from a McDonald's" and fell in love with Pie Town the moment she set her sandaled foot here.

"It's on the same latitude as Malibu, but it's worlds away," she said. Her children have names like Prairie and Autumn, and they also work in the café when they aren't going to school—a 22-mile bus ride. They are beautiful in an earthy, golden, wheat-stalk kind of way. They radiate health, which is a very good thing since there is no doctor in Pie Town, only one who passes through Quemado, 20 miles west on US 60, once a month.

Nita told us her Malibu mother can't understand why her daughter has chosen such a tumbleweed life for herself. Her husband didn't like the isolation either. "He lives out in the valley now," she said.

Kathy has lived in Pie Town for only four years. She was enjoying a successful career in advertising, in Dallas, when she and her then-husband, Thomas Hripko, a radio producer and songwriter, came to Pie Town on a road trip vacation in 1995, intrigued, like us, by the name. When they arrived, the café had closed down and so there was no pie to be had. (The owner of the long-running café had broken both legs in a car accident and never fully recovered.)

The letdown moved the songwriter to write the following ballad, which I pop into my tape player most mornings these days when I sit down to write:

Wild west is on its last ride
Sun is sinking fast in the frontier sky

Town of sixty people gives you no good reason to stay
No city lights, no shopping malls, all the young kids moved away.
Navajo Motor Lodge is closed down
And there's no more pie in Pie Town

Boys took jobs working with the highway crew
To help put in a freeway bypass town and wreck the view
Girls are changing sheets and scrubbing toilets as motel maids
At the brand new Best Western down by the Interstate.

Town of sixty people gives you no good reason to stay
No city lights, no shopping malls, all the young kids moved away.
Navajo Motor Lodge is closed down
And there's no more pie in Pie Town
No more pie in Pie Town

A year later, Kathy and her husband decided to remedy the situation by buying the café themselves. Kathy's mother, a gifted pie baker, came out from California to help run the place and teach her daughter how to roll out a dough. "I was a complete novice," says Kathy. "It had never even occurred to me to make a pie."

At first, they made all their pies with lard, but since they cater to so many health-conscious hikers and cyclists in the area, they quickly switched to a butter-flavored shortening crust. The business was just starting to take off when Kathy's mother had to return to sea level because of her emphysema. That's when Kathy tapped Nita to help with the pies. They meshed instantly.

"Hey, Kathy, show them our 'special' pie," Nita said, grinning.

Kathy returned moments later with a fossilized piece of peach pie à la mode on a glass plate. She held it upside down but the pie didn't budge.

"We found this in the café one day after it had been sitting for a week on a shelf," said Nita. "It's part of our café art." (Nita presses dried flowers under glass when she isn't making pie.)

Most afternoons, after baking, the two women sit on the porch with Sadie, Kathy's missile-shaped mutt with one black eye, and a shaggy cat, and watch the world go by on US 60.

"We peel apples, dream up pie recipes, watch for rainbows and lightning, and try to solve the world's problems," said Kathy. "On really dark nights, we sit out here and watch for star shadows. It's like living in a postcard."

The women liked to talk about the interesting people who dropped by the café, "everyone on their way to somewhere else."

They all came for a slice of pie and for some reassurance that you could still find pie in Pie Town. And they all left crumbs of their far-flung lives behind. "It's a lot of pressure," said Kathy. "We want every pie to be perfect because some people have made a very long journey to have pie here."

Having experienced Pie Town without pie, Kathy explained, she made sure everyone who passed through got a slice.

"We're closed on Sundays, but I'll always open the door if all you want is a slice of pie," she said. A tattered, dog-eared spiral-bound notebook was filled with comments from such visitors—Divide hikers, European road trippers, elk hunters, snowbirds, and other back-road travelers trying to make sense of America.

"Good conversation, beautiful women, and great-tasting pie," wrote one visitor. "Don't tell my mother, but your pie is better!" wrote another.

Kathy practically lives at the café, which doubles as mercantile, community center, and yoga studio. She and her husband have separated, and he remained in Dallas. "We've stayed very close friends, and we're both happy that the other is finally doing exactly what fulfills them," she said.

"I used to make a six-figure salary and take business calls from my swimming pool," Kathy said. "I got a real dose of humble pie when I moved here. A real big dose."

She said she'd blossomed since she shed her fast-paced lifestyle and moved to the high desert. Her cheeks had a creamy apricot glow that you wouldn't find at any counter at Bendel's.

"There's something very gratifying about being out here in the middle of nowhere making pie," she said. "You can have a personal problem weighing on your mind, and you can go in and make a pie, and by the time it's done, you don't even know what was bugging you because you've just finished a labor of love.

"And when you bring people a slice and they tell you it reminds them of home, what could be more gratifying than that?"

The banana cream pie was the only whole pie left in the display case, so Kathy brought it out onto the porch for Kris to take a picture of it in the desert light. We turned our backs for a minute, to watch a house rumble across a highway on a trailer bed. "Someone's going out west to start a new life," Kathy said. And that moment of distraction was all it took for the long-haired cat to dive whiskers-first into the pie's cream topping. Sadie followed suit. In a previous life, Kathy might have reacted. But here, in Pie Town, her laughter ricocheted off the canyon walls.

It isn't all rosy, of course. July brings monsoon rains, you can't order moo shu chicken in the middle of the night, and everybody knows everybody else's business, thoughts, even. And, added Nita, it can be hell cashing checks when your address is Pie Town, USA. "No one believes you when you tell them where you live!"

A thin stream of locals trickled through the café while we visited. A wickedly handsome rancher named Ace tipped his baseball cap and smiled at our quest. "My favorite's coconut cream," he said before climbing back in his truck. Kris was ready to climb in after him. "Every woman in town is in love with him," Kathy said, "but he's a Mormon."

Mary, a rancher, who came to help with the pies occasionally when she wasn't branding cattle, dropped by to visit awhile as did Pop McKee. McKee had lived in this part of the world since 1937, when his father, Roy, drove his family here by tractor from west Texas, after dust and sandstorms pitted their farmland. With his sea-foam beard so long it almost touched his chest, and the two-inch raised vein shaped like an anvil on his right temple, he looked like a character the Joads might have encountered on their journey west.

It was Pop who had brought the apricots from his garden for the pie we'd just tasted. Pop invited us to drop by his house before leaving town. Nita and Kathy encouraged us to take him up on this offer because Pop rarely invited anyone to his home, and, said Nita, "it's something to see."

Kathy gave me her two recipes and the purple bumper sticker, which I ceremoniously applied to Betty Blue's backside while the girls gathered around and belted out a chorus of "Bye, Bye, Miss American Pie." We all hugged, promising to stay in touch.

Pop's front yard was straight out of *Alice in Wonderland*. A bare tree was strewn with cobalt-blue bottles hanging from its branches. Old pie tins were tied to the tall wooden fence, flapping in the wind.

"They got old," Pop said, "so we gave them a new life."

He took us inside the house to show us all the furniture he'd made by hand. As he pointed to each object, I noticed how large his hands were. One hand, fingers outstretched, could easily fill a nine-inch pie pan.

He was particularly proud of his collection of Vicks Vapo-Rub bottles that lined an entire shelf in his kitchen, which reeked of Spicy Taco Mix, and of a rolling pin he'd carved displayed above the kitchen window.

Pop announced that he wanted to give me a present. He disappeared in his shed and came back with a single four-pointed deer antler that had been blasted white by sun and age. If you held it a certain way, point tips up, it actually looked like a cupped hand with fingers outstretched, a hand only slightly bigger than Pop's.

"Where's the other one, Pop?" Teri asked. "You can't have just one antler!"

It was an odd gift, to be sure. I wondered how de Tocqueville reacted when the chief of the Saulter Indian tribe on Lake Superior plucked one of two sacred feathers he wore on his head—as proof that he'd killed a Sioux—and handed it to the Frenchman.

I'm not an advocate of hunting, and if you'd told me a year ago that I'd some day grace my living room with a deer antler, I would have laughed.

But perspectives change out on the open road. Things aren't always what they seem. Sometimes the seedpod from a yucca plant looks like a date.

Sometimes the middle of nowhere feels like the center of the universe.

Sometimes a deer antler is a perfect place to rest a stereo speaker.

KATHY'S APRICOT CREAM PIE
FROM THE PIE-O-NEER CAFE

PIE-O-NEER PIE CRUST

(Makes 5 bottom crusts; the gals at the Pie-O-Neer like to make dough in advance because, they say, it's much easier to work with once it's been frozen!)

5 cups flour

2 cups shortening (Kathy and Nita use butter-flavored Crisco)

2 teaspoons salt

½ teaspoon baking powder

1 egg

1 teaspoon vinegar

1 cup cold water (roughly)

In large bowl, sift together flour, baking powder, and salt. Cut in shortening until mixture resembles peas. Break egg into a liquid-measuring cup. Add vinegar to egg, then add cold water to make 1 cup. Beat slightly with fork.

Add liquid mixture to dry ingredients, stirring lightly with fork until just moistened. Lightly form into 5 equal balls. On floured surface, lightly shape balls into patties. Place patties into plastic freezer bags and freeze. When ready to use, thaw at room temperature, but do not allow patties to become warm. Roll out on floured surface.

Note: Dough may be chilled and used immediately; however, Nita and Kathy find it easier to work with after freezing.

"BASE" CREAM FILLING
(FROM GRANDMA ROSIE)

(enough for 1 pie)
3 tablespoons flour
3 tablespoons cornstarch
1 cup sugar
3 egg yolks
2¼ cups milk (whole milk is better than reduced-fat)
1 teaspoon vanilla

APRICOT TOPPING
(enough for 1 pie)
2 cups ripe apricots
1 cup sugar
About 2 tablespoons cornstarch, plus a little cold water
1 tablespoon butter

Mix together flour, cornstarch, and sugar. Stir in milk and egg yolks.
Bring to boil while stirring constantly. Add vanilla. Continue to

cook and stir until mixture thickens. Let cool and pour into a pre-baked pie shell.*

Bake for about 20–25 minutes, or until pale golden brown. Remove weights and lining before filling.

Cut apricots into halves or quarters, and lay them on top of the cream filling, working from the middle out, so as to form a circle of fruit about three inches smaller than the actual pie. The idea is to let the creamy yellow filling smile through.

For the glaze, stir sugar and 1 cup water in a saucepan. Mix a little cornstarch (about 2 tablespoons) w/cold water in a cup, then stir the cornstarch mixture into the sugar water and cook, stirring often, at medium heat. Add 1 tablespoon of butter and keep stirring until glaze thickens a little. Remove from heat and let glaze cool slightly before pouring over fresh fruit.

big hair, big pie, big lie . . . texas

" 'We are what we eat,' the proverb says. But that is only half true. In some sense, we remain hungry even when stated, because food is an emotional trigger to things long forgotten, trapped in memory . . ."

—EDNA O'BRIEN, *GOURMET* MAGAZINE

---

*When "blind baking" an unfilled crust, you should preheat your oven to 425 degrees at least 20 minutes before baking. Prick the bottom of the crust with the tines of a fork to prevent the bottom crust from blistering while it bakes. Line your empty pie shell with foil or parchment paper and fill it with dried beans or pie weights or uncooked rice.

What makes Kris and me such good friends and road-trip partners is that we both have dual personalities. We are both adventurous, some might even say reckless. On the other hand, we are both self-professed nesters seeking creature comforts. Very independent women who wouldn't mind leaving a little bit of that independence on the side of the road somewhere. Constant seekers who would like to be found someday.

Where Kris and I go different ways is that her "seeking" knows no bounds. Kris believes in extraterrestrials, UFOs, and all things crystal.

And on our way to Texas, she really wanted to stop in Roswell, New Mexico—just to look. "I'm sure we'll find good pie there," she said.

I was pretty sure we wouldn't. "Pie is down-to-earth," I said. "Nothing otherworldly about it."

But since I didn't want to be "the turd in the punchbowl," and since I was still feeling bad about our roadkill row, and since Roswell would not take us too far astray from our next stop, I obliged.

Teri, short for Tarantino, was game. "Great visuals," she said.

We stocked up on bottled water in Socorro and took US 380 right across the Rio Grande, the backbone of New Mexico, and past the White Sands Missile Range, the main missile testing site of the United States Army. We drove within only about 20 miles north of Trinity Site, where the first atomic bomb was exploded in July 1945. It was about 150 degrees outside, but we all got the chills.

As we approached Roswell, Kris briefed us on the mysterious "crash" of 1947: the shallow trench, the scattered debris, the mutilated cattle.

So, you can imagine my surprise and Kris's relative delight when for the first and only time of the trip, we started seeing cow roadkill strewn about US 380.

Of course, this was a main thoroughfare for truckers between Texas, New Mexico, and Arizona, and cattle ranches abound. Still, it was creepy.

As in most American cities, the gateway into Roswell is one big strip mall anchored by a chain of car dealerships. Only here, the Roswell Honda dealership had a green balloon, shaped like a two-stories-tall alien, tethered to its sales office. Green aliens were in every shop window, even the bridal shop in town had a four-foot-tall green alien doll modeling a lacy white dress in the window.

We stopped at the International UFO Museum hoping someone could tell us where to go for pie in this town. Wendy, a white-haired lady behind the welcome counter, was more interested in talking about the crash.

"In those days, if you'd said you believed in something like that, they would have put you in the booby hatch," she said directly to Kris, sensing a sisterhood.

Wendy called over the owner of the museum, Walter Haut, to come talk to us about pie. A strapping guy with the biggest ears I've ever seen, Haut was the public relations officer on the base at the time of the crash. He claims he actually wrote the press release for Colonel Blanchard about the flying saucer—only to have it rescinded a day later.

Haut's memory of the incident is a little fuzzy, as have been his facts in interviews over the years.

In fact, Haut was much more interested in talking about what it was like participating in the Bikini A-bomb tests, something that clearly left some scars. For years after that, he said, some of the other men who'd participated in the bomb-testing would get together and bake pies, for relaxation.

"We were pretty competitive about it, too," Haut said. "Mine were the best." And although I'm sure he made a fine pie, I wasn't sure if I believed his story and I certainly wasn't moved to add his recipe to my collection.

· · ·

At a supermarket on the way out of town, we bought some ice water and fresh fruit for the road, and as we were climbing back into our oven of a car, an elderly Latina woman with saddlesoap skin motioned us over to the supermarket bench where she was sitting. *"Tamales?"* she whispered. *"Seis dolares para doce."*

Fifty-cent undercover tamales sounded divine, so we followed her to her parked van where her husband reached into a box and pulled out a sack with a dozen still warm mini-tamales. No aliens on the wrapper, just grease.

As searing as the temperatures were outside, the spicy tamales tasted great, and the chile peppers were just the kick we needed to orbit us out of the weird Roswell vibe.

We'd been back on the road for about an hour or so, when Betty Blue's temperature gauge shot right up toward the dreaded scarlet zone. I pulled over, turned off the engine, and grabbed the manual.

"DO NOT TURN OFF THE ENGINE," it said in block letters.

Our throats parched and our breath on fire, we stumbled out of the car and popped open the hood. Kris was wearing a short skirt, and to keep her legs from sticking to the leather seats, she had put down some paper towels, which she forgot to remove before getting out of the car.

Our Tarantino was zooming in on those vertical stress lines between my eyes and the temperature gauge on the dash.

"We need a man. We need a maaaannnnn," Kris wailed into the camera. Somewhere, Gloria Steinem's ears were ringing.

Just then, a man rode up in a white pickup truck.

Rodney had zipped past us on his way to his job repairing truck engines, when he spotted us and turned around to help. He wore a black felt hat and a circus-red, heavy cotton jumpsuit, the pant legs tucked into knee-high black cowboy boots with Western stitching.

"You ladies need some help," he said, tipping his brim as he sauntered up to the car.

I thought for sure Kris would faint from karmic and cosmic overload. "We asked and you came," she told the shy Rodney, who was trying to size up our little group.

It didn't take Rodney long to figure out what the problem was, mechanically: some gauge thingie had stopped working and was preventing water from getting into some doohickey. The liquid in the tank had gotten really hot, and, when he unscrewed the cap, lime-green hot goop shot up like a geyser and dribbled all over the tank.

"Ooooh," I said. "It's extraterrestrial green."

"Is that what you gals are here for?" Rodney said, extracting his disappointed face from under the hood.

No, I said, our mission was pie. Rodney was relieved. From under the hood, he reminisced about his mama's pecan pie. His mother had survived cancer then died suddenly of a massive heart attack, he said.

"But she did make some good apple pie." Rodney wasn't exactly Brad Pitt–handsome, but there's something about a cowboy on a rescue mission talking about his mama that gets to a gal. We had to refrain from a group hug.

"You should be fine from here on out, ladies. Just be sure you get your radiator flushed before wintertime."

"Whatever you say, Rodney." And then, with another tug of his brim, he walked away with a slightly bow-legged swagger.

"We should have offered him a tamale," Teri said, reaching for another. Kris patted Betty Blue's dash. "It's our own fault for neglecting Betty," Kris said. Indeed, since Teri arrived, we'd fallen out of our habit of patting Betty's dash each morning for good luck.

Our plan for Texas was to go to a small town called Ponder, where, I'd heard, there was an authentic steakhouse called Ranchman's Café, known for its T-bones and titanic pies.

Since we were going to be in the Dallas area, big-hair country, Teri suggested we hit one of those beauty salons and get our hair teased.

She loved the idea of talking to some Texas hairstylist about pie while she teased my hair. "Great visuals," she reminded us.

"I don't want a helmet head," I told the girls.

This led to a philosophical discussion about Texans and their obsession with all things armor: helmet hair, belt buckles big as hubcaps, mighty American stretch-metal cars. Even the nine-banded armadillo, the Lone Star State's favorite critter, is anything but furry and cuddly. And what about those longhorn cattle?

Pies at the Ranchman's Café, Ponder, TX

Road trips can lead to cheap psychobabble, and we were about to dismiss Texas as a cold and unfeeling state, when we drove past the Texas state sign and smiled. DRIVE FRIENDLY, THE TEXAS WAY, it said.

We decided that meant socializing with some of these truckers in ten-gallon hats. We filled up on gas and fell behind an older trucker with a supershiny rig without those stupid mud flaps bearing a torpedo-breasted bimbo. He was kind of shy, but we did get him to talk to us about the cotton fields we were passing and the dreaded boll weevil wreaking havoc on the fibers. On the subject of pie, he had some firm convictions. No Texas pie was as good as the cherry cream pie they dish out at the TA truck stop in Sweetwater.

"Did you say 'cherry cream,' good buddy?"

"Ten-four, cherry cream. Ten-four."

They were plumb out of the cherry cream pie when we pulled into the TA truck stop close to midnight, having eaten nothing but tamales all day. The waitress with a bushy horsetail and prairie-cut bangs served us up a slice of lemon meringue pie and a slice of peach pie à la mode. I saw it as a bad sign when the back crust on both slices somehow divorced itself from the rest of the pie and fell back on the plate like a windblown picket fence.

The meringue atop the lemon pie was hard and perky, as unnatural and uninviting as breast implants. The peach pie was gelatinous and soupy, and the vanilla ice cream matched the artificial yellow of the Formica counter.

A couple snuggling in the booth behind us asked Teri why she was filming a piece of pie—and an ugly one at that. We got to talking, slid right into the booth with them.

Ken and Deborah had dated ten years earlier and had only very recently reconnected—after a fluke encounter. Ken was a long-haul trucker and he invited Deborah to ride in his rig with him for a few days, to get reacquainted. She had called in sick at work and here they were, on their way to California, eating a late-night burger snack at a Texas truck stop.

They were coming from Dallas where they'd already eaten soul food for dinner at Sweet Georgia Brown's. They'd ordered a piece of sweet-potato pie to go, and, on I-20, she had spoon-fed him the pie for miles, as he drove, positively giddy.

"You have not lived, honey, unless you have had your baby by your side, in your rig, feeding you sweet-potato pie," he said. As it was happening, he'd tortured his fellow truckers by smacking his sweet-potato lips into the CB radio.

Just thinking about the moment made him slide out of the booth and onto one knee. "Deborah, will you marry me?" he said. "I guess so," she said with a casual shrug. And then she moved right on to her mama's extraordinary pie crust.

"What made it so good?" I asked.

The ample-breasted Deborah extended her arms out in front of her like a sleepwalker, and began to undulate.

"It's all in the motion," she said with a knowing smile. "It's all in the motion."

"That's right, honey," said Ken, who was back in his seat and glancing at her sideways. "Uh-huh."

She shot him a disapproving look.

"My mama makes her pies with love," she said. "Pie is all in the love and it's all in the motion."

"Do you think Ken's proposal was for real?" Kris asked back in the car. Teri and I groaned, because we weren't very hopeful.

We found a room in a Motel 6 across the highway, which made me homesick for our kitschy midwestern motels. Teri ducked outside to call Jeff, her fiancé, and she came back grumbling something about a prewedding-jitters spat.

"You didn't tell him we'd been rescued by a cowboy riding a white pickup, did you?" we asked.

"Oy. Men!" Teri said behind her Zsa Zsa Gabor leopard-print night mask.

The next morning, we had breakfast at the Ramada Inn across the street, because that sounded a lot more festive than the stale doughnuts and instant coffee on the card table in our lobby.

We ordered breakfast burritos, which were delicious, and then, I'm not sure how it happened, but one moment the glass globe of the hurricane lamp was in the middle of the table and the next it was pressed against my ear, delivering a symphony of the ocean, and yes, even the call of whales. Kris pressed it against her ear and heard the same thing. Woo, woo, woo, she cooed, sounding more like an owl than a whale.

The young couple at the next table over giggled at our antics, so we struck up a conversation. They were newlyweds and enjoying breakfast with the groom's mother, Judy, a friendly woman with dramatic Frida Kahlo eyebrows.

Since Judy's accent was undeniably Texan, we asked her if she knew of any good pie in Sweetwater or the Dallas area. Judy said they were from Seminole and in town for their annual family reunion—three days of storytelling, domino playing, and cooking up old family recipes in their hotel kitchenettes.

"My mom's chocolate pie is the best in the world," she said. "You really ought to talk to her. She's in the next room playing cards with her sisters."

We settled our bill, returned the hurricane globe to its cradle, and followed Judy into the club room, where her mother, Dorothy Lou, was at the card table with her sisters Ansa Lee, Mary Jo, and Clara May.

Dorothy Lou did not consider her pies one of her most memorable accomplishments, so she pooh-poohed the notion of talking about them in any serious fashion. She said she would gladly share her recipe, but even though she'd been making it for more than fifty years, she couldn't, for the life of her, remember it off the top of her head.

Judy seemed disappointed that her mother wasn't as excited about her pie as she was. The other sisters chimed in with stories about the pies their mother used to make on the dairy farm where they grew up, and about farm living in general.

"Remember when we used to milk the cows, and the rats would

come out from hiding behind the cottonseed bins, and we'd squirt them with fresh milk?" said Ansa Lee, laughing. "We'd wear those silly bonnets so that the cows wouldn't hurt us with their tails." Ansa Lee's husband had passed on recently, and this was her first family reunion without him. Judy seemed happy to see her auntie laughing so heartily.

They all admitted that although—and possibly because—their mother had been a talented pie baker, none of them had learned how to make a pie before they married, and then they learned in a hurry, to keep their husbands happy.

I heard a long sigh of relief and realized it was coming from the soon-to-be-wed Teri.

Dorothy Lou and her husband, Whitt, had met in Fort Worth in 1943, while they both worked at Consolidated AirCraft, assembling B-17s. Dorothy Lou was one of the six million American women who joined the workforce at the urging of Rosie the Riveter, the fictional character created by the U.S. government to coax women to the assembly line.

"Only Dorothy Lou was prettier than that Rosie ever was," Whitt said, finally finding reason to pipe up.

We stepped outside, by the pool, to take some pictures of the four sisters. "Say 'PIE,' " Kris said. And they did.

As we gathered our belongings, Judy pulled me aside to tell me she'd send along the chocolate pie recipe.

"This whole pie thing is kind of bittersweet for me," she said. "On the one hand, I can't think of pie without thinking of my mom's chocolate pie. But then, I know she's not going to be around forever and nobody makes it quite like she does. None of her sisters can. I know, because I've tried theirs.

"So where," she pleaded, "will I get my chocolate pie when my mother is gone?"

The sisters in Sweetwater, TX

We both knew the question ran deeper than that.

And there it was, the meaning of pie in America, delivered pool-side at the Ramada Inn off the interstate in Sweetwater, Texas.

With plans to get to Ponder in time for dinner, the idea of a side trip to Dallas for a big-hair tease grew dimmer. I was crushed.

We headed east, through Shackelford and Pinto Palo counties, on a rail-thin back road, parched and plain as a stale Rye Krisp. We passed a number of small Texas towns, abandoned and fig-dry.

We passed mousy-brown fields peppered with pumping oil rigs, which frantically pecked the bedrock, like giant, gluttonous prehistoric chickens.

When a New York photographer recommended the steakhouse

with good pie in Ponder, I was immediately drawn by the name which, I thought, captured the spirit of this meditative road trip.

He'd described it as the kind of place where "you have to call ahead and order your baked potato." Perfect.

I looked Ponder up on a map. I was doubly thrilled to see that, in fact, it was dead on the path of the Chisolm Trail.

As the three of us drove across the Panhandle Plains, I thought of the thousands of *vaqueros*, cowboys, who led hordes of longhorn steer from south Texas to railheads in Kansas.

When the rail system extended down south into Texas, the cowboys were no longer needed to rustle cattle. Since cowboyhood had already assumed mythic proportions by then, the rodeo was created to keep the myth of the cowboy alive.

Ponder, named for a rich and influential local banker, was famous for its rodeo, which the whole town pitched in to build in 1930. Population dwindled for a long time after the rodeo moved to Denton, but there's been a resurgence lately, with city folk willing to brave the daily commute to Dallas and Fort Worth in exchange for certain amenities, like wide-open spaces and pie every day at the Ranchman's Café.

The café was opened in 1948 by Grace "Pete" Jackson, a pistol of a woman who learned early on that her success would depend on her knowing how every rancher in town liked his steak. Eventually, the oil men in Dallas found their way to the café and now, most weekends, fancy cars sidle up right next to the pickups in the parking lot for T-bones and meringue pies ten-gallon high.

On weekends, a local fiddler plays bluegrass music with his young shy son, who follows close behind, strumming a washboard with a wooden spoon. "Don't let anyone fool you," the fiddler said. "This may be a steakhouse, but people come for the pie. People worship Evelyn around here.

"I've seen people go straight into that kitchen and slip her a $20 bill to thank her for her pies," he said. "I've seen people come straight from the Dallas airport for a piece of pie. I'm telling you, I've seen it all."

So you can see why Dave Ross, the current owner, was worried when Evelyn underwent sextuple-bypass surgery and was out of commission for several long weeks right before our visit. Since Evelyn kept all the recipes in her head, Ross had to scramble to find alternative recipes on the Internet, then make them himself.

"We're really glad to have her back," Ross said. Evelyn had already gone home for the day, after baking about thirty pies, so we decided to relax, enjoy a steak dinner, and return to meet Evelyn after taking Kris to the airport the following morning.

I was already worrying about what the pie trip would be like without my Beaumont, my Dr. Watson, my Ethel. My Thelma.

Kris was sad not to carry the pie journey to the bitter end, but I knew she was ready to get home and sleep in her own bed, and, more important, to eat sushi and bountiful green salads again. And, although she'd never admit it, I think she missed her cool, fast car, too.

We went into the kitchen to select our T-bones, which were stacked on a round, three-legged butcher block. Next to the block was a large plastic bucket filled with ribbons of trimmed fat, which Ross uses to make lye soap. As we ate our steaks and football-size Idaho potatoes, I watched customers file past Evelyn's pies and stare as though they were in a museum. Some pretended to be looking for the bathroom, clear on the other side of the room, so they could get a closer look.

The rustic pies were something to see. Most of the crusts, slightly charred, were shorter than their tins, so their edges curled up, like burning paper. Meringues, toasted-marshmallow brown, were unevenly distributed, the way snow clumps on a fir tree. The primitively beautiful pies looked as though they'd been made on the wagon trail. Real cowboy pies.

After dinner, Ross brought us a twelve-slice sampler plate of Evelyn's pies and cobblers. The pie lineup included mini-slices of buttermilk, pecan, chocolate, and lemon meringue (made with limes in summer). For Kris, it was the pie equivalent of the grand finale at a Fourth of July fireworks display.

That night, Kris handed over the mosquito itch stick she'd hung on to since Ohio, and gave Teri the yellow highlighter pen to chart our course.

Evelyn had already made four chocolate pies and was moving on to a batch of lemon meringue, by the time we arrived the next morning at 9 A.M. She'd also made a batch of thirty crusts.

"No time to waste," she said. "Sunday nights are always busy." Standing in front of an old industrial range, stirring the lemon filling in a tall banged-up metal pot with a long wooden spoon, she was a little wobbly on her feet. And in spirit.

Some of the pie recipes she'd refined over the years but never written down had slipped her mind in the hospital. She hoped it was temporary.

Evelyn never thought she'd become a minor celebrity. "When I was a young girl, I just worked the farm with my brothers and father, and never took the time to wonder what I'd do when I grew up," she said. "I'm just a country girl.

"I don't feel like an artist, but if pie pleases so many people, then it must be an art. Right?"

We nodded.

"I feel at home when I make pie," she said. "I feel good about myself. I didn't have much of an education, but this is something I can do well."

It was Pete, the former owner, who showed Evelyn how to make pies and swore her to secrecy about the crust.

Evelyn took a long, slow drag of iced tea.

"One of these days, y'all are going to look up and you're going to be looking for fresh pies, and you're going to realize there's nobody cookin' them no more."

As we left, a customer who'd overheard us talking pie to Evelyn followed us out into the hot July morning. "If you're looking for pies," she said, "you really should check out the pies at Catfish Haven, near the Oklahoma border. The baker is a neat ol' lady with a beehive."

My friends Doug and Jeanette were expecting us for dinner in Houston, in the opposite direction.

Teri put the key in the ignition. "So, I take it, we're heading toward Oklahoma?"

The first thing you see when you walk into Catfish Haven is a huge center table laden with whole pies, each covered in plastic "to prevent the calories from jumping out," according to a staffer. The next thing you see is D'Ann Davis, the beehive lady, manning the fryers with the dexterity of a foosball champion.

Her beehive shot straight up like a thumb. Only on the sides, which were cut shorter, did strands escape, sticking out like catfish whiskers.

Teri, who still hadn't decided how she'd wear her hair on her wedding day, was transfixed.

(Interestingly, the beehive was created by a non-Texan—Margaret Vinci Heldt of Chicago. Heldt had been the 1954 National Cosmetology Association's hairstyling champion. She owned a posh salon on Michigan Avenue, when the editors of *Modern Beauty Shop* magazine challenged her to come up with a 'do to outdo all 'dos. Inspired by a Moroccan fez hat she'd seen, and armed with gobs of hairspray, she developed the famous high-swirling, round-topped hairstyle. She stuck a pin in the 'do, and an editor exclaimed: "It looks like a beehive!")

· · · ·

When D'Ann finally stepped away from the fryers to come talk to us, her face was wet with sweat, and her dark eye-makeup running so that she looked like a Raggedy Ann doll. She was all smiles talking about pie.

"Why do so few people make pie from scratch?" I asked.

"Cuz it's work, girl," she said, tamping her moist cheeks with a paper napkin.

D'Ann insisted that each and every crust at her restaurant be rolled out by hand. Since they sold three to four hundred pies a week, she and her staff made the crusts in assembly-line fashion in the early part of the week, then froze them. They filled and baked them off as they needed them. Although she had trained most of her staff to make the pies, she said "people can always tell which ones are mine," because of her distinct crimping technique.

While Evelyn's pies were rough-and-tumble, D'Ann's pies were kind of prissy.

"Pies reflect your personality," she said. "If you make a pie, it should be like you."

I asked D'Ann to describe her personality in three words.

"Let's see," she said, staring at the ceiling. "Happy. Satisfied. Contented."

That seemed to describe a lot of the pie bakers we'd met so far.

My eyes kept going back to D'Ann's hive, and I asked her how long it took her to maintain the style day after day.

"I've been wearing my hair like this since high school," she said. "I just say 'get up,' and it jumps up by itself. It's just like my pie recipes," she added. "If something works and pleases people, why mess with it?"

Any advice for people willing to give it a whirl, I asked, meaning the pie, not the 'do.

"Don't get in a hurry," she said, "and don't take shortcuts. Patience makes good pie."

Teri and I bought a slice of cream-cheese pecan, D'Ann's most popular pie. We shared it in the car after a barbecued beef sandwich at Clark's Outpost in Tioga, Gene Autry country.

It was good, but so rich and cloying I was glad hypoglycemic Kris was safe on a plane home.

DOROTHY LOU'S CHOCOLATE PIE

CRUST

1 9-inch prebaked pie crust

FILLING

1½ cups whole milk

½ cup PET evaporated milk

1 tablespoon butter

1½ cups sugar

3½ tablespoons flour

3 tablespoons cocoa

pinch of salt

3 eggs yolks, beaten

1 teaspoon vanilla

In a heavy-bottomed saucepan, heat whole milk, evaporated milk, and butter together. Do not boil. In a bowl, mix sugar, flour, cocoa, salt, and beaten egg yolks. Mix well and add to hot milk-and-butter mixture. Cook over low heat until thick. Add vanilla, stir, and pour into a prebaked pie crust.

MERINGUE

3 egg whites

3 tablespoons water

*1 heaping tablespoon cornstarch mixed with sugar, so they combine to
make ½ cup*

Beat egg whites and water together until stiff. Gradually add the
mixture of cornstarch and sugar, beating constantly, until egg whites
form stiff peaks.

Layer meringue onto hot filling, being careful to completely
cover the pie. Bake in a preheated 400-degree oven until meringue
turns golden-brown—about 15 minutes.

le pays cajun

*"I went to the woods because I wished to live deliberately, to front
only the essential facts of life, and see if I could not learn what it had
to teach, and not, when I came to die, discover that I had not lived."*

—HENRY DAVID THOREAU, *WALDEN*

Mixing bowls aside, I've gathered an odd assortment of mementos
on the pie trip, and the most peculiar one sits on top of my blueberry
iMac computer.

It's an alligator bone. An osteoderm, to be precise—one of the
many bones tucked beneath a gator's handbag skin that give an alligator's back its rough-and-bumpy character. The porous bone looks

like a smooth piece of bleached coral, only it's got a ridge down the middle, like the nose on a face.

When people ask, I say I had to wrestle a few alligators to get the best pie recipes in Louisiana. But the "button," as osteoderms are called, was a gift from Greg Guirard—crawfish fisherman, environmentalist, poet, swamp photographer, and distinguished crawfish pie baker in Catahoula, Louisiana, the heart of Cajun country.

After leaving the creature comforts of our friends Doug and Jeanette's lovely house in Houston, we took the interstate to the border of Louisiana, at which point we slipped on to US 14 to *le pays Cajun*. Teri was so excited to be back in Louisiana, her adopted home state, she squealed for 12 miles past the state line, right past all the "vasectomy reversal" billboards.

Teri grew up in Levittown, New York—America's postwar paradigmatic suburb—and later studied philosophy at Binghamton. So it made perfect sense that her first job out of college would be as a general-assignment newspaper reporter at the *Daily Star* in Hammond, Louisiana.

Her friends and family thought it was odd, but Teri knew she'd landed in the right place when, shortly after she took the job, the paper slapped pictures of a jazz funeral procession for an alligator, known as "Ole Hardhide," on the front page. Ole Hardhide had been the town mascot in neighboring Ponchatoula, which also boasts a giant red strawberry on the police department's roof. Ole Hardhide lived in a cage in the center of town. Apparently, he'd been dead for days before anyone noticed.

Teri tells great stories about the transition from Long Island to Louisiana. Most of them involve big bugs. Our plan was to pass through Hammond on our way to New Orleans, not necessarily for pie, but to visit Teri's dear old friend Claude, a former photographer at the *Daily Star*. It was Claude who taught Teri how to eat catfish, and other basic Southern survival skills.

But first, I wanted to see what kind of pie we would find in Cajun country.

US 14 is a lean road lined with corrugated tin barns, sugar-cane fields, and murky ponds where white egrets stand knee-deep and still on dipstick legs.

We stopped in historic Abbeville, because Doug, our friend in Houston, remembered a killer crawfish pie at a place called Madame Ouida's. Heretofore, I'd really tried to limit my research to sweet pies, but in Louisiana, where rules are meant to be broken, I was willing to bend. Besides, Doug had spent the morning installing a coat hanger as a makeshift antenna for us. Betty Blue's antenna had mysteriously disappeared somewhere between New Mexico and Houston. Near Roswell, no doubt.

From the phone of a corner music store in downtown Abbeville, I called Madame Ouida, who had already closed up shop for the day and had zero interest in letting us drop by to talk about the art of making pie.

"I don't give out my crust to anybody," she snipped.

This was a sign, I told Teri, that I needed to stick to my sweet plan. "If you're looking for dessert pie, you might try the place across the street," said the shopkeeper who'd listened in.

Bollino's Coffeehouse and Café with its loft space, vermilion walls, exposed brick, and oversized cubist-style paintings felt more Amsterdam than stodgy Abbeville. Its pastry case was a veritable pie fun house: turtle pie, grasshopper pie, brandy pecan. All made in-house by the young and bubbly Libby Bollino, who was busy mixing the filling for key lime pie when we walked in.

Libby told us she and her husband, James, had met tending bar in New Orleans, and had moved back to Libby's hometown to start their own business and a family. She said the town was adjusting to the notion of a coffeehouse. Some people still didn't know, for example, that you can't just sit at a table all day without consuming. She smiled.

"But the pies are selling. *Everybody* loves pie."

I asked Libby why that was.

"Look how pretty pie is," she said, pointing to a dark pecan pie with plump, scalloped edges.

"There's something organic, sort of artistic about pie," she said, "and yet unlike most works of art, it's practical, because you know someone's going to eat it."

She stood, hands on her hips, staring at her pies in the display case.

"Or maybe it's the *round* shape that people like. There's something very mystical about a perfect circle. Plus, pie appeals to all the senses: it has a salty crust with a sweet filling and gushiness all around."

Libby said her mother was *not* a pie baker and, in fact, the only pies she remembered from childhood were the chocolate ice-box pies from Piccadilly's Cafeteria. (Remember Sarah Webster in Memphis and her pillbox hat?)

Libby learned to make pie the hard way: practicing—and failing.

The weekend before they opened the coffeehouse, she spent two days making four pies—er, four pies she could sell, that is.

"I won't tell you how many I *actually* made."

"Pie-baking isn't hard, but it does take patience," she said, leaning against the pastry case. "And everyone wishes they had more patience. Don't they?"

Even here, in the Deep South, customers didn't believe her when she told them she made the pies from scratch. "People are really impressed. They don't react that way to a cobbler. A cobbler is about as impressive as a casserole."

Libby was an English major and didn't imagine, when she was staying up nights crafting term papers in college, that she'd return to Abbeville one day and bake pies for a living. But life, like a road trip, takes odd and unexpected twists—if you let it. William Faulkner had always been Libby's favorite author, and I asked her if she saw any parallels between Faulkner and pie. Whip-smart Libby didn't skip a beat.

"Faulkner is all about the triumph of the human spirit," she said. "When he accepted his Nobel Prize for Literature, Faulkner gave this great speech in which he talked about how important it is to write about man not merely *enduring*, but *prevailing*.

"Making pie is *prevailing*," she said. "It's saying, I'm not going to make a simple cobbler, I'm going to make a *pie*." She waved her fist and dish rag in the air. I thought she might break out into a verse of "The Internationale."

I really liked Libby. If I lived in Abbeville, I'd want to hang out at the café with her and make pies and talk books all day. She and James had a baby boy, and they took turns baking pies and caring for him. It sounded like a rich life. One that gave her time to, occasionally, sit down and read.

Libby remembered reading something, in fact, about a parish in Cajun country where the entire community sat down and ate pie on Good Friday, but she wasn't sure where exactly it was.

That was enough to go on, we told her. We'd find it.

We wanted to buy a whole pie to take to Claude in Hammond, but Libby said all the pies were already spoken for, so we bought a slice of each of her pies and put them in the cooler in the car.

We went to a bookstore in Lafayette and sat in the regional-cooking aisle until we found the parish in question: Catahoula. It was getting dark and so late, we decided to stay near Lafayette overnight. We stumbled onto Breaux Bridge, a small, historic town along the Bayou Teche, famous for its two-hundred-year-old footbridge and known as the Crawfish Capital of the World. (Who decides these things, anyway?)

We drove past an old, overcrowded cemetery, its raised tombstones buckling in the moonlight, and Teri, who was driving, pulled over and jumped out of the car. "We *have* to walk in a cemetery in the dark while we're in Louisiana," she said. "It's a tradition."

This being swamp country, all of the tombstones were raised, like osteoderms, something I'd never seen before. An invisible stray cat followed us with a strident cry, as we meandered through the maze of tombstones. Only when we finished our tour did the cat jump out onto our path to reveal itself—in true Faulknerian fashion—as pitch-black. I jumped about three feet in the air. We decided to keep walking through this quaint downtown and get a closer look at the bridge, where colorful crawfish had been painted on the overhead structures. (The bridge was built in 1950, and Ana Belle Dupuis Hoffman Krewitz, a local resident, was the first person to drive across it in her Model-A Ford. Talk about a leap of faith.)

We turned off on a dead-still side street, drawn by a beautiful, vintage Acadian home with a sweeping front porch that reminded me of Buford's in Russellville, Arkansas. A sign said "bed and breakfast," but all the lights were out. A note on the door said: "Call this number if you want a room." So we did. "I'll be right over," said a cheery voice, before we had a chance to inquire about the rate. Mary Lynn must live right around the corner because she pulled into the gravel drive within minutes. Mary Lynn was a big woman. She had to be, to make room for a heart as big as a house: When I explained we were on a no-frills, no-lace budget, she shrugged.

"Just leave what you can in the guest book when you check out in the morning." Her only requirement was that we join her at Café des Amis down the street, for an authentic Cajun breakfast.

A school administrator who had renovated this old boardinghouse as a hobby, she gave us a tour of the place, formerly the Old

City Hotel, where "drummers," traveling salesmen like Willy Loman, had been laying their weary heads since the 1850s. The front part of the house was an original Creole cottage that had been built in 1812, with four-inch hand-hewn beams.

We were the only guests, as the renovation wasn't quite complete, so Mary Lynn let us pick our room. We picked the one with twin poster beds. It opened onto a side porch looking out on the River Teche. After Mary Lynn left us with the key to the place, we retrieved the car near the cemetery, slid Libby's pies in the refrigerator, and then skidded across the hardwood floors, giddy as cats on 'nip.

In the morning, we washed our hair and nursed coffee in rocking chairs on the porch. It was a nice change from the concrete motel parking lots I had been waking up to for weeks. As promised, we met Mary Lynn at Café des Amis where we enjoyed some eggs topped with crawfish étouffée and sweet chicory coffee. We asked Mary Lynn if she knew anything about this annual Pie Day event in Catahoula. Her eyes grew as wide as the biscuits on Teri's plate.

"Why, Tootie Guirard started that tradition," she said. "Her son Greg is a good friend of mine. He can tell you all about Catahoula's Pie Day."

She got on the phone and talked to him, then gave us directions for Catahoula. Easy as pie.

We thanked Mary Lynn for her hospitality, retrieved our pies from her refrigerator, slipped a check in the guest book, and headed toward the *coeur* of Cajun country, St. Martinville, where thousands of French settlers turned up in 1755, after being forced out of Nova Scotia by the British.

The *grand deplacement*, as the exile was called, was the backdrop for Henry Wadsworth Longfellow's epic love poem "Gabriel and Evangeline." Legends of Evangeline can be found everywhere in St. Martinville, where the young woman came in search of Gabriel, only to find the rascal had married someone else. St. Martinville is also where French (Let-Them-Eat-Cake!) aristocrats fled during the French Revolution, which is how the town got its nickname of "Petit Paris."

Once in Catahoula, we had trouble finding Greg Guirard's house and weaved in and out of dirt roads, bordered by reeds and leafy sugar cane, just like the cat at the cemetery.

We pulled over to ask a local in overalls and a straw hat.

"Greg's house isn't really in Catahoula," said the man. "Technically, it's not really *anywhere*."

That was helpful. The truth was that the "house" was on Bayou Mercier Road, a dirt snake of a road that led to the levee and had only recently been given a name—at the local fire department's insistence.

We drove up and down Bayou Mercier Road until we finally spotted a thin opening in the woods that was, indeed, a drive, and took it to the end, where a cottage with green shutters sprouted from the earth amid sweeping cypress trees. Several dogs and even more cats emerged from the chirping, natural woodwork to greet us. Two of the dogs had the signature pale-blue eyes of the Catahoula leopard dog, a breed of warrior dogs brought here by the Spaniards. The dogs eventually mated with the red wolf. No doubt, these were a rich gumbo of breeds. Greg Guirard, a handsome, proud man in his late 50s at least, pushed open the creaky screen door and waved hello. I noticed the crawfish-red workboots planted upside down on a fence post on either side of him on the front porch.

We sat on an outside bench, with the crickets and grasshoppers and frogs attempting to drown out Greg, whose voice was as soft as the lowlands.

There was no small talk because Greg had no time or patience for it. His parents, Tootie and Mr. Jim, as they were known, came from two of Cajun country's most prominent families, the Martins and the Guirards. His parents had camped at this cottage on their honeymoon in the late 1930s, and they liked it so much they eventually moved there, to the surprise of the rich folk in town. His mother, Tootie, now in a nursing home, took Good Friday very, *very* seriously, Greg said.

She believed that you had to really, truly fast on Good Friday— no water, no coffee, no brushing of teeth. But while the church thought the fasting should last until sundown, and the Cajuns thought noon was quite sufficient, Tootie firmly believed that fasting until 10 A.M. was penance enough.

"She's always had her personal theology," said Greg with a smile. "When we were little, she'd wake us up at 6 A.M. on Good Friday with scary stories of two-headed calves or the like, just to get us out of bed to make sure we would get at least four hours of suffering in before breaking fast at 10," Greg said, shaking his head at his mother's antics.

Once that clock struck 10, Tootie was ready to party and to eat until she could eat no more.

The early French settlers had always broken their fast with a "sweet-dough pie"—a simple custard pie—and over the years the tradition evolved into breaking fast with any old pie. For many years, Cajun families would make their pies on Thursday and spend Good Friday traveling from neighbor to neighbor's house delivering and trading pies. One year, more than forty years ago, Tootie decided to put an end to all this traveling and host the annual Pie Day exchange at her cottage in the woods, also known as "the camp."

"The only rule for attending was that you had to bring a pie that was made entirely by hand," Greg said. One year, five Cajun brothers, roving musicians, were camping in the woods near the house. Greg invited them to Pie Day but warned them about the hand-scratch pie rule. "Well, wouldn't you know it, they managed to whip one up on their campfire. And it was pretty good, too."

Tootie always made arrangements for the local priests to come bless the pies before breaking fast and, usually, the priests were happy to oblige.

One particular priest, however, objected to Tootie's celebration, which he deemed sacrilegious on the day Jesus died for our sins.

This priest was so determined to squelch Tootie's annual party that, one year, he organized a competing Catholic ritual to coincide with the festivities. In the seven miles of road that separated St. Martinville from Catahoula, there were twelve old oak trees, each bearing one of the stations of the cross. The priest invited non-pie-eating Catholics to join him on a flatbed truck for a prayer procession stopping at each station of the cross. Not only did the 10 A.M. procession conflict with Tootie's "break fast" party—it blocked the roads for anyone who was trying to get to her house in the woods. "Fortunately," said Greg, "this priest did not stay long in the parish."

Even though his mother was now in a nursing home, Greg said it was vital to keep the Pie Day tradition alive. People continued to flock to the house from all over the country because they knew "it's the one day of the year they are sure to see old friends and family," he said. "Cajuns really like to get together and celebrate life."

Greg said it was especially crucial to keep these cultural traditions alive when so much of the Atchafalaya Basin was disappearing. Drying up. Twisted bayous were now filled with sediment and overrun by trees. Flooding had buried the basin in silt. The catfish and the crawfish fishermen were having to find new ways to feed their offspring. "This may be the last generation of fishermen in the basin," said Greg who had personally planted thousands of cypress trees to replace those razed by loggers. "A lot of them are forced to sell their skiffs."

He devoted his precious free time to photographing the vanishing swamp in all its eery splendor and interviewing the people who'd made it their home for generations, living off of trapping and fishing and even bootlegging, years back. He supplemented his income by talking about the grace of the swamp to passengers aboard the *Delta Queen* steamboat.

His pictures of the vermilion-red swamps and bayous at sunset were almost otherworldly. Greg said it was the burning of the sugar-cane in the fall that turned the sky acid-red. The oaks cloaked in mantilla moss and muscadine vines worked their own magic.

As a parting gift, Greg gave us each an osteoderm, which he used to make jewelry, and sent us down the road to Lillian Blanchard's to see if she would give us Tootie's blackberry pie recipe, which he did not have.

On the short drive to Lillian's house, I stopped to answer nature's call in a sugarcane field, and Teri could not stop laughing when I parted two cane stalks to wave hello and sunk two feet in the mud. I had to ride to Lillian's with my muddied feet hanging out the window, and when I got there, I made a beeline for the garden hose, hoping to rinse off before she saw us.

Lillian caught me, of course, hose in hand. She spoke Cajun French with a heavy Canadian accent, so I couldn't understand much of what she was saying. But I knew she wasn't upset. She talked a bit about Tootie and the pleasures of Pie Day, and then she told us how her mother and aunt had married two men who were brothers.

I thought that was sweet until Lillian said they were also cousins.

Since that wasn't allowed, the parish made each couple pay $10 for the right to marry.

"I guess they thought it was worth it," she said, laughing.

Lillian gave us Tootie's blackberry pie recipe, and we found our way back to the rickety wooden bridge that led to the raised levee, which would take us to Lafayette. We drove "straight off" it, singing "Drove my Betty to the levee but the levee was dry" clear through to the interstate.

On Greg Guirard's advice, after returning to New York, I called Pat Rickels, an English professor and folklorist in Lafayette. Pat hadn't missed a single Pie Day in Catahoula for forty years.

Pat was as warm and friendly on the phone as everyone in Louisiana had been in person. "So, you met Greg," she said, "the Henry Thoreau of the bayou." She was sorry to be the one to tell me that Tootie had passed away since our visit.

"Greg was on the *Delta Queen* when it happened," she said, "and they had to pluck him from the steamboat by helicopter."

I knew this was a great loss for Greg, in the midst of so much loss already.

"Don't worry," said Pat, "in typical Cajun fashion, the funeral was a blast. Tootie would have loved it."

One of Pat's clearest memories of Tootie, she said, was watching her feed *la cuit* to her grandchildren. "First, she'd boil some cane syrup down until it was brown and thick. She'd dip a silver butter knife into the syrup and then dip the knife into a bowl of chopped pecans. Usually, she'd have a grandchild on each knee when she was doing this," said Pat, "and each would take turns licking the sweet crunch right off the blade."

At the funeral, the priest recounted many of Tootie's favorite confessional stories. Like the one about the very loud woman whose sins could be heard by everyone waiting their turn outside the confessional. Tired of asking her to keep her voice down, the priest suggested she jot down her sins on a piece of paper. At her next confession, she slid her list through the small window. "What's this?" he said. "Eggs, milk, butter . . . ?"

"Oh, darn!" the loud woman exclaimed. "I left my sins at the A&P!"

Pat said Tootie was "always aglow" on Pie Day.

"For some reason, it never rains on that day, and all the new babies born that year are there, spread out on a quilt under a tree."

Pat worried about the future of Pie Day, she said, because in recent years, busy people have started bringing "fifty-fifty" pies to the event.

"Fifty-fifty pies?" I asked.

"Yes," she groaned. "Homemade fillings with store-bought crusts—fifty-fifty. It just isn't right. Tootie wouldn't like it one bit."

She paused. "Ah, Tootie . . . She would always watch the clock on Pie Day. And as soon as the priest had blessed the pies, she'd say: 'Let's eat!'

"And then," Pat sighed, "we would all fall into pie."

LIBBY BOLLINO'S RECIPE
FOR TURTLE PIE

1½ 14-ounce bags of caramels

½ cup evaporated milk

1½ sticks of butter

3 ounces unsweetened chocolate

1 cup flour

1½ cups sugar

3 eggs, whole, lightly beaten

¾ cup chopped pecans

1 teaspoon vanilla

1 cup chocolate chips

½ cup pecan halves

Combine the caramels with evaporated milk in a pot and cook at low heat until the caramel melts.

For the brownie layer, melt together the butter and unsweetened chocolate either in a microwave or in a pot on the stove. When chocolate is melted, stir in the flour, sugar, eggs, chopped pecans, vanilla.

Generously grease and flour a 10- or 11-inch pie tin and pour almost half of the brownie mixture into it. Top with a little more than half the caramel mixture, then layer with the rest of the brownie mixture. Spread to cover the caramel entirely. If a little "peeks" out, don't worry. Keep the remaining caramel warm on the lowest possible setting on your stove or reheat when ready to use.

Bake at 350 degrees for 30 minutes. Remove the pie from the oven and let it rest about 5 minutes. Spread remaining caramel over pie and sprinkle with chocolate chips. Arrange pecan halves around edge of pie, then swirl chocolate chips decoratively with a toothpick or a small sharp knife. Refrigerate for at least 1 hour before serving. This pie keeps and travels well. Kids and adults love it.

In the store, we use a sharp knife dipped in very hot water to cut turtle pie. (Use ¾ recipe for 8- or 9-inch pie tins.)

TOOTIE GUIRARD'S GOOD FRIDAY BLACKBERRY PIE

2 quarts blackberries

3 cups sugar

1 crust, plus more dough for the lattice

1 tablespoon flour

2 tablespoons butter

Cover blackberries with sugar and let stand awhile in a bowl. Cook blackberries at low heat until cooked—about 20–30 minutes. Line pie tin with your favorite crust recipe. Sprinkle flour on bottom crust. Pour cooked blackberries into pie shell and dot with butter. Cover top with strips of dough, criss-cross. Bake at 350 degrees for 25–30 minutes. Wait until 10 A.M. before digging in!

let the good times roll

*"He was a preacher . . . and never charged nothing
for his preaching, and it was worth it, too."*
—MARK TWAIN, *THE ADVENTURERS OF HUCKLEBERRY FINN*

Even though we knew Claude was expecting us in Hammond, I did not want to drive past Baton Rouge without at least trying to track down Madear Johnson. Madear was the mother of the shuttle bus driver who'd praised his mother's blueberry pie at JFK airport.

We drove up and down Euclid Avenue and never found the house number Kris had scribbled in her palm. We gave up and pressed on.

Claude had just brought home a floppy black puppy from the local shelter when we arrived. He had not named her yet, so Teri suggested the obvious: Pie.

"I kind of like that," said Claude. "Paaaahhhhhhh it is."

Did Claude really want to commit to a name that would have people scratching their heads?

"Oh, that doesn't bother me," said Claude. "I used to have a cat named Sofa."

We celebrated the naming by eating Libby's slightly weathered pies. Everyone loved the turtle pie best. The edges had softened in travel, but that sweet caramel filling hit a home run—especially with Claude. Claude's best friend Rodney, also an old friend of Teri's, dropped by to take us out for catfish dinner. Rodney was a handsome

man who could charm the skin off an alligator. Teri had warned me about his legendary womanizing. But the only woman he was talking about that night at dinner was his mama. Mama Millsap and her apple pie.

"She doesn't use a top crust," he said with a certain pride. "And she adds whipping cream to the filling to take the edge off the apples."

He licked his lips.

"Nothing can ever top your mama's pie," he said. *"Nothing."*

I had very high pie hopes for New Orleans.

After all, "let the good times roll" refers to a rolling pin, does it not?

We stopped at Café du Monde to get beignets and our bearings. Claude and Rodney said a man named Omar peddled his small sweet-potato pies and pecan pies in the streets of the French Quarter and, with some confectioners' sugar still on our lips, Teri and I set out to find him on foot.

It was dangerously hot. Adultery weather.

On Dumaine Street, one block from the St. Louis Cathedral, we paused in front of a witchcraft shop, and something—supernatural, I'm sure—pulled us inside. A young man named Chesley, with hair dyed violet and cut à la James Dean, sat in a cloud of burning frankincense behind a counter cluttered with potions. Behind him, shelves were lined with old apothecary jars of herbs and roots and powders. His eyes lit up when we mentioned pie.

"I love pie," he said, lowering his voice on the word *love*. Chesley was from Moscow, Texas, originally. Population 200. His fondest memories, he told us, were of picking blackberries along rutted dirt roads so that his French grandmother, Marcelle, could make her famous blackberry pie. More important, he'd recently made a "love pie" for his girlfriend on her birthday. For the filling, he used rose petals, hibiscus, and raspberry jam.

"No one had ever baked a pie for her before," he said. "It must have worked because we ate the whole thing, and she *still* loves me."

Chesley is a true fellow believer in the power of pie. He reached for the *Victorian Grimoire*, the famous book of spells, and read pie passages aloud to us. The Grimoire suggested that baking pie is a wonderful way to manifest your desires. "Concentrate very hard on what you desire while you're making the pie, and then while you're eating it, and your desire will come true."

What if your desire is to learn how to make a flaky, tender crust? I asked. Is there a spell for that?

Chesley rubbed his pointed chin. "I don't have a spell, but I could certainly come up with an herb potion that might do the trick.

"Kava kava would work to relax you before you went into the kitchen," he said. "And valerian and galangal root would both help for courage."

And while we were on the subject of magic potions, I asked Chesley if he had any quick-potion fixes for my unresolved love life. He handed me a tiny red pouch with a black drawstring, filled with a mysterious batch of herbs sure to make me irresistible. I was seeking clarity, not another man, but heck, it was only $3, so I bought it. Even though Teri was getting married in three weeks, she bought one, too. (On her wedding invitation, Teri was described as someone who didn't know "if marriage was a word or a sentence.")

We asked Chesley, who was in his late 20s, why wicca and other forms of "natural" witchcraft were so popular among men and women his age. "I think people of my generation have really lost touch with their spirituality," he said. "They're searching for something, anything, to bring meaning into their lives."

A young man with a goatee came in for a tarot card reading—so we said good-bye. "Good-bye, ladies of pastry," Chesley said. "Good luck on your rolling-pin chronicles."

We'd barely rounded the corner onto Chartres Street, when two city police officers on foot patrol stopped us in our tracks.

"Hey, ladies," said one of the officers. "You looking for a date?"

"Wow. Those pouches are amazing," I whispered to Teri. Then I realized the officers were jokingly offering up a town drunk they were arresting—not for the first time. They were waiting for a patrol unit to come take their handcuffed charge away, killing time teasing tourists. The drunk knew the drill. He was laughing right along with them.

Since these officers worked the street, I thought they might know Omar. They did, but they said Omar was very elusive.

"You just never know where you're going to see him next," the burlier of the two said. "I haven't seen him in a week."

"But you know who else makes really good pie?" one officer began to say. "Carl Dennis." I swear to God, just then, Carl Dennis himself crossed the street. He was also in uniform, though he was a security guard at a museum—not a cop.

"Did I hear someone mention pie?" Carl said, smiling. Turned out, he, too, sold sweet-potato pies and pecan pies in the French Quarter, on his breaks before and after work. "My father's the baker," said Carl. "He's a preacher and he makes them from scratch several times a week."

Naturally, we invited ourselves over to watch later that day.

Minister Edgar had been baking for more than fifty years, and he seemed delighted to be finally baking for an audience. He was wearing a bright white guayabera shirt and had all of his ingredients laid out on the island in the middle of his sunny kitchen. His plan was to make sixteen pies—eight sweet-potato and eight pecan—for Carl to sell in the Quarter the following day, at $2 a pop. Edgar went to school to learn how to cook after a stint in the army, courtesy of the GI Bill, and before becoming a merchant marine, he spent time cooking in a local hospital.

He confessed to having led a wanton life while at sea, but, he said, he'd been walking on very firm ground since he'd come home for good. He credited his wife, Archie Ernestine, for setting him straight.

"Women always take men to church," he said. "Men take women every place else."

Minister Edgar said he was "a preacher, not a teacher," but when making dough, he became both.

In a large stainless-steel mixing bowl, he mixed together flour and shortening, a dash of salt and a bit of sugar. He did not measure any of his ingredients, and bristled when I asked about that. For the next fifteen minutes or so, he held the bowl firmly down with one hand. With the other, he used a fork to mix its contents, working it in tight, concentric circles. How would he know, exactly, when to stop mixing?

"How can I explain in words something you've got to see with your eyes?" he said. "I just can't explain."

I was riveted by his wiry forearms and his hands, especially the one holding on to the bowl for dear life. The thumb was long and thin and capped by the smoothest of nails, as pointed as a papal hat.

The dough resembled gritty cornmeal as he added ice-cold water, one drop at a time. "See how it's holding together?" he said. "*Now* it's ready."

He scooped the dough out from the bowl and onto a circular work board, and pressed all his weight onto the dough mass, working it with his knuckles like a knotted muscle. He pinched a piece of the dough mass, and tossed it from one palm to the other like a Hacky Sack. He'd then flop it on the board to flatten it out with his old rolling pin with loose red handles.

"I've had this rolling pin as long as I've lived in this house—and that's more than 40 years," he said.

It was easy to see why the handles hadn't come off despite years of wear and tear: he didn't use them. The pies were so small, and the pin so long, he griped the pin about four inches in from the handles. He rolled twice back and forth, added a speck of flour, turned the disk, rolled again, twice, back and forth. He picked up the disk of flour and dropped it into an aluminum pan about 5 inches across. Since the dough was a hair short, its edges fluted straight up. He tamed the petals of dough by crimping the edges down with the tines of a fork ("no fancy tools necessary"), and then, with a knife, he trimmed the excess edges so that they curled into a small pile, like wood shavings on a carpenter's floor.

As he worked, he threw in the occasional preacher's pearl of wisdom.

"The trick to a long and happy marriage," he told Teri, who'd brought up her impending wedding, "is respect."

"Let me ask you this. Do you say 'thank you'?" He pointed a floured finger at her. "People don't say 'thank you' anymore out of foolish pride," he said. "But a 'thank you' goes a long, long way. It's all about respect."

The minister continued to roll out his small discs of dough. "Ahem. Uh-huh. Amen."

As I stood there, leaning against the kitchen wall, I thought this was a church I could come to every Sunday.

There was a knock at the back door. Two grade-school girls came looking for "icebergs"—popsicles without the stick the minister made and sold to the kids in the neighborhood for 50 cents a pop. Popsicle sales helped pay for the pie ingredients, Carl explained.

When the pie pans were lined, the minister worked on the fillings. He added melted butter to about two pounds of cooked, peeled, and quartered sweet potatoes. Then he scooped up two generous scoops of sugar from the sugar bucket under the island, tossed some cinnamon into the mix, gave it one good stir, and, pleased with the deep, burnt-orange color of the mixture, poured it straight from the bowl into each pie shell.

"See? How could I learn to make pies? Not only does he not measure anything, he doesn't *taste* anything, either," wailed Carl.

For the pecan pie, Minister Edgar mixed Karo syrup "black or white, it doesn't make much difference," melted butter, sugar, and a handful of flour, which he stirred with a whisk. He dropped a handful of pecans (from a neighbor's tree down the street) into the bottom of each pie, and then poured the sweet filling right on top.

"This gets me every time," said Carl. "Watch how the pecans start at the bottom but then float right to the top."

"It's one of those life mysteries," said Minister Edgar. "It's kind of nice that people don't know *everything* in life."

While the pies baked, filling the house with a warm spicy incense, Archie Ernestine, who had stayed in the living room, finally wandered into the kitchen. Was it the smell that brought her in, I asked.

"No," the minister said. "My wife told me many, many years ago that she likes her sweets walkin' and talkin.' "

Archie Ernestine had also done her part for this country. In the early 1950s, when only 20 percent of the black population was registered to vote in the South, the NAACP launched a massive get-out-the-vote campaign. Archie Ernestine set up a folding card-table on a dock on the river to help rural blacks register to vote. Many of them did not know their own age, and Archie Ernestine helped them figure it out. She was arrested for helping to sign up about a hundred blacks, she said with surprisingly little rancor. "Those were different times."

The minister, clearly, did not want to go there. Didn't want to talk about those times. Not when pies were in the oven.

He swung open the oven door and practically stuck his head inside. He liked what he saw.

"These pies are ready!" he declared. Usually, the minister went to the trouble of naming each pie as he pulled them out of the oven, Carl said, "as if they were hurricanes." The minister did it merely to keep track of them, but on this day, the pies remained nameless, if not faceless. Teri and I bought two of each and dug into the sweet potato right then and there, in the minister's kitchen. The filling was so steaming hot, it burned the roof of my mouth without even touching it.

"They say American as apple pie," said the minister. "But this here sweet potato pie is *Negro* pie."

I couldn't think of a better pie for Teri, who was flying out the next morning, to end her trip on. I was tempted to ask for the recipe, but I knew what the minister would say.

"Some mysteries are better left unknown."

Archie Ernestine shoved an old crinkled envelope in my hand, as we were leaving. "I wrote it long ago," she said. "Take it."

Teri drove us back to our hotel in the French Quarter. It was still light out, but the heat was starting to slink away. I smoothed out the paper in my hand, an old bill-payment envelope from Whirlpool, and read out loud:

Minister Edgar Crawford and "helpers"

To open the door, facing your own future for the first time,
Is quite a frightening thing to your heart, soul, and mind.
When you open the door to your future, you get a chill.
You must pray for strength, placing all things in God's will.
From this day forward, you are beginning on your own.
It is a great step, yet mind-boggling to face all the responsibilities
now that you are grown.
Forge ahead with great determination, do what you must,
It's your salvation.
Don't look back, be firm in things you do.
Remember, every successful person has passed this way too.

"Did she really write that?" Teri asked.

"Teri," I said, "some mysteries are better left unknown."

The day had been as rich as roux, and we couldn't think of a better way to end it than listening to some scratchy live jazz at Preservation Hall.

"Tuba Fats" was in the house that night. The celebrated street musician had lugged his tuba around the world, but this was where he was born to play. After the set, I reached into my purse to leave a tip for the musicians in the designated basket. Instead of my wallet, I grabbed one of Minister Edgar's small pecan pies. I tentatively handed the still-warm pie wrapped in plastic to Tuba. His eyes bulged.

"That's a Carl Dennis pie," he said, extending his open palm.

And I do believe that was the best barter ever made in Ole Louisian'.

MAMA MILLSAP'S
OPEN-FACED APPLE PIE

CRUST

1 9-inch pie crust

FILLING

1½ cups granulated sugar

⅓ cup flour

1 pint tart apples, sliced very thin

¼ teaspoon nutmeg

1 cup heavy whipping cream

Mix the sugar and flour together well. Sprinkle some of this dry mixture on the bottom of the crust. Add sliced apples, sprinkle rest of dry mixture over the apples, then add the nutmeg.

Pour cream over the mixture. Toss gently by hand. Bake in oven set at 400 degrees for 15 minutes. Reduce heat to 350 degrees and bake 45 minutes longer.

the nicole states

(most of them, anyway)

"The very essence of apple pie nowadays is its frozenness . . .
Instead of saying 'as American as apple pie' it would
obviously be more accurate to say: 'as cold as apple pie.'
Who wants our national warmth, charm and
loveability likened to frigid pastry?"

—RUSSELL BAKER, *NEW YORK TIMES*

Nicole had barely buckled her seat belt when she announced that she had a hankering for junk food.

"Bring on the hydrogenated oils," she said.

What is it about the open road that makes a grown woman pine for purple jawbreakers and Tennessee-style barbecued corn chips—stuff we wouldn't dream of buying at home?

"Eating junk food is the whole reason for a road trip," says Nicole.

And the gas stations know it, don't they? The way they cram those goodies right next to the cash register prompting impulse purchases of Bazooka bubble gum, Red Vines licorice, and Slim Jim beef sticks.

In the Rocky Mountain states, gas station counters are lined with jars of buffalo jerky flavored with everything from cherry to jalapeno. In Wisconsin, cheese products in all shapes, and even on a stick, taunt the traveler. And in Alabama, pickled pig lips are the road tripper's snack of choice.

"I've never had them," said the cashier at one Amoco station, of the ballerina-pink hog smackers floating in a murky liquid that looked like formaldehyde. "But we go through two of those tubs a week."

"They go down great with Budweiser," a lanky trucker chimed in as he grabbed a couple pairs to go.

Nicole and Teri had crossed paths in the middle of the night in New Orleans. There was no official passing of the highlighter pen as there had been with Kris and Teri in Ponder, and I was sorry about that.

I took Nicole to Café du Monde for breakfast, and spread the Southeastern states map on the table. Nicole's face went blank.

"I can't read maps," she said.

"HA HA," I said, removing the highlighter pen cap with my teeth.

"No, really, I couldn't read a map if my life depended on it."

How could a woman who knew how to temper chocolate and make beignets as light as baby puffer fish not know east from west, or that the little red arrow meant an exit off the interstate?

"I'll drive, you navigate," she said.

It was probably for the best, since I had done very little advance work for this, last leg of the trip, and would be doing some reporting in the car.

I knew I wanted to find good pie near the White House and, of course, Golden Peach pie in Georgia. But no pie came immediately to mind when I thought of Alabama. We'd play the Yellowhammer State by ear.

Shortly after leaving New Orleans, at a gas station near the Mississippi-Alabama border, Nicole went inside a gas station to use the ladies' room and emerged with a fried peach pie, pleased as Punch. The greasy pie was a belly bomb of the highest order.

"I was hoping to keep my junk food and my pie intake separate," said Nicole. I demonstrated the concept of "Dumpster pie" and we carried on to US 43, which cut straight through Alabama from south to north.

Of all the roads I've taken across America, the stretch of US 43 between Mobile and Demopolis has got to be the creepiest. For miles on end, we passed mysterious industrial complexes, which offered no clue as to what went on inside.

Weird genetic research, we decided.

In fact, our stint in Alabama was creepy from start to finish. It is not a state I wish to malign, so I will spare you the details. Suffice to say that we did not get a good pie vibe. And, if we didn't bail soon, I was worried Nicole might jump ship.

Things improved markedly the moment we left Tuscaloosa and headed for Georgia on Route 78, a lush, wily road that meandered through the Alabama Pine Belt and continued almost straight on through to Atlanta.

Rusted-out dishwashers and disemboweled refrigerators lined the road for a good 20 miles.

"A different kind of roadkill, I guess," said Nicole. We dubbed Alabama the Multitasking State after spotting a gas station peddling chicken wings, and a bait shop that offered cheddar biscuits and tanning beds. Our favorite was the hair sea-lon with inflatable pool toys in the window. "Get a trim while you swim?" asked Nicole.

We crossed the Sweet Georgia sign just as the bruised peach of a sun was pressing into the horizon.

WELCOME, WE'RE GLAD GEORGIA'S ON YOUR MIND.

Late July is prime peach season. The plan was to head to Fort Valley, right in Peach County, to get our hands on some fresh peach pie. But an acquaintance who grew up in Atlanta told me I couldn't leave Georgia without stopping in the capital for some of that white-bean pie, so popular in the black West End neighborhood.

We drove through a bleak, industrial section of town where we watched black Muslim families setting up picnic tables on loading docks in factory parking lots. Sunday picnic amid abandoned cars and brimming trash containers. We talked of the parks and trees we'd taken for granted as children.

My Atlanta friend had told us we could find white-bean pie anywhere in the neighborhood, so we stopped at the first restaurant we saw.

Three black men in colorful African djellabas, who were standing on the sidewalk, said they owned the place, which was vegan, but they'd never heard of white-bean pie.

Perhaps we'd have better luck at Chanterelle across the way, they suggested. Chanterelle was a soul-food postchurch mecca. Men in suits the color of Buicks, and women shoehorned into tight, frilly dresses gathered around the display case examining the goods.

"White-bean pie? Never heard of it," said the chef. "We serve red-velvet cake here." He pointed to a ruby-red frosted cake. Dessert as bridesmaid dress. "Maybe the Jamaican place down the street could help you out."

Taste of Tropical, anchoring a nondescript strip mall, was, unfortunately, closed. I peered through the glass anyway, and noticed a gentleman in a floral shirt sitting on a ladder, changing the licorice-red magnetic letters on the menu board. I rapped on the door, and he scissored his hands in the universal gesture that means "we're closed." But I wasn't about to leave Atlanta without a taste of this mystery pie.

"Do you sell white-bean pie?" I mouthed. His frown melted into a smile, and he stepped down from his ladder.

"How do you know about white-bean pie?" he asked, opening the door. "White-bean pie is a down-home specialty." Joscelyn Crumbery's voice was hilly, and I wished we could pipe him through Betty's radio for those long flat stretches of the road like that dreadful US 43 in Alabama. Shortly after he'd opened this restaurant, Joscelyn said, an elderly Jamaican offered to make the traditional pies for a fair price. Joscelyn tried one of the old man's pies, and they brought him straight to the shade of a coconut tree. A deal was struck.

"They have been flying out the door ever since, mon," he said, slapping his knee. We asked Joscelyn if we could meet the baker, maybe even add the recipe to our collection.

"Sorry, mon," he said. "It's Sunday and that's a sacred day for his family." He pulled a small, individual white-bean pie out of the freezer for us to take on the road. We popped it in the still-broken glove compartment. "It'll thaw by the time we get to Fort Valley," I said.

Nicole hadn't said much all morning. In fact, Nicole could go for hours, it seemed, without so much as a peep. It was where she was in her life, and that was fine with me. I'd absorbed so much in the last few weeks, my thoughts were swirling.

Then, out of the blue, Nicole said: "I don't think I would have ever ended up in an all-black neighborhood on the outskirts of Atlanta, if we hadn't been looking for pie." And, although our first couple of days together on the road had been trying, I was glad she was beginning to see the point.

It took a while to escape the urban sprawl that was Atlanta, but when we entered peach country, everything changed. Even Betty Blue ran better.

Stately pecan trees replaced steely office buildings. They were draped in Spanish moss, *abuelas* going to mass in their mantillas. Spanish moss, also called horsehair, is a relative of the pineapple. It isn't really a moss at all, but an epiphyte with no root system, which lives off moisture in the atmosphere. I wondered why it hadn't started growing in Betty Blue's interior.

We stopped at a McDonald's for a soda, and the woman ahead of us in line was demanding one of their new lemon pies. McDonald's had launched a new pie flavor, and I wasn't informed? McDonald's pie, incidentally, is the only pie in America that comes with a warning label—HOT.

The counter girl kindly explained that they'd run plumb out of the new pies. "As I told you yesterday, lady," the cashier said, "the new shipment won't arrive until tomorrow."

In Perry, we got a room in the stodgy but classic 1920s Perry Hotel. We took a dip in the tiny pool, then dined in the gussied-up coffee shop.

I begged our waitress for something—anything—green.

Nicole may have been craving Pixie Stix, but I wanted vegetables. Sure, you can find a salad in Middle America, but you will have to excavate through a mountain of packaged, cardboard croutons and a heaping cup of creamy ranch dressing before you come across anything green or fibrous that's ever hit dirt.

Vegetables are either tucked in a casserole or deep fried—rarely served in the raw.

At a catfish restaurant in Alabama, the young waitress took a timid step back when I told her I would kill for a side of vegetables, reinforcing all her stereotypes about aggressive New Yorkers. And no, I kindly told her, those itsy bitsy chopped scallions in my hush-puppies didn't count.

"We don't have vegetables, except for turnip greens," she said. She returned swinging a sand pail of turnip greens drenched in a butter bath.

Our waitress in Perry suggested we try the "congealed shower salad," a house—and Georgia—specialty.

When she set the oval dish in the middle of the table, Nicole and I stared at the jiggly pink scoop for a long time, afraid to touch it. The texture resembled grainy watermelon flesh, and it was topped with a dollop of Miracle Whip.

Nicole braved it first. She tasted pineapple, grape, and cherries, before she identified it as canned fruit cocktail that had been Robocouped. What made it a "salad" was the single Iceberg lettuce leaf on which it sat, triumphant.

"Look," said Nicole, "you got something green."

There was pie on the menu. After our chicken-fried steak, we ordered apple and pecan, since peach was conspicuously absent. This was Nicole's first fresh pie slice of the trip and I could read the disappointment in her eyes the moment they arrrived. The crusts were yielding, spongy, anemic. The fillings listless.

"The person who made these doesn't love pie," said Nicole after two bites. The restaurant manager came around like a cat in heat, asking about the pies.

"They're absolutely sinful," I said. I winked at Nicole. No harm. No foul.

Our bellies anchored, we retired to our room to plan the next day's itinerary. I remembered the white-bean pie still in the glove compartment and snuck out in my jammies to get it. It was at the perfect melting point. The gingerbread topping still crunched, and the crust had not lost its spine despite the heat and long drive. The Navajo-white filling was creamy, like a pudding.

"Now *this* is pie, mon," said Nicole.

When the writer M. F. K. Fisher was asked by Richard Sax to describe her most memorable meal, this is what she said:

I was about eight, with my father and my little sister, driving in our Model T from the desert foothills of southern California . . . [Irish Mary had given us] a big peach pie for the trip down past Los Angeles to our little town of Whittier, and beside it in the wooden lug-box, she put a pint Mason jar of thick cream, with three old chipped soup plates and three spoons and a knife . . . once down into the winding mountain roads, live oaks cooled the air, and we stopped at a camp where there were some tables, and ate the whole peach pie, still warm from Irish Mary's oven . . . We poured cream from the jar onto the pieces Father cut for us, and thick sweet juices ran into delicious puddles.

"That's the peach pie experience I'm looking for," I told Nicole over breakfast the next morning, before we doubled back to Fort Valley.

Fort Valley was initially named Fox Valley, but, as the story goes, when the name was submitted to the Post Office in 1825, the illegible cat scratch was misread as "Fort," and the name stuck. Fort Valley used to be a cotton center primarily, but that changed after 1875, when Samuel H. Rumph introduced a new peach variety: the Elberta. Rumph named the clear-seeded peach with yellow flesh and a crimson blush on its cheek after his wife, Clara Elberta Moore.

He'd been experimenting with many peach varieties, but the Elberta was his favorite. It was so firm that when Rumph sent a test shipment to New York, he didn't even pack them in ice. They arrived intact.

The Elberta became the workhorse peach of the area. Back then, and even as recently as 1970, there were thirty peach-packing facilities within 30 miles of Fort Valley. Only six are left. On our way into town, we followed signs toward one of them, advertising free tours.

There were several pans of gooey peach cobbler in the plant restaurant, but not a slice of pie in sight. Maybe one of the assembly-line workers could suggest a place in town for peach pie.

"I'm Bertha Mae and I separate the good from the bad," said a black woman with curlers in her hair, whom we approached in the "sorting" line. Peaches rolled by Bertha Mae at the rate of two hundred thousand per hour, and her job was to spy the ones with flaws and send them barreling down a separate chute.

She'd been with the company for thirty years, had worked "just about every line," but she liked sorting best. She still took pride in her job and even wore dangling peach earrings.

Bertha Mae told us she was more of a cobbler person herself, and she was about to give me the name of a dear friend in town who made a wicked peach pie, when her supervisor ordered her back to work.

Thirty years with a company won't buy you five minutes of chitchat. I apologized on her behalf, but he was intransigent.

I wanted to jump on the sorting machine and hold up a UNION sign but stuck my tongue out at his turned back instead. Bertha Mae laughed behind her hands.

On Main Street, signs like SKIPPER'S PEACH SHOE REPAIR and BRENDA'S PEACH PIANO had me convinced that everything peach was within reach. But neither café had peach pie on the menu.

MaryAnne, a chatty woman behind the pharmacy counter at the local drugstore could help us, but only if we wanted pecan pie, not peach.

Her husband was a pecan broker, she said, and she'd spent years tweaking her pecan pie recipe.

"You want to know my secret?" she said. "I use brown sugar instead of Karo syrup. My husband goes nuts over it.

"Men just love pie," she added. "Steak'll get 'em in a heartbeat, but pie will finish the job."

Georgia, Texas, and Alabama all produce pecans, MaryAnne said, but Georgia's are superior since they get more rain, which makes them more oily and more flavorful.

"Texas pecans tend to run very dry," she said with condescension, "which is why they usually end up in box candies, like Whitman's Samplers."

We agreed Georgia's pecan trees looked particularly regal.

"Don't be fooled," she said. "It doesn't take but a puff of wind to knock one down."

For all things peach, she suggested we talk to Matt Mullis. The young Matt was the man in charge of cooking the gargantuan peach cobbler for the annual peach festival. The cobbler fed three thousand.

Matt, a contractor, was remodeling an antebellum mansion, soon to be the city administrations office. He was taking measurements in the mayor's new digs when we turned up.

He said he'd recently taken over the cobbler responsibility to honor his late mother, famous in the area for her pies, which were as delicious as they were pretty.

The cobbler, which must be stirred with yard rakes, was baked in a pan that was 6 feet wide by 11 feet long and 1 foot deep. It required 90 pounds of sugar and 75 gallons of Georgia peaches.

"Fresh peaches, of course. I won't eat a canned-peach pie or cobbler. When you live here, you can taste the difference."

That is, if you can ever find a slice.

"Maybe we'll have better luck in Savannah," Nicole said, as we left peach country, peach-deprived.

Cemeteries have always given me the willies. So I considered it a real breakthrough that I traipsed through so many of them on this trip. From the power walk in the Wellsboro Cemetery with Kris, to our stroll through the Breaux Bridge Cemetery with Teri, I was learning to appreciate their stillness and grace. So, when Nicole made a request to visit Savannah's Bonaventure Cemetery, the literal midnight garden of good and evil in John Berendt's runaway best-seller, I obliged.

One of the secretaries flat-out sneered when we walked into the musty office, suspecting we were like the millions of tourists who've descended on Savannah since the book's success. I assured her we were not *Midnight* groupies. Intrigued, she sniffed the air like a pointer.

"I just was wondering if you could tell us where to go for good pie in Savannah," I said. "Unless you make a good pie yourself."

She was visibly thrown.

"I . . . I . . . I have a wonderful recipe for sweet-potato pie," she said. Then she stiffened. "But what makes you think I would give it to you? No way. I ain't telling. I ain't telling you about my crust, and I ain't telling you about my filling neither. No sirree. Uh-uh."

Nicole, who isn't big on confrontation, was already backing out the door. I, on the other hand, would not leave until I'd found a soft side to this woman. I asked her which of the tombs in the cemetery was her favorite.

"Everyone makes such a big deal about the little girl on the cover of the book," she said, shaking her head. "But my favorite tomb is the one of Gracie.

"She was a beautiful little girl, and she done died too young."

Gracie Watson was the only child of W. J. Watson, who owned the Pulaski Hotel in town. She was born in 1883 and died of pneumonia six years later. Her parents commissioned a white marble sculpture from a local artist. His sculpture had her in a frilly dress and high-buttoned shoes, sitting on a tree stump, with a wildflower in her hand.

For some reason, visitors have never been able to keep their hands off of Gracie, the secretary said. For years, they stroked her sculpted hair and her legs, so that much of the statue's fine detail had been worn away. A few years ago, a protective fence was finally erected around the tomb.

We told her we'd go take a look at Gracie. The woman smiled. She wouldn't give us her sweet-potato pie recipe, but she'd loosened up enough to suggest we try The Lady and Sons, right downtown. We strolled through the cemetery for a good hour and, as promised, we stopped to pay our respects to the little girl.

Paula Deen, the lady behind The Lady and Sons restaurant, was sitting in one of her restaurant booths, reading glasses pinching her nose, going over the books when we turned up.

"Pie?" she said, removing her glasses. "Haven't you heard? Pie is on the endangered species list.

" 'As American as apple pie'? Huh! Pie's becoming obsolete."

Deen, considered by many to be the doyenne of Georgia cooking, admitted she was just as guilty as the next turncoat, having substituted cobbler for pie at her restaurant. "It just isn't cost- or time-efficient to make pie at a restaurant that serves between four and six hundred people a day.

"It's *first-rate* cobbler, mind you, but it's not pie. And there is a difference." I was glad we were on the same page.

Deen told us she learned to make fried-apple pies and dried-fruit pies from her grandmother. "I was lucky. I had twenty years of watching my grandmother cook, right by her side. Newer generations aren't that lucky. Not a day goes by that I don't tell one of my customers: 'talk to your grandmother!'

"It's so important that children don't let recipes die with their elders."

But that was exactly what was happening with pie, she said. "It used to be that people in the South showed their love and affection with pie.

"When someone moved into the neighborhood, or had a bad day, you'd bake them a pie."

"My big fear," she said, "is that new generations have been weaned on so much processed food that they actually *like* the taste of a frozen-crust pie," she said. "They think that's what they are *supposed* to taste like."

She was right, of course. I thought of my niece, of all the Dumpster pies we'd tasted on this trip, and of the woman near Atlanta, pining for McDonald's new lemon pie.

"I'll tell you, I'd run a country mile for a slice of good homemade coconut cream."

Our visit with Paula had left us deflated. Nicole hadn't really known what to expect on this trip. Truth is, Nicole had never really thought much about pie in her rarefied world of haute pastry.

But I could see it dawning on her that pie was a lot like a neglected spouse. It can be taken for granted for only so long, before it disappears.

I repeated Evelyn's words of caution that she spoke back in Ponder:

"One of these days, you're going to look up and be looking for fresh pies, and you're going to realize there's nobody cookin' them no more."

I think Nicole was starting to share some of Paula Deen's guilt.

"Maybe we should start some sort of national pie movement," she said. "Get people baking pie again."

I needed no convincing. "Yeah. Like when Gandhi tried to get his countrymen to sew their own dhotis," I said.

Dreaming up ways such a movement could work kept us entertained all the way to historic Georgetown, South Carolina, our next stop.

In the lobby of our motel, I looked down and saw that Lafayette had once stood at that very spot—although probably not fumbling for his American Express card.

The liberty-loving marquis's bust was all over historic George-town, which, we learned at the Rice Museum, was once surrounded by rice plantations. The museum ladies with their jasmine-white hair were delighted to help us find pie. They huddled and all agreed there was only one place to go: "the Kudzu Bakery, of course."

"It's not like any bakery you've ever seen," they said.

As we headed out the door, one of the elderly ladies followed us out. "I'm originally from New Jersey," she said. "So, I feel it's my duty to warn you about something."

We leaned in closer.

"OKRA," she whispered. "It's slimy. It's awful. It's everywhere."

Customers spilled out of the Kudzu Bakery screen door with children in tow and white cardboard boxes in each hand. A perfect combination of rustic and modern, homey and hip, the bakery was packed. Behind the curved glass of the display case, classic Southern desserts preened like majorettes: red-velvet cakes with fresh cream-cheese frosting; lemon cakes brushed with a honey syrup and covered with almond-cookie crumbs. And pies. Glorious-looking pies.

Nicole and I spotted the peach pie at the exact same time, and a girlish smile spread across Nicole's face.

"We're not sharing, right?" she said. We each got our own slice and carried it to the pineboard bar that jutted out of a brick wall lined with shelves of elderberry-and-kudzu jelly, pear butter, and fig preserves in the back of the bakery.

The pie had been baked in a quiche pan, so it had a regal, tall collar of a crust. The peach slices were roughly cut, churlish, and tawny. We took one bite and sighed. We weren't on the side of a Southern

California road, there was no cream, and our daddies were miles and miles away, but this was bliss.

I ranked the Kudzu Bakery pie right up there with the apple-blueberry from Mammy's Cupboard and the huckleberry-peach at the Spruce Park Café in Montana. We sought out the owner to tell him so. Joey was at his second shop next door, where he sold kitchen equipment and plenty of pie pans, rolling pins, and mixing bowls in muted retro colors. We were surprised a place as small as George-town could support such a fancy baking retail shop.

"People in town liked the pies at the bakery so much, a lot of them got inspired to make their own," said Joey.

We told him about our visit with Paula Deen, whose bleak pie forecast seemed to contradict Georgetown's pie spirit. Was there hope for pie in America?

"You bet there is."

Joey said the bakery sold twenty pies a day—four hundred the day before Thanksgiving. "We start making them three days before the holiday," he said. "We set up bunk beds in the loft above the bakery, so that the help can catch some shut-eye between shifts." Joey refused to use a pie press, so the staff could make only thirty-four pie crusts at one time.

"I'm a nonsymmetrical kind of guy," he explained, which was why each of his pies looked so beautifully flawed, so unconditionally loved.

We got to talking about the power of pie. I told him about Dave the Montana bear trapper who baked his way out of his depression.

Joey understood full well the power of pie-baking to transform and transcend. A therapist friend of his had once asked him to hire a young woman he knew who was going through a difficult time. She was married with two small children and "struggling with her iden-tity," he said.

"She really had a hard time with the dough at first, but, eventually, she got it, and when she did, she became a much more confident person after that."

So confident, that the woman, Susan, had recently returned to Columbia, where she and her husband planned to open a bakery of their own. We told Joey we'd stop by on our way to North Carolina to visit with her.

"Tell her we all miss her," he said.

He gave us his card, and I noticed the pun, "simply *divine*," under the Kudzu Bakery name and smiled.

Legend has it that in the South, mothers keep a close eye on their sleeping babies to protect them from the mighty kudzu vine, a choker of a broad-leafed weed that can grow at the rate of a foot per day and smother anything in its path. Leave your car in the drive when you go on vacation, and, chances are, it'll be locked in kudzu when you return. Oddly enough, the nonnative plant was brought here by the Japanese as a symbolic ornamental gift for the 1876 Centennial Exposition in Philadelphia.

On our way to Columbia, we fell behind a burnished-red flatbed truck loaded down with two enormous coils of thick wire that looked like giant eyes staring us down.

We lost it when we stopped for gas at a BP in Paxville that advertised great gas prices and "butt meat and liver pudding" to boot.

Under a warm summer rain, we found our way to the bakery in West Columbia, where Susan was working temporarily. She came out wiping her hands on her apron, and, over coffee, she told us how baking had changed her life.

"I was a gifted and talented underachiever who had dropped out of school in tenth grade," she said. She'd married and had children young, she said, and one day she looked up and realized she didn't know who she was.

"I know making pie isn't rocket science," she said, "but there's something about it that is really gratifying.

"Once I conquered my fear of dough, I felt like I had conquered my 20s," she said. "Mastering crust opened the door for more achievement."

On our way to North Carolina, I wanted to stop in historic Pendleton, which, according to my handy AAA guidebook, was known for its craftspeople, namely potters. We stopped at the first potter's studio we found near Pendleton. A woman who had taken up pottery in her golden years let us watch her work in her backyard shed. I spotted a rolling pin on the table behind her and asked about it. "Oh," she laughed. "I use it to roll out my clay, but that doesn't mean I can make a pie."

For pie, she suggested we head to a bakery in downtown Pendleton, near Mechanic Street. That was perfect, since Betty Blue needed another oil change. "All the pies are handmade from recipes that come from the owner's grandmother," she said, visibly impressed.

I felt good leaving Betty Blue in the care of the elderly man who ran the garage. If he treated her as well as his perfectly pressed uniform, she'd be fine.

We walked along a shady path of dogwoods down the road to the bakery, on the first floor of an old, turn-of-the-century home. A crape myrtle tree in the side yard was afire with fuchsia blossoms. Vintage school desks were lined up on the wide front porch. With its rocking chairs, crocheted lace runners, and old photographs, the front parlor reminded me of a movie set. The woman behind the register seemed to be in character. She was dour and wore her hair in a granny bun though she appeared to be only in her late 40s. We asked about her orchard pie and when she told us it was house-made we each ordered a slice.

"We only sell the pies whole!" she snapped.

As she slid the whole pie into a box, we asked her about Grandma's special crust. Was it lard or butter? She mumbled something about the crust being made off-premise. So, we asked about Grandma's special filling. Well, that came delivered, too, she said under her breath.

"Oh, so the pies are *not* made here," I said, just to be clear. "Some are, but some are just assembled here," she said, never looking up at us. We took our whole pie on the porch and each ate a slice, sitting in the old wooden school chairs. The pie wasn't half bad, and the fruit in the filling—we guessed pear, blueberry, cranberry, and apple— stayed whole and flavorful. But there was a distinct cheapness to it. It had no integrity. This was one recipe I did not want.

The husband came out on the porch to chat and maybe make up for his wife's rudeness. When he found out we were researching pie in America, he was eager to tell us about the recent Pillsbury bake-off pie "scandal." Apparently, the most recent winner of the national competition had, er, uh, "lifted" her winning recipe from their bakery, he said, hoping to rouse some anger.

We shrugged our shoulders.

"What goes around, comes around," I said to Nicole as we headed back to the garage.

The mechanic was pinching my blackened air filter between his thumb and forefinger and showing it to a regular customer of his, when we returned.

"I've never seen one this bad," he said. "We had to order one from Clemson. It should be here in about an hour."

We handed him the leftovers of our orchard pie and decided to walk off the "bad karma" slices while we waited for Betty. This last pie had really gotten to Nicole, had wounded her and her craft. There was only one way out of her funk.

"Let's buy some crap," she said, spotting a corner market.

We walked out loaded down with hot tamale candies, bubble gum, and corn chips for the drive to Pittsboro, North Carolina, where my friends Wayne and Sally would take us in for the night.

Near the state line, in a town called Gaffney, we passed a water tower with a giant peach painted on it. It looked like a large woman's blushing behind.

An old pie safe is the first thing you see when you walk into Wayne and Sally's house, set back in the woods, off a gravel road. It's a funky, comfortable house. A house that says happy people live in it. Lots of cats and a scruffy, low-to-the-ground dog, too. It's quite a step up from the shack they lived in for many years after they were first married, which still sits on the property.

This was a pit stop, not a pie stop, but Sally wanted us to meet their pie-loving friend Laura before we left town, just the same. Laura had been baking in New Orleans and had recently come back to Pittsboro and taken a job as Wayne's Gal Friday for a change of pace, Sally said. I suspected heart trouble. Laura had no place to live, and Sally and Wayne offered up their love shack. Laura had only been there a few nights when a thick black snake slithered down from the rafters. When Laura realized the snake was merely curious, she learned to live with her roommate over the next few weeks.

Just when you've got yourself convinced you're a pretty tough cookie, someone like Laura comes along to make you feel as flimsy as a Georgia pecan tree. We met Laura for lunch the following day at the K & W cafeteria in Chapel Hill. I expected a woman who looked like she could wrestle snakes. I was way off.

She was 30 but could pass for 17. She wore her long brown hair in coiled side-braids, cinnamon buns. She wore shorts with platform shoes, and her legs were no quitters. Lolita and Princess Leia wrapped into one; all eyes were upon her in the long cafeteria line that slithered right out the door.

"A long wait means you have plenty of time to check out the goods," she said, craning her long, thin neck to inspect the Jell-O salads which, this day, ranged from indigo blue to antifreeze green. "I just love this place . . . It's like Christmas every day here."

The stacked pie display was even more impressive than Piccadilly's. As I stared at the vast assortment, it dawned on me that in my time on the road, I'd actually tasted most, if not all, of the varieties of pie on display.

And while Laura kept talking to Nicole and Sally about the glories of the K & W, I savored my own delicious, private moment of victory.

"It's not the best pie you'll ever have," I heard Laura say, "but it's good enough pie. And good enough pie is better than no pie at all, isn't it?"

Something to think about.

Laura recalled the time she made a lattice-crust apple pie for a beau. She was so nervous, she forgot to put sugar in the filling. "He ate the whole pie anyway."

"Sounds like he was a keeper," I said.

"If only love were as easy as pie," she sighed.

The K & W pies were just like Laura said: good enough. Not bad, but not memorable. Certainly not as memorable as the peach pie at the Kudzu Bakery or Minister Edgar's sweet-potato pie in New Orleans, I said.

When Laura learned we'd been to New Orleans, she dropped her jaw.

"You did go to Dick and Jenny's for their lemon meringue pie, right?"

I shook my head.

"Dick and Jenny's lemon meringue is the best pie you'll ever have," she said. "The first time I tried it, I was with my best friend," said Laura. "We normally share everything, but she wouldn't give me a bite of this pie. She made all sorts of sounds when she was eating it and so, finally, I got my own slice and I figured out what all the fuss was.

"This pie is so good that you could have just broken up with your boyfriend and about halfway through your slice, you'd forget his name. Forget he even existed.

"You've got to turn around and go back," she said. "You've just got to."

And when I started this trip, I just might have gone back to eat lemon meringue pie and forget.

But not now. I was headed home.

Laura and Sally climbed into Laura's pool-bottom blue pickup truck. Behind the wheel, Laura kissed her fingertips, then reached up and tapped the hood of her car to wish us good luck.

"Happy trails," she said.

virginia is for
lovers . . . of pie

*"Everyone on the trail dreams of something, usually sweet and gooey,
and my sustaining vision had been an outsized slab of pie. It had
occupied my thoughts for days, and when the waitress came to take
our order I asked her, with beseeching eyes and a hand on her forearm,
to bring me the largest piece she could slice without losing her job."*

—BILL BRYSON, *A WALK IN THE WOODS*

In Virginia, I could have headed to Charlottesville, the home of Thomas Jefferson, to find some pie with historical meaning, some crust with a solid constitution.

But I headed for the Shenandoah National Park instead. I had just read Bill Bryson's *A Walk in the Woods*, chronicling his adventures hiking the Appalachian Trail and remembered Bryson saying the "AT" was at its most beautiful as it meandered through the park in Virginia.

As a fellow pie seeker, Bryson could surely be trusted.

We drove toward Shenandoah by way of Staunton, the oldest town west of the Blue Ridge Mountains. Staunton was allegedly named after a woman, and she must have been a head-turner, because as we came up on a hill that gave us an overview of the steepled downtown, we gasped at how beautiful it was.

Nicole had been quiet all morning. Mulling something over, I could tell.

She'd been thinking, she said, that she should start a collection, too. But she wasn't sure what to hunt for.

"It'll happen organically," I said. One day, she'd see something in a junky old shop that would make her heart flutter. And she'd know if it was something she could spend a lifetime discovering.

Given our current restraints, it had to be something manageable, I told her. Grand pianos were out. "How about old cake stands?"

Boring, she said.

We parked in downtown Staunton, for leg-stretching and coffee, right in front of an antiques shop that was having a white-elephant sale.

On the sidewalk stood an old library newspaper rack—something every journalist should have.

"Maybe I could use it to hang towels?" I said. In the nick of time, a young couple interrupted.

They'd spotted Betty Blue's license plate, and, as pie lovers, they had to stop and ask. They, too, were going out for coffee, to go over final details for their upcoming wedding.

She owned a vintage clothing shop in town, and, yes, she said, she would be wearing a vintage wedding dress. "It came from an Indiana bride, circa 1952, complete with shoes and handbag." The dress had been on display in her shop window for weeks for the whole town to see, even the groom.

She would have gladly gone on talking about the wedding, but he was intent on getting to the bottom of this pie-themed car. Turned out, the groom, a contractor, had a thing for pie. Not just eating it, but hearing women say it.

Specifically, women from the South. Women who say "paaaaahhhhhh" instead of "pie."

It sounded a little kinky to me. But the fiancée found it charming.

"The lady at the bank has a really strong Southern accent, and she says it for me as soon as I get to her window," he said. "A few of the waitresses in town say it for me, too."

It would be irresponsible to write an entire book on pie and not address, at least in passing, this strange attraction men have to pie, particularly in the wake of the movie *American Pie,* in which, I hear, hormones and pie go hand in hand.

I'm no Freud. But, my guess is, it has something to do with pie's dual nature; the fact that pie is both sensuous and maternal. Sweet yet sensible.

Pie just may be the Madonna-whore of the dessert world.

We were getting close to home and I had it in my head that I needed to find some last great bowls and maybe even a pie safe, like the one I'd seen at Wayne and Sally's.

We stepped inside an antiques shop and I immediately saw four pie safes I wanted. Setting my sights on something smaller, I found two butter-yellow mixing bowls, nesting.

"I have a pie story," said the shopkeeper, who'd spotted Betty's license plate and was following me around his shop. "Want to hear it?"

He used to milk cows as a boy, he said, and he'd always have to watch the milking-barn floor for those nasty rat-tail maggots, just to make sure they didn't find their way into the milk.

"Fascinating," I said, wondering where this was going and where Nicole had disappeared.

He hadn't thought about those maggots in about fifty-odd years, until recently, when his wife decided, out of the clear blue sky,

to make a mulberry pie. He was delighted, until he bit into a mulberry stem.

"It reminded me so much of those rat-tail maggots, I spit it out
and gagged. I couldn't take another bite," he said. "Told the wife to
throw that pie right out."

Nicole appeared just in time. Wearing an ear-to-ear grin.

"Cookie jars," she said.

Loaded down with two more bowls and a cookie jar in the shape of
a pig with a chef's toque lid, we pressed on toward Shenandoah
National Park. My plan was to find some hikers on the Appalachian
Trail who, like Bryson, had lusted after—and found—good pie on
the AT.

We parked at a pull-out on Skyline Drive and hiked in a ways to
join the trail. In no time at all we felt worlds away from the road.

At the first shelter, we came upon a mother and daughter who'd
just pitched camp and were enjoying a healthy dinner of corn bread
stuffing mix and herbal tea. It was their first day on a four-day back-
packing trip. A butterfly kept landing on the mother's head, and her
daughter kept trying to wave it away. It was a nice moment. I found
myself really missing my mother, though we spoke nearly every day
I was on the road. The chemo seemed to be working. But she was
tired. So very tired.

They had no pie recommendations, they said, because, frankly,
said the daughter, "no one makes better pie than my grandmother's
blackberry."

We continued hiking on the trail for almost an hour and never
saw another soul. I was starting to get nervous. About bears, not pie.

We were about an hour's hike from Skyline Drive when I swore I
heard a grunt. Nicole, or a chipmunk, no doubt. But I got it into my

head this was a grizzly who sensed I'd been around huckleberries. I kicked into high gear, started power-walking back to the car.

Nicole tried to distract me by describing some of more fabulous desserts she'd created over the years. "Did I ever tell you about the caramel-roasted figs with hazelnut phyllo, and a crème fraîche risotto I made for a Share Our Strength dinner?"

"Nice try," I said, "but I don't think it's such a good idea to be talking about sweets with a B-E-A-R in our midst."

"I'm thinking of making an old American classic called a 'fool,'" shouted Nicole, who by now was 40 paces behind. "Have you heard of it?"

Our hunt for pie-hungry hikers had been a bust, so, on the advice of a park ranger, we headed to the Big Meadows Lodge where Clara, the hostess, raved about the restaurant's cobbler.

I explained to Clara about our "issues" with cobbler.

"What about our blackberry *ice cream* pie?" she asked.

That would do.

We sat on the restaurant deck looking out at the Blue Ridge Mountains and although the pie wasn't great (more texture than flavor), the view was definitely worth hiking for days and even braving bears for.

I was about to ask Nicole if this dessert "fool" really existed, when I heard a *rat tat tat* against the windowpane behind my Adirondack chair. I turned to see an elderly couple, both in rocking chairs, inside the restaurant lounge, ogling my pie.

"How dare you eat that right in front of us!" I could faintly hear the woman say through the glass. That was a dare if I ever heard one, so I gathered my plate and went inside to offer her a bite.

Jim and Edna, both in their mid-70s, said they were waiting for a table and didn't want to spoil their appetite. "We're just having fun with you, because we both love pie," said Edna.

I asked Edna if she made pie herself, and Jim jumped in:

"Of course she does. That's why I'm *marrying* her." I'd heard right. Edna and Jim had met only four months earlier and were planning to marry in the fall. I asked them how they met, and ushered Nicole over so she could hear, too.

Edna had gone to a furniture store in Charlottesville, where she lived, to buy a new mattress. It had been a while since the long-divorced Edna had had to buy a mattress, and so she was nervous. She found a mattress that seemed just firm enough for her back. She asked Jim, the manager of the store, if he wouldn't mind lying down next to her to make sure it didn't "dip" in the middle.

He obliged. And by the time they stood upright again, Jim and Edna were fast friends. She had learned that he was recently widowed and quite lonely. He'd taken a second job, working at McDonald's in the evenings, to kill time. She'd been divorced for twenty years and had also recently lost her longtime companion.

He asked for her phone number and when he called her the very next day, she invited him over for dinner.

"She made me a strawberry-rhubarb pie that was out of this world," Jim said, pressing her hand in his. "I was hooked."

Edna and Jim had just gone apple-picking at a nearby orchard the day before to make some apple pies over the weekend. On a lark, she'd suggested they drive up to the lodge for a romantic Friday-night dinner.

The two couldn't keep their hands off each other.

This wasn't the first time on my journey that a pie made from scratch had led to nuptials, I told Nicole as we drove back down into the valley, toward Washington, D.C. Nicole contrasted Edna and Jim's story with a recent episode of *Sex and the City*, in which Miranda's elderly cleaning woman tries to convince the hot-shot lawyer that she must own—and learn to use—a rolling pin, to lasso a husband. Aren't rolling pins a sign of rolling back? Miranda asks Carrie. Carrie wouldn't know: she uses her oven for storage.

What a difference a couple of generations makes.

When Kerouac took to the highways, pie made from scratch was ubiquitous. Wherever he looked, apple pie was there. I, on the other hand, had to dig, and drive, sometimes hundreds of miles, to find a pie that was made by the person who served it. But while old-fashioned pie has largely disappeared from the American landscape, the mythology of pie lives stronger than ever. That's because pie is a symbol of something bigger than Mom and her way with desserts.

Look into the face of a pie, and you'll see many of the traits Americans pride themselves on. Resilience and determination. Stick-to-it-iveness. They are all there. You'll see the first pioneers who built supper around nothing more than lard, flour, and prairie oysters. People like Deborah Tyler who sold porch pies to pay the bills. Dave the bear trapper who baked his way out of a dark cave. Laura, in Montana, who worked through searing pain in her fingers by rolling out dough.

Pie speaks to our nation's competitive streak: an already famous George Eastman who wanted his lemon meringue to be the best; two colleges arguing over whose students first flung a pie tin in the air for fun. Generations of women vying for blue, red, and white ribbons at county and state fairs. Women like Louise Piler, of Rolfe, Iowa, who, as a young farm girl, watched her father show cattle and hogs, and now boasts her own flotilla of coveted blue ribbons from the Iowa State Fair.

It took years, and lots of collapsed meringue pies, before Louise tasted victory, she says. One day, a deflated Louise and her husband were driving home from the fair in Des Moines, and Louise announced she was hanging up her rolling pin for good.

"My pies just aren't ever going to be pretty enough," she said.

Her husband stopped the car. "Honey, you just swallow your pride and try again," he told her. Not long after that, she won "sweepstakes"—the prize for the most blue ribbons won at one fair. She headed straight for the nursing home to show her ailing father, 86, the bright purple satin (sweepstakes) ribbon.

"I walked in his room and he said: Did you win?" That was the sweetest victory of all, she said. Louise said baking was a salve from her job as a cardiac-intensive-care nurse. Which just goes to show that working women can make pies, too.

You don't have to be unsophisticated or unadventurous to enjoy making pie. Aunt Anne in tiny Bernard always made three pies by noon Sunday, and still made time for things like India in her life. Pie speaks of patriotism, yes, but more important, it speaks of a slower time, when things weren't so complicated. When there was always someone home to greet a child after school. When prairies didn't need to be saved. When firemen had time to help coax a cat down a tree.

Juanita, in Munith, managed to live on that kind of time. She baked, nearly every day, to show her friends and neighbors how much she cared.

"It's a way of paying respect," she said. Exactly the kind of respect Minister Edgar talked about while baking pecan pies on that sweltering day in New Orleans.

"Respect the art of pie," wrote Susan Bright. I wonder what she'd think of the diner in Iowa City I read about in the paper that tosses pie in a blender and calls it "a pie shake." No time to bake pie. No time to sit down and eat it properly with a cold glass of milk.

Today's pace isn't a pie pace.

We work so hard, we think, to make life easy, but easy never comes. Not with families and friends so spread out and splintered. People move, clear cross-country, for more money, a better job. Pretty soon, the only time they see their families is on the holiday. Everyone around the table stares at a pie, hoping the pie can fill the void for all that has been lost.

That's a world of pressure to put on a pie—and its baker. No wonder no one bakes anymore.

Easy as pie?

Not so easy when there's no one around to show you how easy it can be. Paula Deen, in Savannah, Georgia, was right. Based on the countless cheap-thrill pies we tossed in the Dumpster, a surprising number of Americans have never tried a genuine slice of home-sprung pie.

The quintessential American pie, be it apple or sweet potato or Mary Baumbach's cherry, sits in the cupboard of our collective consciousness. We know, intuitively, what a plump, juicy berry pie in a golden flaky crust should taste like, but we've learned to settle for less; for those "fifty-fifty" pies banned from Tootie Guirard's annual Pie Day in Catahoula. I haven't resolved in my heart whether Laura was right when she said that "a good enough pie is better than no pie at all." I remember so fondly Susan's banana cream pie made from a dry mix in Gold Hill, Colorado. But I also remember the delicious discovery of Doris Kemp's apple-blueberry pie. You can tell when a pie has been made by hand and heart. Like Ty said, "you just know." In many ways, pie in America has met the same fate as the handwritten letter, supplanted by e-mail. E-mail isn't just quicker. It expects less of the sender. Words weigh less, it seems, when they travel at the speed of light. I think of the rush I get on those rare occasions when I open my mailbox and find a handwritten letter. In our crazy, whipstitch lives, it seems inconceivable that anyone could take pause, pull up a chair, and sit down with their thoughts . . .

As Edna did, just a few days after our brief encounter in the shadow of the Blue Ridge Mountains:

Dear Pascale,

I thought I would write to you to tell you what happened to Jim and me on Monday, Aug. 7. We had decided to go to the court house to get our marriage license so we could start making plans for the wedding.

Got to the courthouse and clerk was filing forms, etc., when a judge from Richmond popped his head in the doorway asking, "Anyone want to get married?"

I looked at Jim and said "Why not?" He said, "No," and I said, "We could get it all done here and now."

He: "You want to do it?"

"Sure," I said, motioning to the judge.

He came over and said: "Come on out, I'll do it in the court-yard," and then he led us outside, toward a garbage can.

"Not here," I said. So he led us over to the front of the courthouse on Market Street to the stairs between two cannons, a statue, and two piles of cannon balls, where he conducted the ceremony. People stopped to watch from the street and many people observed from the windows of the courthouse.

Jim had given me his wedding ring on Friday, which I had on my right hand. I took it off and he placed it on my ring finger. We kissed, and then the judge led us to a park bench where he filled out the certificate. We drove to JC Penney's at the mall where he purchased me a one-carat diamond ring. It is gorgeous.

Oh, I took Jim to The Nook in the mall and bought our lunch of vegetable soup and toasted cheese sandwich. Today is his last

*day working at McDonald's. Jim is a former Baptist minister.
He is the most gentle, caring, compassionate man I've ever
known. I know we will enjoy our union together for many years.*

Good luck to you on your pie "booklet."

Most sincerely, with love,

Edna Francis Cox

Bless her. She'd included her recipe for strawberry-rhubarb pie with
a woven lattice crust.

EDNA FRANCIS COX'S
STRAWBERRY-RHUBARB "IT'S-NEVER-TOO-
LATE-TO-FALL-IN-LOVE" PIE

CRUST

2 cups flour

½ teaspoon baking powder

1 teaspoon salt

⅔ cup shortening or lard (Edna uses lard)

6 tablespoons ice water

¼ cup milk

FILLING

¼ cup Town Crier Flour

2 tablespoons cornstarch

1½ cups sugar

⅛ teaspoon salt

1½ cups diced rhubarb

2 cups strawberries (cut in half)

1 tablespoon butter

1 egg white or a little water

Sift 2 cups flour, measure, and sift again with baking powder and 1 teaspoon salt. Cut shortening into the flour mixture. Add just enough water to hold pastry together. Roll out on a board that has been brushed with flour. Roll out enough dough to fill a 9-inch pie pan. Cut the remainder of the dough into 1⅛ inch-wide strips or bands, for lattice crust.

Brush the pastry with milk.

In a bowl, mix ¼ cup flour, cornstarch, sugar, and ⅛ teaspoon salt, for the filling. Sprinkle ¼ of this mixture into the bottom of the pastry-lined pie pan. Mix remainder with the rhubarb and straw-berries. Toss well. Pour into pie pan. Dot with butter.

Moisten the rim of the bottom crust with cold water and lay half the strips across the face of the pie. At the outer edge of the pie, take the first cross strip and weave it through every other bottom strip. Use this as your guide strip. Fold every other bottom strip halfway back over the guide strip. Place the next strip down near the guide strip over the strips that are NOT folded back. Unfold the others over the new strip. Keep alternating folding strips back as you weave across to the edge of the pan. Using sharp scissors, trim the strips so that they hang over the edge about ½ inch. Moisten the dough under each strip with egg white or water and tuck the overhang under the border of the bottom crust. Press firmly to make it stick. Crimp edges. Bake at 450 degrees for 10 minutes. Reduce temperature to 350 degrees and bake 50 minutes. Let cool before serving.

capital pie

*"I confess that in America I saw more than America; I saw the image
of democracy itself, with its inclinations, its character, its prejudices,
and its passions, in order to learn what we have to fear
or hope from its progress."*
—ALEXIS DE TOCQUEVILLE

It was so early when we arrived in Washington, D.C., on Sunday
morning that we scored the prime parking spot closest to the White
House.

Two security officers promptly stepped out of their booth to take
a look, and who could blame them? We looked just like the Clam-
petts driving up to the gates of Bel Air. The tarp covering the wicker
table I'd been hauling since Meadville, Ohio, was shredded, like
Ellie Mae's denim cutoffs.

Betty hadn't seen the inside of a car wash since New Mexico, and
her wooden rolling pins, still hanging on for dear life, front and back,
were carpeted with bugs. We'd lost Doug's wire-hanger antenna
somewhere in Catahoula, but the duct tape was still there, flapping
in the wind.

And, after about 19,500 miles, I wasn't feeling exactly daisy-
fresh myself. I had hoped there might be some activity at the White
House, a press conference on the lawn, or some visiting dignitary
photo op, so that we might wrangle a pie recommendation from
someone official.

But three months away from the interminable November 2000 election, not a creature was stirring on Pennsylvania Avenue. So I stepped up to the grim-faced security officer at the Southeast Gate and asked him point-blank: if he could go anywhere in D.C. for a piece of presidential pie, where would he go?

You'd think that a guy with a name like Tyrus Ezekiel would have a sense of humor. He sat stone-faced.

I'm sure Tyrus went through hours of training to learn how to spot nut jobs in the crowd long before they try and scale the fence or start wildly firing shots. We didn't exactly fit the "wacko" profile, and that threw him. He looked us up and down, then down and up, and up and down again. Then he scanned the parking lot for a tour bus.

Then Tyrus must have remembered a warm pumpkin pie from his youth, because he finally cracked a smile.

"Why don't you ladies try the Old Ebbitt Grill just around the corner," he said. "They make good pie and they use berries from local farms."

When de Tocqueville arrived in Washington—which happened to be his final stop as well—he wrote that he was struck by the "openness" of the White House. Indeed, he and Beaumont apparently waltzed right into Andrew Jackson's salon on "visiting day," and the president even offered them a glass of madeira.

No doubt the adventurous de Tocqueville and Beaumont would have also ended up at Old Ebbitt Grill, had it been open at the time. But the famous bar did not open until 1856. Since then, a long line of presidents, including McKinley, Grant, Andrew Johnson, Cleveland, Theodore Roosevelt, and Harding, have all tossed back a few at the Ebbitt's bar. The Ebbitt has moved several times before setting down roots in its present location at 15th & H streets, kitty corner from the Office of the Treasury. Weeknights, the long galley bar swarms with journalists, political insiders, government staffers, interns, and, of course, lawyers. Lots of lawyers.

But on this Sunday morning it was fairly quiet, which gave us lots of time and room to admire the warped wood floors and the mounted stuffed-bear head, a war trophy gift courtesy of Teddy Roosevelt himself.

Blackberry was the pie of the day, and I was delighted to end the trip on a dark-berry pie, since I'd started my journey with an olallieberry pie in Pescadero, California.

Full circle I'd gone.

The pie arrived on a fancy china plate, which had been decorated with a spiderweb design of blackberry coulis as tangled as the pie itinerary. It came with a side scoop of French vanilla ice cream.

Only three bites of the filling, dark, cool, and musty like morning woods, and I was five again, in the backseat of my uncle's car. We were on our way to meet my great-grandmother for the first time, in a rural, forgotten pocket of Brittany. Her one-room thatch-roof house, which had no plumbing or electricity, sat at the very end of a narrow dirt road bordered by blackberry bushes with brambles so thick and overgrown they scratched the car as we passed, treating me to my first set of goose bumps.

My great-grandmother sat on a wooden bench inside her deep stone fireplace, making coarse buckwheat crêpes for us in a cast-iron skillet. She'd picked the wild blackberries for the filling herself, and had the arm scrapes to prove it. She filled each crêpe with the cooked, sweetened blackberries, then she folded the crêpe in a half circle, and once over again, so that the large circle became a triangle.

She offered me the first crêpe. My father had to give me a push, because this primitive woman with hair on her chin and no working toilet scared me.

They all watched as I took my first bite. I was too young to know I was tasting heritage. But I knew that the deliciousness of the moment went beyond the sweet, purple juice dripping down my chin.

"Too bad about the crust," said Nicole, yanking me out of my reverie.

It had gone completely soft. Had lost all spine or will.

Nicole was quick to jump to the baker's defense. Clearly, she said, the pie had been baked on Friday, then kept refrigerated—a capital offense. The perfectly sweetened filling was remarkably good, each berry independent, and had we eaten it out of the oven, we'd be singing a different tune.

"The kitchen had all the right intentions," she said.

Isn't that so often the case in politics, I thought.

On the way back to the car, I asked Nicole to snap my picture in front of the White House. And, although there are few things that irk me more than sidewalk cell-phone usage, I dialed up my parents to tell them which particular stretch of sidewalk I was calling from.

It was early in California, and my father was in the kitchen, making coffee for my mother who was still sleeping.

"*Papa, devines ou je suis* [Guess where I am]. *Devant la Maison Blanche* [In front of the White House]."

"Wait one second," he said, resting the receiver on the kitchen counter. I heard his worn leather slippers shuffle across the linoleum as he went to get my mother. They like to be side by side for significant moments. And ordinary ones.

"How exciting," I heard my mother say, as she made her way into the kitchen. "Does that mean she's done? Can she stop driving now?"

crumbs . . .

"A man travels the world over in search of
what he needs and returns home to find it."
—GEORGE MOORE, "THE BROOK KERITH"

Shortly after Ty moved to New York, we flirted, briefly, with the notion of buying a small house. We couldn't really afford it, and our relationship wasn't the least bit solid enough. Still, it soothed us somehow to wander through empty homes and imagine a future life together, as settled as sifted flour.

Happily, we'd found a realtor, Elena, who was willing to indulge this flight of fancy. Elena was twice my age (though she'd never admit it) and in frail health. At this stage in her life, she was more keen on making connections than commissions.

We looked forward to our Sundays with the eccentric Elena, who still carried herself like the stage actress she'd once been. Sensible was not in her wardrobe. Bangles and boots and rich fabrics that flowed, were.

Elena refused to let us drive, preferring instead to chauffeur us around the Hudson River Valley in her rusted, cornflower-blue Volvo station wagon, puttering at 20 miles an hour. She liked taking "scenic" detours just to point out a striking hydrangea bush or a pretty curve on a bay window.

We had other things in common, Elena and I. For years, we'd lived right around the corner from each other in Santa Monica—

without knowing it. We liked barn-wood floors and we both collected old mixing bowls.

One day, Elena invited me to her home in Tarrytown, where she lived with her husband, Jesse, to show me her collection. Most were the expensive yellow-ware bowls that are beyond my reach. She'd found them at tag sales, long before they were trendy.

"What is it about bowls?" I asked Elena. We were sitting on her living room floor, surrounded by six of her favorites.

"It's because they're *iconic*," she said, clutching a buttercup-yellow bowl as wide as the green bowl my mother used for her floating-island dessert. "It means we're *nesters*. Round receptacles are maternal, they are like cocoons."

Pies are cocoons, too, I thought.

"So, when are you and Ty going to have a baby? You're not getting any younger, you know." With every wrinkle on her face, Elena felt she'd earned the right to speak her mind.

So, when she learned a few months later that Ty and I were taking a break from the relationship, she let it be known that she did not approve.

Flaws? Some of the prettiest bowls in my collection have flaws, she said.

We didn't see Elena for many months after that.

I went back out on the road to pie, and Ty took a long journey of his own. And when we finally came back together and decided to marry, that these two islands were tired of floating, Elena was one of the first people we wished to tell.

Elena had gotten very sick in the interim. An illness so grave she couldn't bring herself to name it. "This *thing* I have," she'd say, rolling her navy-blue eyes. She spent most days confined to the upstairs bedroom of their old carriage house on Sunset Way, down the hill from where Mark Twain once lived.

Ty and I brought her French tulips, color of plums, for her nightstand. As an engagement present, she gave us the wide, wheat-yellow carved bowl I'd once admired in her bony hands. And I noticed the bowl was indeed imperfect. Beautifully so.

Inside the bowl Elena had dropped a brief note: "Dear Pascale and Ty: *Remember to triumph over the bumps. The joys will outnumber them.*"

My wish is that some day soon, the bowl will grace the mantel or sill of a funky old house Elena will have found for us. But I know better.

So, for now, the bowl is going in the refrigerator overnight.

I want it to get nice and cold. Because tomorrow, I'm finally going to bake a pie. From scratch. For Elena.

I do believe I have everything I need: Ty's jay-blue pie plate, a long wooden spoon from Pennsylvania Dutch country, and plenty of rolling pins to choose from. More important, I have sound advice and encouraging words from bakers like Elva, Edgar, Laura, and even young Darrell.

I've carved out the whole morning for nothing but this, because, I've learned, you really have to stop your life to make a pie. That is what makes it the ultimate gift. It is a gift of yourself. A gift of time.

A marriage pie is what I'll make: huckleberry and peach, like the one we loved at the Spruce Park Café in Montana. The California peaches have arrived in my local supermarket. I'm hoping they'll take Elena back to her sunny Santa Monica days. I had to order the purple huckleberries special. Elena could use a whiff of fresh mountain air. Besides, I'm told Montana hucks can pull you through some pretty rough patches.

I will wake up very early, before the cardinals even, to give myself plenty of time for mistakes. And, if the first batch of dough doesn't take, I will "press on," as Calvin Coolidge advised, and try another.

(His ode to persistence, copied from the wall of the Mill Pond Bakery in Munith, Michigan, hangs from my fridge.)

Naturally, Ty has offered to help with the crust. Though I see many joint pies in our future, it's important I tackle this one solo. I've driven more than 20,000 miles chasing tradition. Time to start my very own.

"Il faut mettre la main à la pate," my mother would always say whenever we danced around a challenge. This French expression literally means: "It's time to put your hands in the dough."

Time to surrender to pie.

Dear Pascale,

I would be so grateful if you could include my great-grandmother, Nan, in your book. I am 19 years old and just recently lost my nan in June. She was 88.

My Nan was an amazing woman. My fondest memories revolve around eating her homemade apple pie. I wish that you had had a chance to taste this work of art because words cannot describe it.

Nan never entered contests, never won any awards. She was told time and again to open a bakery. But Nan didn't want to sell her baked goods, because she made them out of love.

She made her crust from scratch and used only the finest apples in the bunch. The crust was always moist and flaky, the perfect color of gold, and the apples never too sweet. She always had a piece ready for me when she took it out of the oven.

I don't know how I am going to survive the upcoming holidays without her and her pies.

I think that anyone can make a good pie with practice, but it takes love to make it perfect. The smell alone of one of her pies baking filled me with such a warm feeling. What I wouldn't give . . .

I thought it would be a nice way for me to thank Nan for everything she baked into her pies by having you include her in your story. I would give you her recipe if she had one, but the thing is, she never used one.

And every pie came out better than the last.

Thank you for your time,

Sincerely,

MORGAN COLE-HATCHARD
Stony Point, New York

on the pie trail

The recipes kept coming, even after the book was out. Readers sent in recipes and even handed them to me at book signings. I've included a few here. Go forth and bake!

Disappointed that I couldn't find any peach pie in the Peach State, Gloria B. Smiley, a food stylist in Atlanta, Georgia, shared the following recipe for peach pie.

GEORGIA PEACH PIE

CRUST

1 9-inch pie crust, prebaked

FILLING

3 cups peaches, sliced (preferably fresh)

1 tablespoon lemon juice

½ cup sugar

2 tablespoons cornstarch

pinch of salt

¼ teaspoon almond extract

1 tablespoon butter

TOPPING

1 cup whipped cream
½ cup raspberries or blueberries

Preheat oven to 400 degrees. Sprinkle peaches with lemon juice and sugar; let stand for 1 hour. Drain the accumulated juices (should measure about 1 cup) into in a small non-stick saucepan, and boil the liquid until syrupy and slightly caramelized. Meanwhile, transfer peaches to a bowl and toss them with the cornstarch, salt, and almond extract.

Pour syrup over peaches, tossing gently. Arrange peach mixture in pie crust and dot with butter. Bake at 400 degrees for 20–25 minutes, or until top starts to brown slightly. If edges of crust start to brown too quickly, cover with foil, shiny side up. Remove pie from oven and cool completely. To serve, pipe with whipped cream and garnish with berries. Serves 6–8.

Andrea Cohen, a former cop from Tallahassee, Florida, sent me an old, yellowed recipe for rhubarb custard pie that she gleaned from her husband's grandmother's collection.

HERITAGE RHUBARB CUSTARD PIE

CRUST

1 9-inch double-crust

FILLING

2 ½ cups unpared rhubarb, cut in 1-inch lengths
1 ½ cups sugar
¼ cup flour

2 eggs, slightly beaten

2 teaspoons lemon juice

pinch of salt

2 tablespoons butter

1 tablespoon sugar, for sprinkling

Preheat oven to 450 degrees. In a large mixing bowl, gently combine rhubarb, sugar, flour, eggs, lemon juice, and salt. Moisten edge of bottom crust with a little water and line pie plate. Turn filling into lined pie plate and dot with butter. Fold top crust under edge of bottom crust. Use your fingers to press edges together and seal so juices cannot run out. Turn edge upright to form a standing rim and crimp edge decoratively. Sprinkle with a tablespoon of sugar.

Bake at 450 degrees for 10 minutes. Reduce heat to 350 degrees and bake for another 30 minutes. Serves 6.

This is a great starter pie for the uninitiated or for children learning how to cook—especially if you use the vanilla pudding mix as recommended. For those of you who want to work a little harder for your pie, I'm including a simple recipe for classic vanilla pudding I found in the 1905 *New England Cook Book* I picked up in an antiques barn in Vermont.

BANANA CREAM PIE

1 box Nabisco Nilla wafers

1 package instant vanilla pudding and pie mix (or vanilla pudding recipe below)

2–3 bananas

fresh whipped cream (optional)

Layer a 9-inch pie pan with the wafers straight out of the box. Prepare the pudding mix per instructions. Layer pudding on top of the wafers. Slice bananas and arrange them on top of pudding.

Repeat above steps until your pie pan is filled. Top with the fresh whipped cream. Serves 6–8.

CREAM-PIE PUDDING FROM *THE NEW ENGLAND COOK BOOK*

4 tablespoons cornstarch
1 tablespoon cold milk
4 egg yolks
6 tablespoons sugar
2 pints scalded milk
1 teaspoon vanilla

Wet the cornstarch with the cold milk. In a separate bowl, beat the yolks and sugar until slightly creamy and pale yellow in color (about 2 minutes). Add this mixture to the scalded milk. (Scald milk by heating it until just below boiling). Stir well. Add the wet cornstarch and vanilla. Stir well. Let cool and set before putting in pie crust.

At a book signing—in the Bay Area, I believe—a woman handed me this recipe for coffee toffee pie. Hold on to your rolling pin. Flavors here are intense.

COFFEE TOFFEE PIE

CRUST

½ package pie-crust mix

¼ cup light brown sugar, packed

¼ square unsweetened baking chocolate, grated

¾ cups finely chopped walnuts

1 tablespoon water

1 teaspoon vanilla

FILLING

1 12-ounce package semisweet chocolate chips

4 tablespoons sugar

6 tablespoons strong-brewed coffee (espresso is nice)

7 egg yolks

2 teaspoons vanilla

7 egg whites

TOPPING

1 cup whipping cream

6 tablespoons powdered sugar

2 tablespoons instant coffee

½ cup chopped walnuts

Preheat oven to 375 degrees. Combine pie-crust mix with brown sugar, walnuts, and grated chocolate. Add the water and the vanilla. Mix until blended. Grease a 9-inch spring-form pan. Press ingredients against sides and bottom of pan. Bake at 375 degrees for 15 minutes.

Mix and blend together chocolate chips, sugar, and coffee over a double boiler. Let cool, then beat in the yolks, one at a time, and the vanilla. In a separate bowl, beat the egg whites until stiff. Fold chocolate mixture into the beaten egg whites. Pour the resulting mixture into the baked, cooled pie crust.

Combine whipping cream with the powdered sugar and instant coffee. Refrigerate one hour. Beat until stiff. Decorate pie with topping. Garnish with chopped walnuts. Serves 8–10.

James Sharshan of Cape May, New Jersey, received *American Pie* as a birthday gift from his daughter when he turned 68. Over the years, Sharshan has collected 150 postcard recipes—recipes printed directly onto postcards for mailing—from 18 states. He sent along several pie recipes from his collection, including this postcard recipe for Dixie Pecan Pie, which is not as sweet as your run-of-the-mill pecan pie.

DIXIE PECAN PIE

CRUST

1 9-inch pie crust, unbaked

FILLING

3 eggs

½ cup dark Karo syrup

½ cup heavy cream

1 teaspoon vanilla

3 tablespoons Bourbon

1 cup sugar

⅛ teaspoon salt

2 tablespoons butter, melted

2 cups chopped pecans

TOPPING

Whipped cream, or vanilla or coffee ice cream

Preheat oven to 375 degrees. In a large mixing bowl, beat eggs well. Beat in all other ingredients until well-blended. Pour into pie crust. Bake on cookie sheet for 40 minutes, or until center is set. Cool to room temperature and then refrigerate. Serve with whipped cream, or with vanilla or coffee ice cream. Serves 8.

Diane F. from Green Bay, Wisconsin, sent along her family's easy (and healthy) recipe for pie crust. (Her husband's cholesterol is 399!) This crust has a "crumbly" consistency, like shortbread.

WATCHING-OUR-CHOLESTEROL CRUST

(Makes 1 10-inch double crust)

3 cups flour

1 teaspoon salt

1 tablespoon sugar

1 cup oil

4 tablespoons milk

1 sheet of wax paper

In a large mixing bowl, mix together dry ingredients. In a smaller bowl, blend oil and milk together with a fork. Combine with dry ingredients. Work the mixture with your fingers into a smooth disc, then divide it into 2 smaller discs.

To roll out each disc, sprinkle a few drops of water on a smooth surface, like a granite or Formica counter or a smooth kitchen table. Place a sheet of wax paper on the surface. (The water drops prevent it from shifting.)

Drop your pie dough disc onto the wax paper and fold the wax paper over it before rolling it out. (The wax paper makes it unnecessary to dust your rolling pin or rolling surface with flour.) Gently peel back the top sheet of wax paper. Lift the bottom sheet with rolled-out pie dough and flip it into the bottom of your pie pan. Peel off the bottom sheet of wax paper. Voilà! Serves 6–8.

Marguerite Couvillion confidently passed along this recipe for the "World's Best Apple Pie."

WORLD'S BEST APPLE PIE

CRUST

1 9-inch pie crust, unbaked

FILLING

1 cup sugar

2 tablespoons flour

½ teaspoon cinnamon

6 cups apples peeled and sliced (roughly 4–6 apples)

2 tablespoons butter

¼ cup heavy cream

1 egg yolk

Bake pie crust as directed; let chill. Preheat oven to 400 degrees. Combine sugar, flour, and cinnamon in a small bowl. Mix well. Place apples in a large bowl and pour cinnamon mixture over them, tossing until apples are evenly coated. Spoon into pie crust, creating a mound in the middle. Dot with butter. Bake at 400 degrees for 30 minutes.

Remove pie from oven and lower temperature to 350 degrees. Beat cream with egg yolk; drizzle evenly over apples, pressing them down lightly with a fork so that cream oozes down into filling. Return to oven and bake for 15 minutes. Can be served warm as well as at room temperature. Serves 6–8.

How I wish I could have met the original owner of this tattered cookbook. She obviously loved to spend time in the kitchen: all the blank pages between chapters are filled with additional recipes she's penned in her distinct whimsical script or clipped from the newspaper.

Since so many readers ask me about lemon pies, I couldn't resist adding this recipe she jotted down in lavender ink.

MYSTERY WOMAN'S LEMON SPONGE PIE

CRUST
1 9-inch pie crust, unbaked

FILLING
1 cup sugar
1 tablespoon flour
juice and rind of 1 lemon

2 egg yolks

1 ½ cups sweet condensed milk

2 egg whites

In a large mixing bowl, stir together the sugar, flour, lemon juice and rind, and the egg yolks—in that order. Add the condensed milk and mix well. In a separate bowl, beat the egg whites until frothy. Fold them into the milk mixture, and mix thoroughly. Pour into pie crust. Bake at 350 degrees for about 45 minutes. Serves 6–8.

A number of pie lovers have asked me if I ever encountered "vinegar pie" in my travels. I never did, but curiosity led me to this modern spin on what was apparently a quick and economical Regency-era classic. The pie's top "crust" is cookie-crisp, and the flan-like filling is much sweeter than the name suggests.

This is a Plain Jane pie, so I strongly recommend topping it with whipped cream or a meringue.

PLAIN JANE (BUT NOT SOUR) VINEGAR PIE

CRUST

1 9-inch pie crust, unbaked (deep shell, preferably)

FILLING

1 ½ teaspoons cane vinegar (balsamic vinegar works just as well)

4 eggs

¼ cup melted butter

1 ½ cups sugar

1 teaspoon vanilla

TOPPING

Meringue or whipped cream (optional)

Preheat the oven to 350 degrees. In a blender or a large mixing bowl, mix the vinegar, eggs, butter, sugar, and vanilla. Stir thoroughly. Let sit for 10 minutes. Pour the mixture into an unbaked pie crust. Bake for about 45 minutes or until firm. Allow to cool. (If you are going to top it with a meringue, layer it on top of the pie 25 minutes after putting the pie in the oven.) Serves 6–8.

After hearing me on the radio, Susan from Grand Rapids, Michigan, wrote to say she had a delicious and foolproof recipe for pie crust that was so easy her daughters mastered it by age 10! Her grandmother had plucked the recipe from the 1958 Punxsutawney, Pennsylvania, cookbook *Cooking with the Groundhog*. Indeed, this dough is unbelievably pliable and forgiving.

PENNSYLVANIA DUTCH PIE CRUST

3 cups sifted flour

1 teaspoon salt

1 ¼ cups shortening

5 tablespoons water

1 egg

1 teaspoon vinegar

Sift flour into a large mixing bowl. Add salt and cut in shortening. In a separate bowl, beat together water and egg. Add vinegar. Stir wet ingredients into flour mixture. Gather into a ball.

Turn out the dough on a floured board, and roll it out to fit pie pan. If your recipe calls for a prebaked pie shell, bake it for 10–12 minutes at 425 degrees. Makes 3 9-inch pie crusts.

No excuses now . . .